The Criminal Law of
Ancient Rome

The Criminal Law of Ancient Rome

O. F. Robinson

The Johns Hopkins University Press

Baltimore, Maryland

First published in the United States of America by
The Johns Hopkins University Press
2715 North Charles Street
Baltimore, Maryland 21218-4319

Library of Congress Cataloging-in-Publication Data

Robinson, O. F.
    The criminal law of ancient Rome / O. F. Robinson.
      p.   cm.
    Includes bibliographical references and index.
    ISBN 0-8018-5318-4
    1. Criminal law (Roman law)   I. Title.
KJA3340.R63   1996
345.37—dc20
[343.705]   95-24849
                                                         CIP

A catalog record for this book is available from the British Library.

Printed in Great Britain

Contents

Contents

Preface

This book is primarily concerned with the substantive criminal law, as the field in most urgent need of treatment. Historians and romanists have written much on the court structures, on jurisdictions, etc.; readers may even be relieved to learn that this book contains no discussion of *provocatio*. I hope I have given in the first chapter enough background against which to set the substantive law. Also, there is no discussion of penalties as such; I hope to treat them in another book in a more general context of crime and punishment. A brief outline of the penalties normally applicable is, however, given at the end of the discussion of each crime. My concern is the criminal law of Rome; I make no attempt to consider criminal jurisdiction in the provinces, or even the problems of criminal jurisdiction in Italy, except where they are – as often in the Later Roman Empire – not readily distinct.

Any attempt to state the substantive law must, for the most part, fail to apply strictly to any period. The generally cumulative nature of the legislation on which the Roman criminal law was built up makes for a blended picture. While it is quite clear that the nature of penalties changed between Republic and Empire, other changes in the law, which are not explicitly recorded, are more difficult to detect. Moreover, to provide the detail necessary to prove them would not be in place in a work trying to give a general picture. Thus the problem of interpolations is not quite ignored, but a conservative attitude has been generally taken.[1] Moreover, it seems quite likely that criminal law was relatively static. I take the *Pauli Sententiae* as reflecting late classical views reasonably accurately. The Digest is reporting mainly the state of affairs in the later second century, with some interpolations of Justinian's time, and also with references back to an earlier state of affairs. The Codes give us dates, even if not always reliable, for changes, particularly in the later Empire. But certainly I can only portray the criminal law as interpreted by the jurists, not as it was in the original statutes.

I have tried to provide fairly full citations of the legal texts, while giving only examples from Cicero, Tacitus and other literary authors; exhaustive citation would have been impractical, and the reader is more

---

[1] For a well-argued recent view against radical changes, see Watson (1994).

likely to pursue a handful of texts in a note than half a page's worth. When dealing with the Later Roman Empire I have usually cited the Theodosian Code in preference to Justinian's because it normally gives a fuller version; further, it is available in a fairly accurate translation, that of Pharr. Dates are all AD unless otherwise specified.

The citation of modern literature is mostly confined to recent work, since that will normally list earlier treatment of a theme, but this is not always possible; in particular, Mommsen's *Strafrecht* remains the platform on which any worker in the field of Roman criminal law must build. But notes referring to modern literature are more often designed as a general guide than as signposts to the interpretation of specific texts.

I have not given references for events to be found in any history of Rome; I assume the reader will have access to such a work, or at least to the *Oxford Classical Dictionary*. And the same applies to fundamental legal institutions, such as *patria potestas*, where I have assumed that the reader will have access to an elementary treatise on Roman law,[2] or perhaps to A. Berger's *Dictionary of Roman Law*. Nevertheless, there is a Glossary of Technical Terms at the end of this book, although this is not intended to compete with the Index.

I owe thanks to many people, but particularly to Sebastian who has read all my drafts and compiled the Index of Sources.

---

[2] E.g. Buckland (1963), Lee (1956), Nicholas (1962), Thomas (1976), Watson (1970b) or (1991).

I

The Framework of Criminal Procedure

Early Roman criminal law is both obscure and hotly debated. We only begin to approach reasonable probabilities around 200 BC, the period from which contemporary evidence – Plautus, Cato, and others – survives. Criminal procedures of the period comprised the domestic jurisdiction of the *paterfamilias*, private criminal actions, the exercise of their powers by the *tresviri capitales* (minor magistrates with police functions), and the jurisdiction of the assemblies of the people, i.e. trials before one of the *comitia*. In the year 207 BC the Senate ordered a special commission, a *quaestio*, to investigate the conduct of certain Italian allies arising from the Second Punic War,[1] and such commissions were relatively common in the second century, supplementing the comitial jurisdiction. However, when in 171 BC the provincials of Spain asked the Senate for redress against their governors, the Senate ordered the praetor to whom the Spains had been allotted to appoint *recuperatores* from among the Senate,[2] but this was a procedure of the private law, without a penal element. Then in 149 BC the *lex Calpurnia* was passed, concerned not only with reparation but also punishment;[3] it established a permanent court of senators as sworn jurors to deal with claims of provincial extortion.

Thereafter, both the senatorial special commissions and also the jurisdiction of the assemblies began in their turn to be superseded by the creation of *quaestiones perpetuae*, permanent jury courts, whose structure, if not purpose, was modelled somewhat on the *lex Calpurnia*. While there remain arguments about the early manifestations of individual courts, it is clear that under Sulla (in his dictatorship 82-81 BC) a system of these standing jury courts was established.[4] It is on this system that the juristic development of the criminal law was predicated,[5] and without this system a criminal jurisprudence would not have been possible. It would not have been possible because special commissions were by definition ad hoc, and to use an assembly (whether *comitia centuriata* or *concilium plebis*) as a court inevitably brought in political issues. (Admittedly, most trials we hear of had political roots anyway.) Trials before an assembly of the people ceased to be held when there was a competent jury court. Arguably the last attempt at a comitial trial had, anyway, been in 56 BC, when Clodius, then curule aedile, accused Milo of *vis*, perhaps before the people.[6] And there seem to have been only two cases of *quaestiones extraordinariae* in the Ciceronian age, the trial of Clodius in 61 BC for incest after the *Bona Dea* affair,[7] and those – including the trial of Milo – founded on the *lex Pompeia de vi* after the near anarchy in which 52 BC opened.[8]

The system of the *quaestiones perpetuae*

It seems true that in the Republic there 'never developed anything resembling a judicature act, and each [criminal] court depended on a special *lex* or *plebiscitum* for its validity and its forms'.[9] This approach, rather than limited rules of interpretation, explains the Republican habit of developing some offences by the passage of a new statute, as was markedly the case with *ambitus* – but there, of course, political considerations were always dominant. New statutes also provided for variations in the penalty. Nevertheless, there was a definite family likeness among the courts. The *quaestiones perpetuae* provided, each for its own offence or range of offences, a framework. This framework was adjusted, but not significantly altered, by the struggles over the composition of the juries of these courts;[10] these were a matter of political rather than juridical importance, and were finally settled by Augustus' *lex Iulia iudiciorum publicorum* of 17 BC. Augustus' role was undoubtedly important in confirming the system of the *quaestiones perpetuae*, but that is what he did – confirm the system that already existed, while adding the new public crime of adultery.

Although there were problems of judicial corruption and bias in the operation of the *quaestiones perpetuae*, and although they had a relatively short effective life, it was the establishment of the system which enables us to consider the substantive criminal law. This system became the norm, the *ordo*, from which other courts differed as being *extra ordinem*, and its influence continued even into Justinian's law.[11] It was the framework which the jurists clothed, whether with their learned opinions, or through resolutions of the Senate, or by advising emperors; it provided the 'convenient signposts'[12] which endured throughout Roman law.

There was, however, one pre-Sullan *quaestio perpetua*, set up by the *lex repetundarum* which is known to us from the inscription on the *tabula Bembina*; it has been commonly called the *lex Acilia*.[13] This is worth mention since we have nearly the full text of this law, and from it we can fairly safely supplement our information about the Sullan courts, the more so if it is some two decades later than has been generally assumed. We know little of the details of the other pre-Sullan standing jury courts; all were effectively subsumed into his work.

Sulla's reforms produced courts dealing with the forgery of documents and coining,[14] with murder and banditry and poisoning,[15] with assault,[16] and also with treason,[17] extortion,[18] and embezzlement of public funds.[19] The suggestion that Sulla created a court for electoral corruption,[20] although supported only by one source, is not impossible; it would have been overshadowed by the *lex Calpurnia* of 67 BC. The argument for his having created a court for adultery is weaker, resting only on the statement in a late source that Augustus' *lex Iulia* abrogated many previous laws.[21] His *lex Cornelia de aleatoribus* was not the subject of a *quaestio*.[22]

Political interests led to the amendment of some of Sulla's statutes or to the creation of further *quaestiones* dealing with public life, such as, on *ambitus*, the *lex Calpurnia* already mentioned,[23] a *lex Tullia* of Cicero's in 63 BC,[24] and the *lex Licinia de sodaliciis* of 55 BC,[25] and – probably a permanent court – the *lex Pompeia* of 52 BC.[26] The *lex Papia de peregrinis* of 65 BC[27] was concerned to check false claims to citizenship; while the court it created may have been a *quaestio perpetua*, it did not in any case long endure. Offences which were against public order, springing often from roots in the civil wars, as well as motivated by private gain, were attacked in the *lex Plautia de vi*,[28] dating from between 78 and 63 BC, and the *lex Fabia de plagiariis* (before 63 BC[29]). Pompey was responsible for a law specifically on parricide,[30] but the crime probably continued to be taken before the *quaestio de sicariis*.[31] Julius Caesar's role in the development of the jury courts remains somewhat uncertain,[32] because the Julian name makes confusion easy with Augustus' legislation. Then came Augustus to put a final stamp on the system with the *lex Iulia de ambitu* and the *lex Iulia de adulteriis coercendis* of 18 BC, the *lex Iulia de vi* (?17 BC) and the *leges Iuliae iudiciorum*, and, perhaps in 8 BC, the *lex Iulia maiestatis*, the *lex Iulia peculatus* (*et de sacrilegiis*) and the *lex Iulia de residuis*.[33] No more *quaestiones perpetuae* were created and, with judicious interpretation, all major offences could be fitted into their framework; as we shall see, the offences outside the norm established by the *quaestiones perpetuae* were all relatively minor, or were the result of criminalizing what were also delicts. The one real exception to this division was the *lex Iulia de annona* of ?18 BC, which confirmed the jurisdiction of the Prefect of the Grain Supply; this offence should not be classed as minor, since the Prefect could impose a fine of 20,000 sesterces and, further, accusations of fraud on the *annona* were permitted to slaves even against their owners.[34]

Procedure in the *quaestiones perpetuae*

One of Sulla's constitutional changes was to retain the praetors[35] in the City for their year of office, sending them out thereafter with pro-praetorian *imperium* to govern provinces. As before, one held the office of

Urban and another of Peregrine Praetor, but the others presided[36] over *quaestiones perpetuae*, assigned by lot.[37] This annual allotment meant that courts could be combined, if this seemed convenient, under one praetor when a new court was introduced;[38] moreover, it seems likely that a praetor could be re-assigned to another court, perhaps only temporarily, to help an over-burdened colleague, as was the case with Domitius in 56 BC.[39] When a court was sitting without a praetor a *iudex quaestionis*, normally an ex-aedile,[40] presided instead;[41] he was perhaps chosen or elected from the jury panel. The term *iudex quaestionis* – the presiding *iudex* as opposed to a *iudex* who was merely a member of the jury – may have covered a praetor, but it is clear that not all presiding *iudices* were praetors; the term *quaesitores* may be specially applicable to these others.[42] A *quaesitor*, like a praetor, took an oath to observe the statute he was administering,[43] and his powers to conduct a trial, for instance by deciding before *nominis recepticio* (accepting an indictment) that there was a case under the statute to answer, seem to have been on a par.[44]

The jury panels originally consisted of senators; they were replaced by equestrians under C. Gracchus' legislation. Sulla doubled the size of the Senate, from which the jurors were again chosen under his system, but in 70 BC the *lex Aurelia* (which may also have abolished the verdict of not proven[45]) created a reservoir of jurors from the three orders of senatorials, equestrians and *tribuni aerarii*. (These last may have comprised the second class in the *comitia centuriata*, with a census wealth of 300,000 sesterces, as opposed to the equestrians' 400,000, but they were clearly closely akin to the equestrians.) With modifications, this membership prevailed throughout the life of the *quaestiones perpetuae*, with the jurors being drawn from three decuries, defined by property qualifications.[46] Jurors had to be between 30 and 60 years old, and to live in or near Rome.[47] There were, or came to be, recognized excuses from service.[48]

The size of the jury was initially regulated by the statute setting up the court,[49] with a right of challenge given to both accuser and accused.[50] Cicero tells us of 32 *iudices* giving verdict in the trial of Oppianicus in 74 BC,[51] but this was a Sullan jury. After the *lex Aurelia* the album, the list of potential jurors, was much bigger, with the numbers chosen from the two lower classes by the Urban Praetor[52] dependent on the number of senators available; we hear of 300 or 360 senators on the panel,[53] since magistrates and others engaged elsewhere on the business of the *res publica*, as well as those chronically ill, had to be excluded. The size of the jury, itself selected by variations of the lot, may have been fixed by the *lex Aurelia* at 75 (25 from each order),[54] for the numbers recorded are mostly close to this.[55]

A request for permission to prosecute could be made to the president of the relevant court by any adult male citizen;[56] it was a duty open to any member of the public, except in the case of *iniuria*.[57] However, technically only one accuser was permitted for each offence; if there were several claimants, agreement had first to be reached on who should bring the prosecution.[58] The accuser had to take the oath of calumny that his prosecution was in good faith.[59] The charge was then formally laid – *nominis delatio* – at which the accused had to be present; contumacious absence could be deemed to be voluntary exile. The accuser then signed the *inscriptio* drawn up by the president, and thus bound himself to follow through his prosecution or risk the penalties for *tergiversatio* or *praevaricatio*; the *inscriptio* also defined the limits of jurisdiction in the particular trial. The prosecutor was allowed a reasonable time to prepare his case, the *inquisitio*;[60] the minimum seems to have been ten days.[61]

Anyone, free or slave,[62] male or female, could be accused, with the exception of magistrates in office and certain others engaged in public business, including (normally) serving soldiers. One who was himself the subject of an accusation could not, at least by the second century of the Empire,[63] bring a charge against someone else. A citizen in good standing was left free during the period of the *inquisitio*, which he used for preparing his defence. During the Republic, to go into voluntary exile at this stage seems to have pre-empted the trial, and led simply to *interdictio aquae et ignis*.

On the day fixed for the start of the trial the case was at once dismissed if the prosecutor was absent; by this stage, the absence of the accused did not stop the proceedings, although Augustus laid down that, in such cases, the condemnation must be unanimous.[64] An accused's reasonable excuse for absence, such as holding a magistracy, absence on the business of the *res publica*, appearance on the same day in another court, and – more reluctantly – illness, was grounds for adjournment. The jurors were sworn. The prosecutor, who was normally required to conduct his case in person, customarily began with a long speech detailing all the charges; it was this which Cicero omitted at the trial of Verres. There was then a set speech on behalf of the accused, who was customarily represented by more than one advocate.[65] The prosecutor then introduced his evidence, to be followed by that of the defence. The prosecution witnesses were obliged to appear under a mandate from the presiding magistrate, although there was a limit to the number of compellable witnesses.[66] Personal appearance, written depositions, and relevant documents were all acceptable, but the first weighed most heavily. Character evidence was most important; the absence of *laudatores* was in itself damning. The defence could only ask, or beg, its witnesses to appear. The witnesses were examined by their own side and cross-examined by the other. At least in trials for *repetundae*, the time for the closing speeches followed a compulsory adjournment – *comperendinatio* – but this was probably not required in other trials.

The verdict of the jurors may well have followed a period of deliberation. The rule, despite a Sullan interruption, was that the verdicts were given by secret ballot, but the different classes voted separately, so that it was possible to say the senators had condemned, the equestrians absolved.[67] The jurors, at least before the *lex Aurelia*, had the third choice of *non liquet*, not proven, probably given effect by smoothing out both the *A[bsolvo]* and *C[ondemno]* sides of their wax covered tablets and scratching in these letters; just to deface the *A* and *C* counted as no vote.[68] A majority verdict was required for condemnation; an equality of votes meant acquittal, while, unlike the Scottish rule, *non liquet* meant a renewal of the trial *ab initio*. The president pronounced the judgment, and, where it was for conviction, gave the mandatory sentence laid down in the statute governing the court and its offence; in cases of *repetundae* and *peculatus* there was a need for the jury to go on to estimate the damages to be awarded. The issue of calumny or *praevaricatio* would be voted on at this point in the case of an acquittal.

Penalties proper to the system of the *quaestiones perpetuae* were a fine or *interdictio aquae et ignis*; death could perhaps be inflicted for the murder of close kin (*parricidium*). Infamy of various kinds and temporary exile (relegation) were penalties for *ambitus*. Prison was not a penalty of the *iudicia publica*, although persons might be left indefinitely in prison, as in the case of the playwright Naevius, or a certain Cornelius.[69] (Condemnation to forced labour was a penalty that early in the Principate became regular for *humiliores*; it necessarily involved a degree of confinement. There is perhaps not much difference between condemnation to prison with hard labour and condemnation to forced labour with deprivation of *de facto* liberty.)

No appeal was possible against a verdict or sentence, but it is likely that tribunician *intercessio* could be used against the preliminary stages in which the presiding magistrate was acting on his own.[70] A legislative act of the sovereign people could restore, grant pardon to, a convicted man.[71]

The coming of the Empire

The establishment of the Principate brought a change in the criminal courts. The disappearance of the *quaestiones perpetuae*, or of most of them, seems to have taken place fairly early, although some may have survived into the second century; it was a matter of desuetude, not abolition. New crimes tended to be brought before the Urban Prefect (who had acquired a general criminal jurisdiction by the time of Severus, and probably well before) and other new officials. Further, in some cases the emperor himself exercised jurisdiction, and in others the Senate.

The *quaestiones* were certainly not abolished; after all, Augustus was concerned to regulate and add to them.[72] Tiberius seems to have been endorsing them shortly after his succession in AD 14; this must have been his meaning when he said that the laws, the statutes, must continue to operate.[73] We are told explicitly of the existence of the *quaestio de sicariis* in AD 54 and of the *quaestio de falsis* in AD 61.[74] Quintilian, who died in 96, speaks of them as a living institution, but he is not altogether reliable.[75] Pliny's evidence is ambiguous;[76] Sherwin-White reasonably suggests, in the absence of evidence: 'Probably the growth of the criminal jurisdiction of the Senate, for certain forms of crime involving the upper social classes, had led to the grouping of two or three of the obsolescent *quaestiones* under a single praetor to deal with offences affecting lower ranks of society'.[77] Nevertheless, certain of the courts, such as those for *maiestas* and *res repetundae*, disappear totally from the record after the beginning of Tiberius' reign; from Suetonius and Tacitus we could reasonably expect notices of their operation, had they survived. It would not be particularly surprising if what happened was that the courts for political crimes disappeared while those for ordinary offences, such as adultery, murder and forgery, continued.[78] It may be significant that the formula given for an indictment is an accusation of adultery,[79] and that so much juristic discussion of adultery is preserved in the Digest; or this may simply reflect the Christian Empire's interest in sexual crimes and have nothing to do with the forum. The possibility of the two alleged parties to an adultery being accused simultaneously by separate accusers[80] suggests that Ulpian was thinking of *cognitio*, trial before an official (such as the Urban Prefect or a provincial governor) sitting alone as judge, since in making charges before one *quaestio* (even if, like the Republican murder court, it met as several sessions) this should readily have been controlled. Severus, as Dio tells us, set out to repress adultery and consequently there were so many indictments that when Dio became consul he found 3,000 entered on the docket – *en to pinaki* – but this is no evidence for a continuing *quaestio perpetua*.[81] Paul's statement that the capital courts of the *ordo* had fallen into disuse may well be truly his, although it could be interpolated.[82]

Senators[83] had exercised some sort of judicial function in the Republic, both collectively in cases of national emergency,[84] and as members of the juries. The Senate was regularly operating as a court throughout the first century AD.[85] The *SC Calvisianum* of 4 BC reveals the Senate dealing with non-capital charges; it is possible that capital charges might already have been heard before a full Senate under the presidency of the consuls. It is arguable that the consuls held the *iudicii publici exercitio*, the same right as the jury courts of inappellable jurisdiction, since there seems to have been no *provocatio* from them.[86] All recorded trials before the Senate were in fact *crimina iudiciorum publicorum*, charges which would have been competent before the *quaestiones perpetuae*. The base of its authority as a court could hardly have been a *lex*; to remove all traces of such a statute would be purposeless as well as difficult.[87]

The Senate normally exercised jurisdiction over its own members (at least, after the desuetude of the *quaestiones perpetuae*), but it also heard charges of crimes against the state brought against equestrians;[88] it even sat in judgment on client kings from time to time,[89] when the emperor presided. But, not surprisingly, the evidence for its jurisdiction over non-political offences seems largely confined to senators and their families.[90]

Constitutionally, the role of the assemblies in elections was early in the Principate replaced by that of the Senate, and, theoretically, the same constitutional replacement seems to have been true in the criminal sphere. A logical consequence of this was that the Senate was never seen as subject to the norms established by the *quaestiones perpetuae*; its jurisdiction was always *cognitio*,[91] and indeed the political element was also part of the continuity. Hence, from the beginning, penalties were not fixed.[92] But the framework of the *quaestiones perpetuae* was preserved, as in other developments of *cognitio*;[93] Pliny shows clearly that departure from the norms of the system required justification.[94] We find a rather loose use of near-synonymous terms – *subscriptio, postulatio, delatio, accusatio, inscriptio* – for the citizen laying his complaint before the consuls;[95] *libelli accusatorii* seem not required since the Senate's proceedings were normally activated orally. The accusation was accepted, *receptio inter reos*,[96] sometimes after discussion by the Senate, sometimes by the consul alone; at this stage the imperial tribunician *intercessio* was possible. Holders of magistracies were immune;[97] death normally ended the cause.[98]

A sort of *divinatio*, to establish the best right to prosecute, might be held;[99] supporting accusers could join themselves to a principal's case.[100] When there were several accused, or several charges, it had to be decided whether to try them separately or together;[101] even at this stage, charges of new crimes might be accepted.[102] A day was then fixed for the trial, and time allotted for the *inquisitio*, the period for collecting evidence.[103] As with trials before the *quaestiones perpetuae*, oaths must be taken against calumny and other procedural wrongdoings.[104] Speeches had to be made within time limits, and evidence was led; there followed a debate, and voting on the verdict then took place. Subsequently there might be debate on the disposal of the convict's property, or the fate of a failed *delator*; sometimes, especially in *repetundae* trials, the Senate as a body appointed a committee who were to establish the size of the reparation to be made.[105] On a capital conviction, after the immediate execution in AD 21 of Clutorius Priscus for a defamatory writing of a very mildly treasonable nature,[106] a ten-day stay of execution was established. Later, the emperor may have confirmed all capital sentences.[107] The emperor could use his *intercessio* to stop a trial or quash a verdict, until appeal from the Senate's decision was forbidden by Hadrian.[108]

Of particular importance, although technically incidental to the exercise of jurisdiction, was the development by resolution of the Senate of the interpretation of the *leges publicae* which had set up the *quaestiones perpetuae*.[109] This seems to have arisen in the course of trials as much as through consultation – the jurists were normally members of the Senate – and, at least during the first century, appears to have been far more frequent than development and interpretation by the emperor.[110] The Senate as an independent court probably disappeared in the early third century.

The emperor's jurisdiction

Naturally enough, the emperor's own jurisdiction was a new development. The early stages of his acquiring a formal jurisdiction are obscure, and purely anecdotal.[111] There is no evidence for the first actual death sentence imposed,[112] but it seems probable that Augustus must have been held to have had the *iudicii publici exercitio*, although there is nothing recorded on this point. One argument to explain the acceptance – not the reality – of his role is the jurisdiction of a *paterfamilias* over his *familia*, and Augustus was given the title 'father of his country' in 2 BC; nevertheless, imperial procurators, who should technically count within his *familia*, were sometimes tried before the Senate rather than by him.[113] Another argument is that the emperor was commander-in-chief of Rome's armies, and he thus had *imperium* in the old sense, the power of life and death over all citizens, even if technically this only applied *militiae*. Furthermore, he had permanent tribunician power, with a right of *auxilium* as well as *intercessio*, and presumably of making accusations, and this could have justified his interventions. Yet some cases put before the emperor do not seem to have fitted any such pretext, such as the accusation against a leading provincial on a non-specific charge of vilifying the emperor, or the woman who claimed that her son had been poisoned by his freedmen.[114] The relationship between imperial decisions and the rule of law certainly became formalized, but of its nature it was not governed by law.[115]

Procedure in trials before the emperor was formally unregulated, save by custom, but a custom shaped by the *lex Iulia iudiciorum publicorum*. His private *consilium* was of importance although, as had always been the case, lacking in authority.[116] Imperial decisions, whether as *decreta* in individual cases before him, or as rescripts when was consulted, must normally have been the work of the jurists on his personal *consilium* or in the Senate, which constituted a formal *consilium* for him as it had for the Republican consuls. However, some decisions on grounds of 'public interest' presumably stemmed directly from the imperial will,[117] just as did some developments even in private law.[118] But it was delegation by the emperor, not his own exercise of jurisdiction nor, as yet, his interpretative function, which provided the Principate's major changes in criminal process. The increasing role of officials not known to the Republic, in particular the Urban Prefect and, later, the Praetorian Prefect, was among the most obvious of these changes. Another was the increased importance of this aspect of the provincial governor's function, an increase which led to his being commonly referred to simply as '*iudex*', because that had become the most important aspect of his duties. Direct legislation by *edicta* was not of much importance until the end of the second century;[119] it became supreme and without rival in the Later Empire. The use of rescripts to develop the law as well as expound it also became marked from the Severan period; in the Later Empire they were much less important as sources of law.[120] As Honoré has said: 'For three centuries Roman law had been case law, drawn either from the *responsa* of jurists or from imperial rescripts. With the compilation of the new codes [of Gregorianus and Hermogenianus, under Diocletian's orders] it was implicit that henceforth the law could grow only by general legislation.'[121]

The move to *cognitio* by the emperor or his delegates also, by definition, meant a move away from the use of the *quaestiones perpetuae*, and this permitted an increase in the number and importance of *crimina extraordinaria*.[122] Theft – but this was surely partly for socio-economic reasons – became normally treated as a crime whereas before it had been classed primarily as a delict,[123] and special categories of thief were identified;[124] this was jurisprudential rather than administrative development. Other crimes, from the profession of Christianity[125] to cornering grain,[126] violation of sepulture,[127] and *stellionatus*[128] appeared, some on the margins of private law, as with the *crimen expilatae hereditatis*.[129] Even where a crime fell within the scope of the statutes establishing the *quaestiones perpetuae*, a judge exercising *cognitio* had discretion over the penalty, though this discretion was not unfettered.[130]

The Urban Prefect had some criminal jurisdiction in the City from the start[131] and, by the time of Severus at the latest, within a hundred-mile radius of Rome.[132] The Prefect of the Night Watch had a considerable, if limited, jurisdiction over petty crime.[133] The Prefect of the Grain Supply was very important in his particular sphere of office; its significance for the well-being of the City was indicated by the special relaxations on the right to make accusations in this field.[134] By the time of the Severi, the Praetorian Prefects had jurisdiction in Italy beyond the hundred-mile radius; they had started as military commanders of the Praetorian Guard, but from the late second century the post acquired judicial functions.[135] These functions came to the fore, and were indeed their only ones in the Dominate. Their own jurisdiction was obscure, but the emperors came to delegate to them their appellate function,[136] and they sat *vice sacra*, in the emperor's stead, in the Later Empire.

The emperor, naturally enough, could always delegate his powers. Other officials, however, could only do so if they held through their own proper office such powers as they wished to delegate; a delegate could not further delegate.[137] Appeal was always possible from someone with a delegated jurisdiction to his principal's authority, hence *appellatio* replaced *provocatio*, but not where an inappellable jurisdiction had been delegated;[138] in that case the only recourse was an appeal for clemency, through the emperor's tribunician *intercessio*, or, later, his plenitude of power.[139] The Senate, as we have remarked, had become inappellable, perhaps from Hadrian on.[140] There were penalties for frivolous appeals; for reasons of expediency, some convicted persons (e.g. brigands caught in the act, stirrers of sedition, leaders of gangs, or those who had confessed) were not allowed to appeal.[141] After the *constitutio Antoniniana* of 212 (when virtually all free inhabitants of the Empire became Roman citizens), appeal followed sentence rather than arrest,[142] save in the case of decurions and imperial officials, but, on the other hand, it was by that time normally available to any free person because all were citizens. Appeals also became possible, through *cognitio*, from those who were not acting as delegates, such as *recuperatores*.[143]

In all the courts procedure became gradually standardized. The original freedom and discretion of *cognitio* became regulated, as for example in the treatment of proofs,[144] or the imposition of penalties. In the provinces, the *ius gladii* ceased to be a military power; it turned into the *merum imperium* now exercised by all governors, but only by them. A governor's *legatus* must remit capital cases to his superior, and had not even the right *atrociter verberare*.[145] However, at least until AD 212, criminal law in the provinces remained largely distinct from the exercise of Roman law over Roman citizens,[146] and the focus of this book is on Rome itself and its surroundings (and to some extent Italy). Appeals did, however, flow in to Rome (and later Constantinople), so that the higher Roman courts had some concern with provincial business.

The Dominate

In the Later Empire, that is administratively (although not jurisprudentially) from the reign of Diocletian, there was no specific Roman law distinct from what was available in the provinces; even Italy was classed among the provinces. The new administrative structure split up the traditional provinces; for example there were at one stage five where there had been one in Britain.[147] Each group of these new provinces was classed as a diocese, nearly always under a vicar, and the dioceses grouped into four (Praetorian) Prefectures (Oriens, Illyria, Italy, Gaul). Rome, and shortly Constantinople, with their surroundings, were alone outside the new structure. The emperor was now deliberately a figure of awe, remote from his subjects, garbed in purple, and carrying an aura of the divine.[148] However, although competence, procedure and penalties in criminal law had all changed, the substantive categories of the system of the *quaestiones perpetuae* remained, from conservatism, and for ease in interpretation.[149]

In the Dominate the Senate was no longer a regular court, but the *iudicium quinquevirale*,[150] five senators under the presidency of the Urban Prefect, had jurisdiction in capital cases involving senators, so a vestigial jurisdictional role remained. Justinian invited all senators to sit in his *consistorium*; senators might be appointed judges of appeal.[151] (After Constantine, a senator who was not of the highest grade[152] lost the privilege of being tried only in Rome – or Constantinople – because he was no longer required to have his domicile there; most senators thus, for the first time, became justiciable in the provinces.[153]) Emperors seldom gave public and personal justice.[154] Imperial jurisdiction was exercised in particular by the Praetorian Prefects, each *vice sacra iudicans*.[155] The Praetorian Prefects were inappellable, but *supplicatio*, an appeal for imperial clemency, was possible.[156] Other imperial jurisdiction was delegated to the higher officials in the capitals, in the provinces, and in the palace, who heard persons of high rank at first instance, as well as appeals; they too could delegate, but their decisions could also be appealed to the emperor (or the Praetorian Prefect). The importance of the imperial household jurisdiction was enormous, because it covered the whole civil service.[157] The jurisdiction of individual functionaries, particularly the Urban Prefect, seems to have become wider.[158] (However, the *vicarius urbis Romae* was not his deputy, but the head of the diocese comprising the southern Italian provinces.[159]) Over the Empire at large, apart from the conflicts where military or fiscal courts claimed jurisdiction,[160] we find nearly everywhere the hierarchy of prefecture, diocese, province.[161] In the cities of the Empire *defensores civitatum*, with petty criminal jurisdiction, replaced, at least partially, the municipal magistrates; major matters continued to be remitted to the provincial governor.[162] The Church began to play a role; while having only powers of arbitration, the *episcopalis audientia* acquired official status.[163] We hear of the *forum ecclesiasticum*; and the clergy emerge as a particular, and privileged, class.[164] Asylum, under the protection of the Church, was a more regulated affair.[165]

There were specific changes in procedure. State prosecution – *inquisitio* – often replaced accusation by a member of the public (but we should remember that an investigation must usually be triggered by an individual complaint), although the victim of a crime did not lose the right of accusation.[166] Once a charge was accepted by a court, it was put into writing, and this *inscriptio* or *libellus accusationis* was signed by the accuser and the accused and entered on the court register; no oral accusations were accepted, at least for serious crimes.[167] Much emphasis was laid on the safeguards against abuse of procedure, even when the accused was a slave.[168] Since all jurisdiction was *cognitio*, there was judicial discretion over the control of proceedings, but we find much legislation trying to prevent improper influences on the judge.[169] Other legislation was directed to bringing accused persons to trial within a reasonable time.[170] Because there were clearly so many prisoners on remand,[171] there were attempts to improve prison conditions, restricting the fetters that might be imposed, and ensuring light and food by regular inspections; the sexes were to be held separately.[172] Torture was now regularly used on an accused and even on witnesses, unless they were of the *honestiores*;[173] no rank however high was protection against torture when the charge was one of treason, and then it might even be used on the accuser.[174] Appeals were restricted, in the interest of speedier justice generally.[175]

There were changes in penalties. It seems unlikely that punishments were any more cruel than they had been in the Principate:[176] indeed crucifixion was abolished, and Christians forbidden to be sent to the arena.[177] It is possible that there was a wider use of forced labour.[178] Severe punishment seems, however, despite attempts to restrict capital penalties,[179] to have been more widely used, and on a much higher proportion of the population.[180] Conviction for treason carried a blood taint,[181] although in other cases the emperors were careful to leave something for the family of a convict whose property had been confiscated.[182] There were restrictions on judicial discretion. Lower judges ceased to have discretion in sentencing,[183] and could not revoke a sentence once passed.[184] No death sentence or sentence of total confiscation could be passed without imperial confirmation.[185] When, presumably through judicial or administrative incompetence, persons had been held in prison instead of being sent into exile, they were deemed to have served their prescribed sentences.[186]

There was also some development of substantive criminal law. We find the teaching of the art of ship-building to the barbarians forbidden,[187] and also the keeping of private prisons.[188] Various disabilities were imposed on pagans, Jews and heretics;[189] the Christian state was more concerned with belief than the pagan one had been. Far more striking is that a whole new field of offences arose, when almost any failure in their duty by officials could be interpreted as a crime;[190] there were also many straightforward official crimes.[191] It became the duty of an office staff, whether provincial or central, to report their chief's misdoings.[192] The function of the *agentes in rebus* and *curiosi* was primarily to act as inspectors in an attempt, however vain, to maintain standards in the administration.[193] *Ambitus* now, strangely, became an internal crime, an attempt to climb faster or hold a rank longer in the civil service than the regulations permitted.[194] New criminal legislation in the Dominate was fragmentary, and not always consistent. Legislation, in other words, was markedly reactive; for example, the term *maiestas* could be extended to cover such offences as keeping a private prison, or coining.[195] Little regard was paid to any requirement of *dolus* or *mens rea*.[196] Calumny lost the element of motivation, of intention; merely to make an unsustainable accusation brought punishment.[197] In rape the woman was presumed at fault, and it must have been hard for her to prove otherwise; however, the power of an owner or father to prostitute a girl in his power was limited.[198]

The Later Empire was a savage period; the arbitrary exercise of power was, in a sense, increasing.[199] The criminal law of the Principate was hardly refined compared with the private law, but the norms of the rule of law, of jurisprudence, seem usually to have prevailed; an innocent man – at least, one of standing[200] – need not, outside politics, fear that he would be dragged before the courts. In the Christian Empire there were no safeguards in practice, except perhaps through the Church. The statement of the jurist Paul that in criminal matters the more favourable interpretation should be taken, and that of Hermogenianus that interpretation should be used to soften rather than harshen the penalties of the laws,[201] were empty words in the Later Roman Empire. Justinian preserved in the Digest both Trajan's statement that it was better to let the guilty go unpunished than to condemn the innocent, and also Ulpian's stress on the importance of the distinction between design and accident in fixing the proper penalty,[202] but the literature of the period tells another story.[203]

II

Criminal Liability

Any person involved in a crime, whether as accused, as accuser, or as witness, might be differently treated, depending on sex, age, social status, legal status, and state of mind, as also the time, place and nature of the crime.[1] Equality before the law was not a Roman concept. There were, however, some general norms about intention, *actus reus*, complicity, and defences, and also about prescription, which we shall consider in this chapter.

Domestic jurisdiction

The *paterfamilias* had power of life and death over all those in his *potestas*, and also the power of noxal surrender – although this may never have applied to daughters in historic times. A woman *sui iuris* was in early times presumably subject to her male agnates, perhaps joined by her husband. In later days a woman condemned by a public court might be handed over to her family for execution or exile.[2] (The *pontifex maximus* had a familial jurisdiction over Vestal Virgins.[3]) In domestic jurisdiction over free persons a family *consilium* seems to have been required by convention for the legality of a sentence but, since there does not seem to have been any right of appeal anywhere, this was not enforceable.[4] Slaves, and even freedmen, were originally subject to domestic jurisdiction, primarily if not exclusively.[5] In the course of the Empire, in the interests of public order, the State developed a concern with the criminal behaviour of all who lived within its frontiers, and slaves became subject to public criminal process,[6] and also to some extent protected by it, in that killing a slave could ground a murder charge. Of sons too we are told that a father should not kill his son without a proper hearing but should accuse him before the Urban Prefect.[7] Constantine restricted the owner's right to punish his slaves, although death following inadvertently from a beating was not to be viewed as homicide.[8] Subsequently domestic jurisdiction over free persons was confirmed, but limited to other than serious crime.[9]

There must be a guilty party

The accused must be a living person, with certain exceptions, most notably high treason, *perduellio*, where the serious nature of the crime came to allow the accusation of a dead man.[10] In cases of *repetundae*, and other offences where there was a delictual element, the heirs could be pursued for the unjust enrichment of the estate, though not, of course, for the crime itself; and, similarly, if *litis contestatio* had taken place or the charge had been accepted.[11]

Infants, those under seven years, were excluded from penal liability, as being incapable of *dolus*, of forming a guilty intention.[12] Children up to puberty had a presumption in their favour, but this could be rebutted;[13] their age would also normally protect them from torture.[14] But politics could lead to mere assassinations or exceptions in form of law, such as the sad case of Sejanus' daughter.[15]

Lunatics also were not capable of committing a crime, though the Romans had the usual difficulty of deciding whether there was true insanity or if it was only feigned, and intermittent insanity also posed problems.[16] But a lunatic might have to be kept under restraint, even in chains, for the public safety.[17] While it may not be a true story, we are told that a lunatic slave who attacked the Emperor Hadrian in a friend's garden was simply restrained by Hadrian himself and then not punished but handed over to the physicians' care.[18]

It was only persons falling into these categories, the dead, the young, the lunatic, who were actually relieved of all responsibility. Other persons, magistrates in office who had *imperium*, were totally immune from criminal accusations during, but only during, their term[19] – so too were emperors, but this is moving outside the realm of law in any meaningful sense. In other cases, extenuating circumstances might modify the penalty, but there was criminal responsibility.

For the commission of a crime, as opposed to an unfortunate accident, guilty intention – *dolus*, or what we call *mens rea* – was normally required; *fraus* was also a common term.[20] An accident did not impose criminal liability.[21] As far back as the Twelve Tables, crimes such as pasturage by night on another's land presume such a guilty intention; one would not put out one's beasts at night in the normal way of honesty. But the intention was specifically relevant in cases of incendiarism and death; an objective standard, that the deed was done, may have been enough to create liability, but it was a lesser liability.[22] Later law, classical Roman law, demanded a subjective standard,[23] although reckless conduct (as under the *lex Aquilia*) might still deserve some punishment.[24] Ignorance of the law, unlike ignorance of the facts, was culpable;[25] it was the duty of the citizen to know the law. Liability could not therefore properly be retrospective except, of course, on political grounds.

There were groups whose liability was sometimes accepted as being diminished; these included women, minors, and country dwellers.[26] They might be treated more gently when ignorant of the law; this applied particularly, in the Principate but not in the Christian Empire, to the female partner in an incestuous marriage.[27] Other cases of lenient treatment for women occur in the contexts of forgery and procedural offences.[28] Widows and pupils were specifically protected from the presumption of complicity if counterfeiting took place on the property on which they lived, but without their knowledge; pupils were not to be punished even if they knew, although their tutors might be liable.[29] Minors (those over puberty but under 25) might perhaps also get some benefit from their lack of full age.[30]

Non-citizens cannot have been presumed to know the law, but they had no formal protection against the *coercitio* of magistrate or official, nor could they claim any entitlement to due process. It is not clear what did happen to offending non-citizens at Rome. One can assume most of them would have been dealt with by the *tresviri capitales*, or later the Urban Prefect or the Prefect of the Night Watch. Our information about free non-citizens is, not surprisingly, concentrated on the provinces (and too much of it concerns the early Christians); after the general grant to the free inhabitants of the Empire of citizenship in 212 the problem must have disappeared, as it has from our legal sources. There, the only category of concern is that of those who escaped from their place of exile;[31] the reinforcement of a penalty imposed on a citizen was a matter for due process of law.

Roman criminal law knew humans only as individuals.[32] It was not a *collegium* that was prosecuted, but the individual members of it; the nearest approach to corporate liability was the military penalty of decimation. (This, of course, did not exclude political penalties imposed on cities, such as the sack of Corinth, but that was war not law.) And animals were not held criminally liable, although their conduct might impose the need for reparation on their owner.[33]

The *actus reus* and attempted crimes

For a crime to be constituted, there must be a fact, a deed, an *actus reus*; there could be no crime in a thought.[34] A dolose *animus* was necessary, but it had to find expression.[35] Speech could count as an act in some circumstances, such as defamation; this particularly applied to treason. The clearest statement is ascribed to Claudius Saturninus: 'There are punishments for things done, such as thefts and killings, or for things said, such as insults or false pleadings, or for things written, such as forgeries and defamatory publications, or for things counselled, such as conspiracies and the guilty knowledge of robbers.'[36]

This text does not, however, make clear how the things counselled would become known, other than by speech or writing. If performance has not been completed of a criminal act, there is often no act.[37] Thus it was held that the edict binding someone with jurisdiction to abide himself by his own rulings was not applicable if he had ruled something where he did not in fact have jurisdiction; there was no valid act.[38] In testamentary law, where there was no will recognized by law there could be no forgery or other related crime;[39] however, the invalidity of a particular disposition did not relieve a dishonest person from criminal liability.[40] Again, when a man had arranged for organized abuse against someone but it did not take place, he was not liable under the *lex Cornelia* on outrage.[41]

An additional problem is that where there was a detectable act of attempt, this act must vary with the crime attempted and what has actually been achieved.[42] The usual case on which to hang a discussion of attempted crime was in fact delictual: Titius solicited my slave to steal from me for Titius' benefit; my slave reported this to me and, wishing to catch Titius in the act, I told my slave to go ahead. On strict logic, as given by Gaius, no delict has been committed because Titius did not handle my property against my will, and my slave was not corrupted.[43] Justinian, with an Empire to rule, allowed both actions in order to discourage such attempts.[44] On similar grounds of expediency, any attempt at treason was in itself treasonable. (It seems probable that the curious case of pardon being granted to those who struck *'falsam monetam'* if they did not intend a complete likeness, referred to commemorative medallions and such like, rather than actual coinage.[45])

One approach is to hold criminal the conduct necessary for the attempt itself; being in possession of a drug to be used for homicide was specifically brought under the *lex Cornelia*, just as possessing a weapon *occidendi hominis causa* was itself held an offence.[46] Similarly, the view was taken that to advise a slave to run away was not theft but the corruption of a slave.[47] A second is to interpret a crime so widely that any visible attempt is likely to fall under the interpretation. This would seem the justification for making liable to the penalty of the *lex Cornelia testamentaria* the opening of the will of a living person.[48] A third is to develop a doctrine of attempt, and make that in itself a crime. Specific prohibitions of attempts, whether to solicit promotion in the civil service or to make pagan sacrifices, appear in the Codes,[49] whereas the jurists of the classical period of law seem to have preferred to talk of intention.[50] It was a capital offence for a soldier to intend to desert.[51] Yet the outcome was relevant as well as the intention, so that a deed done even by a most inoffensive person might still earn punishment.[52] This question of outcome seems also to have been the rationale when different penalties were stated to be suitable for a completed or uncompleted seduction.[53]

The problem of attempted crimes was perhaps minimized for the Romans in two ways. While theory did not distinguish between completed and half-completed deeds, once *cognitio* was normal, with discretion in sentencing, the penalty could be varied in practice. *Coercitio* was always available to repress any breach of the peace, such as threatening behaviour, which did not fall under the *lex Cornelia de sicariis*. Certainly, there was no general crime of incitement or conspiracy[54] to provide a non-specific ground by which people could be made liable for a non-deed.

Accomplices

Those partaking in a crime *ope consiliove* – art and part, in Scots legal terminology – were accomplices; the terms were no longer, in developed law, applied to the principal.[55] While there was argument at one time whether the words should be taken as linked or alternate, Paul followed Labeo in holding that there were thus two kinds of complicity;[56] the terminology developed so as in general to define a *socius* as a partner in the deed, a *conscius* one with guilty knowledge, and a *minister* a tool.[57] (In contrast, the Church lists nine ways of partaking in another's sin.[58]) There must be a principal and he must commit an illegal act.[59] In classical law anyway, an accomplice to be so categorized must have a guilty intention;[60] hence one incapable of *dolus* could not be liable as an accomplice.[61] To know who was a thief and not to point him out did not create liability for theft, but in other, more serious offences, such as parricide or brigandage, silence did create liability.[62] The notion of there being a duty to prevent something (without a previous assumption of care) seems to have remained unknown to the civil law, but it was accepted into criminal law.[63] The savage *SC Silanianum* was the consequence of the positive duty of all slaves to guard their owners at the risk of their own lives; they were seen as accomplices in the crime if they failed to prevent their owner's murder.[64] In late law, in cases of treason even intercession on behalf of a suspect could amount to complicity.[65] Some behaviour that does not seem immediately connected with theft was nevertheless viewed as partaking of the theft, such as knocking coins out of someone's hand if they were then seized by somebody else, or waving a red flag which frightened cattle into flight and enabled them to be seized by a thief.[66] Enabling a theft, not for gain but from ill-will to the victim, made one art and part in the theft.[67]

Mere exhortation to someone to commit a crime did not create criminal liability,[68] except, of course, for treason. Complicity *consilio*, by advice, must be specific, by persuasion, direction and instruction;[69] it could also, however, take the form of acquiescence to, ratification of, the deed.[70] A request to someone to do something illegal also created liability.[71] In cases where an order was given to commit a delict or a crime by someone having the authority to give orders, an owner to his slave or a *paterfamilias* to his son, the owner was seen not as an accomplice but as a principal;[72] the same was true when he did not forbid an intended crime he knew of.[73] Where he did not know of his slave's conduct, he was not criminally liable but noxally liable in delict.[74] Obedience to the order of a judge was a necessity, and there could be no *dolus* in such conduct.[75] We shall consider the defence of the slave who alleged he must obey his owner in the next section. Moreover, complicity could be negative; actively to conceal a crime or a criminal did create liability,[76] as did accepting bribes not to apprehend brigands or not to make an accusation of adultery.[77] In some cases there seems to have been a presumption of complicity applied to the owners of land on which counterfeiting was carried out, or heretical practices observed, or brigands sheltered;[78] this could be rebutted or a defence made, as we shall shortly see.

An accomplice was normally held equally liable with the principal offender,[79] indeed, it was not always clear whether there was a distinction;[80] one who learnt magic was as guilty as one who taught it.[81] All accomplices were held equally liable.[82] In the Christian Empire more emphasis was sometimes laid on subjective responsibility, and with this a graduation of penalty; leading heretics might receive more severe punishment than those they led.[83] Again, *cognitio* of its nature allowed for a greater discretion, except where confined by imperial decree.

Defences and pleas in mitigation

We have already discussed the categorical cases of diminished responsibility in women and others. There were various generally recognized defences, which relieved, wholly or partially, from the penal consequences of a deed. Self-defence was one such, but it must involve minimum force.[84] Hadrian laid down that a man who had killed someone making a forcible sexual assault, whether on himself or on a member of his family, was to be discharged.[85] A rather curious edict of 391 gave all men unrestricted right to resist ravaging soldiers and others, in the fields or on the highways.[86]

Defence of superior orders was important in a slave-owning society, and one with serious paternal power; we have mentioned it in the context of complicity. Pleas of this nature can shift responsibility for the deed itself or for the penal consequence.[87] The conclusion one must normally draw is that obedience provided a plea in mitigation rather than a true defence; liability for the crime subsisted, but liability to the penalty was reduced or remitted.[88] A clear example is the case where the Senate remitted the penalty of the Cornelian law on forgery to a man who had offended directly against the *SC Libonianum*, because he had acted on his father's order, and was still young; moreover, he was allowed to take his inheritance.[89] As a defence it was based on the assumption that the intention of the slave or son actually involved was not criminous.[90] It was important that the person who gave the order had the right to do so,[91] but even so, the slave had no right to obey an order to commit a clearly illegal act; if he did so he could be prosecuted in his own person, whether still as a slave or after being freed.[92] Duress was presumably a somewhat similar defence, perhaps linked with necessity.[93]

There were other pleas for the defence to make. Passion might be taken into account to reduce the penalty, but it did not affect the liability. The man who killed his wife on catching her in adultery was generally accepted to have mitigating circumstances to plead;[94] indeed, her slaves did not fall under the *SC Silanianum* if, in these circumstances, they failed to resist a master with a just resentment.[95] Family ties, the claims of blood, could on occasion mitigate the penalty, as with those who sheltered brigands who were their own kin.[96] Drunkenness too might be a plea in mitigation.[97] The Romans do not seem to have recognized, in this context, hallucinatory or other drugs. And, at least under Aquilian liability, the act of the victim could relieve the doer of blame – the intruder on the firing range.[98]

Prescription of criminal liability

The final area to be discussed is the prescription of crime, the lapse of a period after which prosecution was not possible. There appear to have been no such limits in the period before Augustus' revision of the *quaestiones perpetuae*.[99] In some statutes prescriptive periods were laid down, for example five years for an accusation of adultery[100] or of *peculatus*;[101] five years was also the limit for bringing a charge, in the context of the *SC Silanianum*, that a man's will had been opened before the investigation of his death.[102] For other offences there was explicitly no prescriptive period; these included parricide, or the introduction of a suppositious child into a family (which fell under *falsum*),[103] or serious heresy, which, like treason, could even be charged against the dead.[104]

A generalized prescriptive period of twenty years was, on the face of it, introduced by Diocletian, in the context of *falsum*, to apply where nothing else was specified.[105] This vicennial period has been argued to be Justinianic, but not very convincingly.[106] The vicennial period appears to have been familiar to the classical jurists in the context of fiscal proceedings.[107] Once procedure was all *extra ordinem*, governors and others with jurisdiction, such as the Urban Prefect, will have tended to conflate the various forms of process, since civil, fiscal and criminal matters were so often brought to the same court. It seems inherently likely that the same jurisprudence that introduced a vicennial term in civil and fiscal procedure also laid it down for criminal process; I am therefore inclined to attribute its introduction to Severus and Antoninus, or their advisers. The later second century was a period when there was clear juristic interest in the administration of the criminal law.[108]

III

Theft and Related Offences

It is a safe guess that the great majority of crimes committed in Rome, as in modern Europe, were theft, assault, and damage to property. In Rome, however, these crimes were primarily – at least in the juristic sources[1] – treated as delicts. This approach, in a slave-owning society where owners were noxally liable for the delicts of their slaves,[2] probably meant that there was often a fair chance of reparation for the victim of a theft. It also meant that theft was not included among the crimes of the *ordo*, those dealt with by the standing jury courts; it was always repressed *extra ordinem*.[3]

Theft

The compilers of Justinian's Digest elected to distinguish among certain sorts of theft (of which *rapina*[4] had had an independent existence since the earlier first century AD) as well as identifying some closely related offences, such as the pillaging of an inheritance[5] or the ancient Twelve Table delicts of *tignum iunctum*[6] and *arborum furtim caesarum*. Concerning this last, whether from the simple economic centrality of fruit-bearing trees as food, or echoing the age-old importance of Ceres, those who *furtim* – as though they were thieving – cut down trees, and particularly vines, were said by Gaius to be punished as though they were bandits.[7] Elsewhere we are told more specifically that to cut fruiting trees by night incurred a spell of forced labour for most offenders and for *honestiores* a fine or removal from the *curia* or relegation.[8] The compilers also created Digest titles devoted to the strict liability of *nautae caupones* and *stabularii*, theft by a group of slaves within the *familia*, rustling, resetting, thieving at the baths, and burglars and breakers-in.[9]

The greatest part by far of the consideration of theft as a delict was taken from the works *ad Sabinum* of Paul and Ulpian; there was a very limited overlap with the texts, even from the same jurists, concerning theft as a crime.[10] The compilers' separation seems therefore to have been in accord with the approach of the jurists. Further, in Justinian's Code the title on theft and the corruption of slaves[11] was not classed with criminal law in Book 9, but placed between the treatment of fugitive slaves and of freedmen's services. And the congruence of the attitudes of the compilers and the classical jurists is in general confirmed by such post-classical works as *Pauli Sententiae* and the *Collatio*.

Nevertheless, theft was always a crime as well as a delict.[12] The choice, in the Empire, between a civil or criminal action for theft lay with the victim, who could go to the civil courts or '*in crimen subscribere*' – lay a charge;[13] if he brought the thief before the *praefectus vigilum* (or the governor in the provinces) he was taken to have preferred a criminal remedy.[14] While theft was indeed a crime, in the vast majority of cases there would be no reason for the authorities to intervene if the victim was being compensated, and the thief punished by the multiple penalty of the *actio furti*. Moreover, until well into the Empire, domestic jurisdiction was fully recognized. This explains sufficiently why it was aggravated thefts which fell in the public criminal domain; primarily it was when something outrageous needed to be marked for public disapproval that the state intervened. Certain classes of thief were identified as posing a greater threat to society because of their audacity, or the frequency or scale of their operations; the enhanced threat was to be met with an aggravated penalty. Hence in the crime of rustling, *abigeatus*, it is not clear that a choice was allowed to the victim,[15] though presumably a *vindicatio* (or the *condictio furtiva*) would always lie, even when the penal *actio furti* was excluded by the principle of *bis de eadem*.

In the Republic the *tresviri capitales* dealt with thieves, in particular, one must suppose, when no owner could be found. It is argued whether their jurisdiction extended over free men; it seems to me highly likely that there was a legal presumption that anyone who could not account for himself was either a fugitive slave or a foreigner. In the Empire, the *praefectus vigilum* exercised a jurisdiction over thieves; the option of criminal proceedings against thieves in the classical period has been amply demonstrated.[16] In the Later Empire, the blurring of the distinction between civil and criminal jurisdiction (and in the latter the disappearance of the reality of the distinction between the *ordo iudiciorum publicorum* and treatment *extra ordinem*) meant that the problem was rather whether the victim could hope for reparation even though the thief was to be punished,[17] for the punishment might remove from the criminal his means of reparation or put him into another world.

It seems clear from the texts that there was no legislative development of the crime of theft; theft was part of the *ius civile* in the narrowest sense, developed solely by juristic interpretation. The praetor's edict was simply the means by which the penalties were adjusted from those of the primitive period.[18] (His edict, however, was the source for the liability of *nautae*, *caupones*, *stabularii* and in cases of theft by a group of slaves within the *familia*, and also of course for *rapina*, which will be treated after theft.) Nor does there seem to have been any attempt to develop either the content or the scope of theft as crime; the elaborate jurisprudential development of the delict will have been more than sufficient for the simpler needs of those whose duty it was to enforce law and order. Further, the definition of the boundary with *stellionatus* and *falsum* was of relatively little importance in proceedings *extra ordinem*; this was even more the case with matters of fraud which were not quite within the definition of theft.[19]

Taking away another's property was the commonest form of theft, but it was possible to steal one's own property from someone who had currently a better right to it, such as the pledge creditor.[20] Also, one could steal without any intention permanently to deprive the owner of his property.[21] The doctrine of *contrectatio* (dishonest meddling) could be used to penalize attempted theft; it seems to have been extended to cover inducing a debtor to pay someone misrepresenting himself as the creditor or the creditor's procurator,[22] or someone who kept part of what he should have disbursed under a mandate.[23] Land could not be 'stolen', essentially because it could not be taken away, but perhaps also because the typical theft is a secret act.[24] Only *res in commercio* which had an owner could be stolen; where there was no owner an alternative way of repression must be found, as with the *crimen expilatae hereditatis*.[25] The place from which the thing was taken might determine whether there was theft or sacrilege.[26]

Particular forms of theft

Abigeatus or rustling

While rustling is of its nature a country pursuit, and therefore not found in the City of Rome, it was intermittently prevalent in Italy[27] and not necessarily remote from the capital. Rustling was distinguished from theft solely by the number of animals involved: 'Quantity distinguishes the thief from the rustler; for the man who steals one pig is punished as a thief, but he who takes a herd as a rustler.'[28] Carrying arms might aggravate the offence, but its essence remained the number of beasts taken. The clearest statement is given by Paul: 'Rustlers are those who steal one stallion, two mares, and as many oxen [or cows, presumably], ten sheep or goats or five pigs. Whatever is driven away under this number incurs the penalty of theft ... .'[29] Callistratus also named ten sheep as the dividing line, five or four[30] pigs, and a single horse or ox.[31] His failure to distinguish between stallions and mares, and his classing of the taking of a single ox as rustling not theft may have sprung from a sterner view of the law, held either at the time he wrote or, more likely, by the compilers.[32] He also explained that repeated cattle-lifting or sheep-stealing, even of single animals, amounted to rustling.[33] Ulpian was less definite about numbers: rustlers take horses or oxen, but one who takes a single pig or goat or wether (probably meaning any sheep) ought not to be punished like one who drives off the larger animals;[34] this implies that for him too one or two horses or oxen would be sufficient to constitute the offence of rustling.

Heinous rustlers were those who drove off horses or flocks of sheep (whether from a stable or from pasture) either habitually or when carrying arms or with a hired gang.[35] The place from which the beasts were taken was not usually of itself important.[36] However, the man who drove off a stray ox or horses left in an uninhabited tract was not a rustler but rather a thief.[37] Here it was possible that the animals were abandoned or had been left behind by bandits, or they might be lost. The one who drove them off had clearly come upon them by chance, rather than setting out with an intention to drive them off; his succumbing to temptation was insufficient to make him guilty of more than theft.

Hadrian laid down in a rescript for the province of Baetica (in southern Spain) that rustlers there were to be particularly harshly punished, by being put to the sword. But they were not everywhere to be punished so harshly but only where this class of wrongdoing was rather common; elsewhere they were to be sent to forced labour, sometimes only for a limited period.[38] Rustling was not a crime of the *ordo* but rather a theft; but rustlers often carried offensive weapons, and if they were arrested in such circumstances, it was customary for their crime to be severely punished.[39] In these cases of aggravated rustling, the penalty would usually be death or the mines, but sometimes forced labour was held sufficient.[40] Although Hadrian laid down as penalties forced labour, condemnation to the mines or even death by the sword, these were not held suitable for the well-born, who were to be relegated or removed from the *curia*. Presumably upper-class rustlers, unlike others, were not sent to the beasts for doing their rustling armed.[41] Resetters who received the rustlers' plunder were, according to a letter of Trajan, to be relegated from Italy for ten years;[42] this implies that they were likely to be of the land-owning classes.

When beasts which were the subject of an ownership dispute had been rustled, there should be civil rather than criminal proceedings; but only as long as the claim seemed to be based on good faith.[43] Although such a case was likely to be one of self-help, *vis* was not mentioned, and Paul stated that in such circumstances there was a double or triple penalty, as for a thief.[44]

Expilatores, effractores, derectarii, saccularii, and thieves by night and at the baths[45]

Some types of thief were singled out for specific comment. *Latrones*, bandits or brigands, were in effect outlaws, and could even be of the Robin Hood kind.[46] Certain rather heinous thieves were described as *expilatores*; interestingly, Ulpian seems to have expected some of their number to come from the upper classes.[47] Pillaging dwellings and country houses, breaking into them and plundering them, was how they particularly manifested themselves; in the Digest such conduct was also classed under *vis privata*.[48] *Effractores* were burglars; they broke into places – and presumably out again. They were particularly prevalent in blocks of flats – the houses of the rich would have guards at the door – and in warehouses, where men deposited their riches; those supposed to protect the warehouses might be punished too, presumably as accomplices rather than for negligence.[49] Marcus Aurelius took jurisdiction over a burglar of equestrian status who made a hole through a wall and stole some money in this way;[50] the burglar was banished from Africa, his home province, and also Rome and Italy, for a five-year period. The emperor presumably dealt with this case because of the rank of the criminal; normally at Rome burglars, like firesetters, thieves, muggers and resetters, fell under the jurisdiction of the *praefectus vigilum*.[51] *Saccularii* seem to have been those who light-fingeredly cut purses or picked pockets. *Derectarii* were those who entered – without force is implied – other persons' lodgings with intent to steal.[52] Baths obviously offered opportunities to the thief, as do modern sports centres, and thieves there were specifically noted;[53] moreover, the jurisdiction of the *praefectus vigilum* extended to the changing-room attendants if they were not honest with the clothes entrusted to them.[54]

The penalties for such thieves were not necessarily very heavy. *Expilatores* were normally condemned to forced labour, for a fixed period or in perpetuity; those of higher status were removed from their rank[55] or banished.[56] However, when the pillaging was done with an armed mob, it was a capital matter.[57] According to Ulpian, no special penalty for *expilatores* was laid down in the imperial rescripts, and so dealing with them, whatever their status, was at the full discretion of the judge who had cognizance, after he had heard the case.[58] Burglars, along with *saccularii* and *derectarii*, were to be similarly punished, according to the gravity of the offence, provided that for the lower orders it did not go beyond forced labour and for the upper classes banishment.[59] Paul agreed that forced labour, preceded by a beating, was the normal penalty for burglars, but held that those who burgled by night were sent to the mines, also after being beaten.[60] Ulpian maintained that forced labour was the maximum penalty, even for nocturnal thieves (but perhaps these were simply casual thieves who picked up what was left lying about, without breaking into anywhere or entering other people's houses or cutting purses), unless they defended themselves with weapons when, like burglars who committed an assault in the course of their thieving, they were to be sent to the mines, or relegated if of higher status.[61] It is possible that nocturnal thieves were always treated criminally – otherwise why would Marcian have remarked that thieves in the daytime were liable to civil proceedings?[62] A soldier caught stealing at the baths – whether public ones or those in his barracks is not made clear – was to be discharged with ignominy.[63] Other thieves or muggers at the baths were often sent to the mines rather than to forced labour; the frequency of the offence was relevant here.[64]

Reset and harbouring

Reset, colloquially 'fencing', receiving goods knowing them to have been stolen, was a form of theft which seems regularly[65] to be distinguished not only from the actual stealing but also from being art and part in the original theft. As Marcian said, resetters were the worst class of men because without them bandits could not long survive; it was laid down that they should therefore be punished as bandits themselves.[66] Paul made the same point about identity of punishment, adding that, if resetters were removed, the greed of footpads would be put to an end.[67] Ulpian pointed out that recipients of stolen goods were not always resetters; to be liable they must be in bad faith.[68] Those who could have apprehended bandits, but took money or part of the plunder to let them go free, must be viewed as resetters.[69]

Harbouring bandits was a similar offence, but the Romans seem here to have recognized the claims of kinship as a mitigating circumstance. Relations who sheltered a bandit were not to be reckoned guiltless, but they were not to be severely punished; for it was held that the offence of those who received the persons of bandits, but not anything of gain from them, was not on a par with that of resetters.[70] This attitude continued: those who harboured bandits in the hope of sharing their loot with them were indeed to share their punishment; however, simply to shelter them, or to refrain from surrendering them to the court, was penalized by corporal punishment or a fine, according to status.[71] The Emperor Marcian seems to have envisaged a landowner, doubtless one of the *potentiores*, sheltering his over-zealous servants.[72]

Vis and *rapina*[73]

Vis as a crime had several aspects; it covered abuse of office, sedition and public disturbance, armed robbery, and physical (including sexual) assault; it will be treated more fully in the chapter on offences against the state. Moreover, the details of the crime's scope are somewhat obscure because of its confusion with the delict of rapine. *Vis* began as a circumstance, a circumstance which separated *rapina* from theft, but it became a crime; *rapina* in its turn rejoined the criminal sphere as something close to *latrocinium*, banditry. Further, the interdicts *unde vi* and *de vi armata* were possessory remedies, but the behaviour which gave rise to them lay at least on the margins of the criminal law.[74]

Although the early legislation on *vis* was almost entirely concerned with sedition, it seems probable that the *lex Lutatia* of 78 BC (perhaps in its fourth chapter) forbade the usucapion of property seized during seditious events,[75] while the *lex Plautia* extended the jurisdiction of the *quaestio de vi* to cover offences against private individuals which were *contra rem publicam*.[76] The successive *leges Iuliae* on *vis* of Caesar and Augustus dealt with all forms of *vis*; this is why the Institutes of Justinian, like the Theodosian Code,[77] simply, and correctly, refer to the *lex Iulia de vi publica seu privata*. However, by late classical law at least, the distinction drawn between *vis publica* and *vis privata* was that the former was committed by magistrates or officials, the latter by private persons.[78] This is certainly easier to understand than the distinction drawn in the Digest,[79] where the real problem is to decide why the compilers produced two titles, but then failed to differentiate between the two concepts. The title described as concerning *vis publica* refers to the possession of arms at someone's home, to the seizure of anything (except building materials) from a fire, to rape, to cases involving problems of ownership and possession as well as *vis*,[80] and also to violence linked with public office or civic duties. *Vis privata*, according to the Digest title, concerned stealing from a shipwreck, assault when a gang had been collected, or even when there had been no assault or robbery but there was a gang (a threat in itself), and self-help.[81] It was here defined as essentially a lucrative crime, aimed at seizing the property of another, but the list given by Paul is very close to that of Marcian, classed in the Digest under *vis publica*.[82] But *vis* was also constituted by the carrying of arms, even by a single person, or a calumnious conspiracy to share the profits of a civil action; the reference to arms was dropped by the compilers when they edited Ulpian's explanation of the relationship between the delict and the crime.[83] The normal penalty was exile, but there were milder penalties for certain kinds of behaviour which nevertheless fell under the statute; Ulpian, or the compilers, thought that there were different penalties for public or private offences of *vis*.[84]

The delictual action *vi bonorum raptorum*, or *rapina*, had, unlike theft, a specific origin in the praetor's edict, and it was thus classed as a separate delict.[85] In the unsettled conditions which followed the Social War and the disturbances after the death of Sulla, Italy seems to have been infested with armed bands. In the praetorship of an Octavius,

around 80 BC, an action was provided for fourfold damages for deprivation of property by violence or threats of violence.[86] Then in 76 BC the
praetor[87] M. Terentius Lucullus promised an action to recover financial
loss caused by the violence of armed gangs. This latter edict may have
been aimed at damage to, rather than theft of, property, but an additional clause, inserted before the time of Labeo, dealt expressly with
violent theft, whether committed by a gang or not.[88] It was this violence
which grounded the offence commonly known as *rapina*. The practical
distinction from theft was that an action for property taken by force
gave fourfold damages (even in cases where there was not technically
manifest theft) if the action was brought within the year; if it was
brought later, it provided only simple damages. Nevertheless, apart
from the necessary violence involved, its constituent elements were
identical with those of theft, except that not only the owner but anyone
from whose lawful detention something was forcibly taken, such as the
depositee, had the action.[89]

Rapina became widened and more closely linked with *vis* by Marcus
Aurelius, who provided that if someone seized property, even in enforcement of what was accepted as a well-founded claim, that claim was
thereby forfeit.[90] Some two centuries later the loss of the right when
someone resorted to self-help instead of due process was confirmed; it
was enacted in addition that if his claim was unfounded the claimant
must restore what he had taken together with its value,[91] and this was
applied to land as well as to moveables.[92] Such actions as seizing a wife's
property as a pledge for her husband's debt – the one person for whom
she could in no circumstances be surety – could be treated as *vis*, or
knowingly looking after property taken by violence, or imprisoning
someone to force them into handing something over.[93] Very similar (and
also allied to the *crimen repetundarum*) was *concussio*, extortion with
menaces, such as making some gain by purporting to have the provincial governor's authority to act, or seizing pledges (to sell) without the
authorization of the governor.[94]

Offences related to theft

Pillaging inheritances[95]

This was not theft, quite simply because theft required an owner to be
the victim and pursuer.[96] The word *'expilatae'*, moreover, seems here to
have been used only metaphorically, and not to have had the connota-
tion of violence that we find, for example, in the Digest title *de effracto-
ribus et expilatoribus*[97] – after all, an inheritance was an abstract, even
if the things within it were concrete. The offence does not seem to have
applied to the seizure of these concrete objects; in such a case the heir
would be given an action for theft or damage when he entered, as he

then succeeded to the rights of the deceased. It was the appropriation of the inheritance as a whole, its use or abuse as though the appropriator were indeed the heir, that was penalized as a threat to public order more than a vitious intromission. One can imagine such harm being done as the neglect of the farm accounts, the selling off of the best horses, the ploughing up of the formal gardens, so that when the heir did enter he found affairs in a state of disarray.

Since it was neither a theft nor a formal crime, the only recourse was to the extraordinary jurisdiction of the provincial governor[98] (or at Rome the Urban Prefect). Marcus Aurelius laid down in a speech to the Senate that those who thus pillaged inheritances should be punished *extra ordinem* on the accusation of the inheritance[99] – probably the heir when he entered, but perhaps a charge which could be made by a slave of the estate. Septimius Severus and Caracalla, in a rescript, wrote that a choice could be made between proceeding criminally before the Urban Prefect or the provincial governor and claiming the estate in the ordinary courts from those who had seized it.[100] Ulpian stressed that *furtum* and the charge of a pillaged inheritance were mutually exclusive, although he held that an action for production was possible if there were things the pursuer wished to vindicate.[101] According to Hermogenianus, however, the connection between pillaging an inheritance and theft was sufficiently close that a wife could not be charged with the crime, because she could not be accused of theft.[102] This situation required, therefore, for reasons of expediency, that the residual power of a magistrate be invoked *extra ordinem* to cope with a legally unsatisfactory situation, a situation in which usucapion in bad faith was technically possible.[103] A formal accusation must be made, but it was not a crime of the *ordo*.[104]

Sacrilege

Sacrilege in pagan Rome was not an offence against the honour of the gods; the stealing of private property left for safekeeping in a temple was simple theft, not sacrilege.[105] Similarly, treasure buried in a tomb remained subject to secular law; Marcian says that this was because imperial mandates forbade the interment of money,[106] but it seems rather that treasure is by definition something that someone hopes to recover and so is not dedicated to the gods, above or below. Sacrilege was the theft of money or other things dedicated to the gods or to sacred or religious purposes;[107] this did, of course, aggravate the offence, but it was not blasphemous.[108] We shall look at it again later.

Swindling (*stellionatus*)

Stellionatus, swindling, was another offence which required the making of a formal accusation, but was definitely not included in the *ordo*;[109] as Papinian said, it fell under neither public nor private process.[110] Ulpian remarked that condemnation did not involve infamy, and that punishment was *extra ordinem*.[111] Since it was within the competence of the provincial governor,[112] it will at Rome have been in the Urban Prefect's jurisdiction. Withdrawing an acusation of swindling did not incur the penalty of the *SC Turpillianum*,[113] presumably because it was not truly reckoned a crime but closer to a delict; nevertheless, such conduct brought punishment at the discretion of the court.[114]

It was clearly a vague crime, a catch-all for the dishonest, comparable with the delict of *dolus*; Paul described *stellionatus* as a means of persuading someone to hand his property to another.[115] It was as this kind of safety-net against criminals that we find it received into both Scots and French law.[116] Just as the *actio de dolo* was residuary in private law, so in the criminal field *stellionatus* could be charged wherever there was fraudulent dealing which, nevertheless, did not fall within any other crime, such as forgery or theft. Examples given are pledging the same thing twice, or pledging another's property as though one's own,[117] or imposture, or withholding wages;[118] also classed under *stellionatus* was a case of perjury, where someone swore in a document that something was his own when in fact it was only pledged.[119]

The penalty for so fluid a crime could hardly be a fixed one. Ulpian said that the penalty should not exceed the *opus metalli* for plebeians, and relegation for a period, or removal from the decurionate, for those of some status.[120]

Kidnapping (*plagium*) and the *lex Fabia*

Kidnapping almost certainly was a crime of the *ordo iudiciorum publicorum*.[121] Jurisdiction was at some time before the Severan period, and maybe much earlier, transferred to the Urban Prefect in Rome and its environs, or to the provincial governor;[122] the Praetorian Prefects, presumably after the general Severan reform, exercised jurisdiction in Italy beyond the hundredth milestone.[123] Imperial procurators also assumed this jurisdiction, in the City as well as in the provinces. At Rome these would presumably have been procurators in charge of a significant force, such as the *procurator aquarum*, but their jurisdiction did not supersede that of the Urban Prefect. In the provinces it was linked to their exercising the powers of a governor, but Caracalla permitted it even where they had no general capital jurisdiction.[124] An accusation under the *lex Fabia* was available to anyone, even women, where the injury was to their own kin.[125]

The *lex Fabia*, passed some time in the late Republic,[126] may originally have covered simply the stealing of slaves, for Apuleius mentioned
that there had been a *lex Cornelia* dealing with the sale of a citizen as
a slave.[127] However, liability under the *lex Fabia* became extended to
anyone who hid, sold, chained or bought a freeborn Roman citizen, a
freedman, or the slave of another,[128] and to any accomplice in doing
these things.[129] According to Ulpian, the first chapter of the statute was
limited to free persons; this kind of treatment of slaves fell under the
second chapter, as did persuading someone else's slave to escape his
owner.[130] This last must mean something other than that the proper
owner lost his slave; it must surely involve the slave's moving to fresh
employment, so that the kidnapper has acquired an addition to his
work-force. It was made clear, in the fuller version of the statute given
in the Digest, that hiding someone meant hiding him (or her) – from his
family or his true owner – against his will; obviously being locked up or
chained[131] would be reckoned as against the victim's will. It was also
made clear that buying a free person, or a slave not the property of the
seller, must be done knowingly and dolosely if it was to be criminal.[132]

Kidnapping was distinguished from the theft of a slave,[133] although
not always convincingly, but the jurists were not happy to call mere
persuasion to run away theft.[134] The man who took away for sexual
purposes a female slave who was not a prostitute was liable for theft,
unless he concealed her, when he fell under the penalty of the *lex
Fabia*.[135] Hadrian wrote in a rescript that the distinction must be
settled on the facts; in another rescript he held that 'the man on whose
premises are found one or two runaway slaves who have hired out their
services for food, particularly if they have previously done such work for
others, cannot rightfully be called an abductor'.[136] The distinction here
would seem to be based on the landlord's lack of the element of confinement, although it was possible that the existence of a contract demonstrated his innocence despite appearances.[137] As well as the seller, the
knowing buyer of a free person was liable for kidnapping;[138] there was
an implication that the free person had already been kidnapped, as with
other men's slaves stolen for resale. Such a purchase, however, might
well be inadvertent; we know of the prevalence of the *bona fide serviens*.[139] The prohibition on the sale of a free person was extended, by the
jurists it seems, to cover barter, gift, and giving him as dowry.[140]

The seller of a fugitive slave was liable under the statute, as amplified by resolution of the Senate.[141] We are told that to sell one's own
slaves who were merely absent (even without leave? *erro* rather than
fugitivus?) was not criminal; nor was it illegal to give someone a
mandate to recapture a *fugitivus* and then sell him, for he would by that
time no longer be a *fugitivus*.[142] To try to claim that one had title to a
fugitive slave, whom one had concealed, was very unlikely to be accepted as a defence to a criminal charge.[143] A bona fide possessor,

whether of a fugitive or simply someone else's slave, could not be liable, because he was in good faith, and this point was stressed by Severus and Caracalla; nor was the person who shut up a slave whom he knew to belong to another, if he thought this was at the owner's wish.[144]

Diocletian legislated considerably on the topic. He stressed that selling a free person was sufficient to ground the crime; he talked of the seduction of a free person. He allowed the victim a choice between criminal and civil proceedings. He accepted completely the cohesion of statute, resolution of the Senate and juristic interpretation for the definition of the crime. Moreover, not much later a landowner on whose property a slave was found became absolutely liable, to a fine of 20 *solidi* or a beating if his means were insufficient to pay the fine.[145] There does not seem to have been any further development in the Later Empire; Justinian simply said that the Fabian Act on *plagium* was one of the *iudicia publica* and that sometimes, in accordance with imperial enactments, it carried a capital penalty, sometimes a lighter one.[146]

The original penalty, when the offence was tried by a standing jury-court, was a fine, perhaps of HS 50,000;[147] the same fine was applicable to an owner who knew that his slave was committing this offence.[148] As with the other penalties of the *iudicia publica*, there was a harshening associated with the jurisdictional changes of the Principate, and we find the *crimen ex lege Fabia* described as capital in a text attributed to Ulpian.[149] Under *cognitio* the humbler classes were sent to the mines or crucified, the upper classes fined half their property and relegated permanently, while a slave who committed the offence without his owner's knowledge was specifically sent to the mines.[150] Ulpian ascribed these penalties, varying with the heinousness of the deed, to explicit imperial legislation.[151] In the Digest we are told that, while the punishment varied in accordance with the degree of the wrongdoing, offenders were mostly condemned to the mines.[152] That the penalty could be less appears from the ruling that a slave who had been convicted under this statute – although apparently having acted on the orders of his owner, who had been held liable – was not to be freed within ten years;[153] he must have been still in private ownership (perhaps of the original owner's heirs) for manumission to be possible. Had he suffered any earlier penalty? such as a flogging from the magistrate before being returned to his owner? Perhaps it is comparable that a slave bought from a professional slave-hunter could not be manumitted within ten years of the sale against the wish of his former owner.[154]

The penalty for dealing in fugitive slaves, forbidden by a resolution of the Senate, seems to have remained a fine,[155] but this was a relatively minor offence, although formally assimilated to *plagium*.[156] Runaway slaves themselves were to be arrested and held by the *stationarii*; those unclaimed were to be sold off through the office of the Prefect of the

Night Watch.[157] Any caught escaping to the barbarians were to have a foot amputated or be sent to the mines.[158] Apparently responding to an outbreak in and around the City, Diocletian and Maximian ordered the Urban Prefect to impose capital punishment for the sake of deterrence.[159] Constantine, writing to the vicar of Africa, viewed the mines as the normal penalty, but in aggravated cases of kidnapping he ordered slaves or freedmen to be sent to the beasts and the freeborn to be made gladiators.[160]

Corruption of a slave

This was essentially a delict introduced in the praetor's edict, as an *actio in factum* for double damages, towards the end of the Republic; it was the owner's right to sue for his interest in the making worse of his slave.[161] But some aspects of the delict could come under the criminal law; we are told that one who persuaded someone's slave to seek asylum at an imperial statue, in order to bring the owner into disrepute, would be punished severely.[162] In general, however, this delict was not criminalized because by its very nature – persuading a slave to run away or to thieve, or otherwise harming his body or morals[163] – it concerned solely an owner's, not the public, interest.

Wrecking, fire-raising, etc.[164]

This area of the criminal law, *de incendio ruina naufragio rate nave expugnata*, is distinguishable from *vis* and *rapina* in the stress on natural disaster. The fire has been alight, the building has collapsed, the ship or raft[165] is wrecked, and an opportunist has looted, stealing and perhaps damaging. The offence was defined by taking advantage of the confusion caused by the fire or collapse, and was not restricted to the actual premises collapsed or on fire. But the time was of relevance; hence taking from a wreck meant during the confusion of the event, not removing things washed up on the shore later, which was merely theft, and akin to taking what had fallen from a vehicle.[166] The praetor in a special edict, as with *rapina*, gave fourfold damages for an action brought within the year, although only simple damages thereafter; resetters were also liable. Public interest was, however, involved and a criminal prosecution would be allowed.[167]

In contrast, setting a fire in a town in order to rob was a capital offence, whereas doing so to rob a farm or villa brought, for the lower sort, condemnation to the mines or to forced labour, and relegation to an island for the upper classes.[168] To set fire to a block of flats from sheer malice was a capital offence.[169] Firing crops from vandalism was also treated severely, by condemnation to the mines or relegation to an island, depending on status, whereas an accidental fire simply grounded delictual liability for reparation.[170]

Forgery

It is not absolutely clear whether Sulla passed two laws, one on forging wills and the other on forging money, or whether the one *lex Cornelia nummaria testamentaria* provided for both sorts of offence to be heard by the *quaestio de falsis* which it created.[171] It does seem certain, however, that it was Sulla who established a single *quaestio perpetua* for forgery (*falsum*),[172] and that, until the time of Constantine or later, *falsum* of both these kinds continued to be seen as two aspects of one crime. (The forging of money is dealt with in chapter 6.) The Digest takes this unitary approach, but for the Code the compilers must have found the imperial enactments of the Later Empire sufficiently distinct for several titles to be more appropriate. Forgery was a normal crime of the *iudicia publica*, with accusation open to all free men, and to free women where their interests were concerned; we even hear of a slave being allowed to bring a charge of the suppression of a will when it had included his manumission.[173]

There was very considerable extension of the scope of the *lex*, both by resolution of the Senate and by imperial development.[174] The commonest method, as elsewhere in the criminal law, was to extend the penalty of the statute to conduct which was interpreted as constituting *falsum*, rather than tampering with the Sullan definitions. (This approach must have been convenient for provincial governors, who might not have had the text of a statute before them.) The first major elaboration of the statute was by the *SC Libonianum* of AD 16; so closely were they linked that the Digest title concerns both. Under this extension of the statute it was the very act of writing oneself in to the text of a will that was penalized,[175] and it is clear that there was by no means always a dolose intention in the scribe, despite other texts insisting on the need for bad faith if there was to be a crime.[176] For example, someone had been left a legacy of a slave, but the slave was actually manumitted in the will; the legatee was liable when he cut out the manumission, even although at the wish of the testator.[177] Although the statute, or more likely the *SC Libonianum*, made provision for a testator's authorizing his son or slave to write in something to his own benefit,[178] this privilege seems to have been treated with great suspicion by jurists and emperors.[179] This resolution of the Senate applied even to soldiers' wills.[180] It may also have extended the penalty of the *lex Cornelia* to the forgery of documents other than wills.[181]

The emperor Claudius issued an edict extending the penalty of the *lex* to cover codicils; perhaps it was only in this edict that persons writing in legacies for themselves, as opposed to instituting themselves as heirs, became liable to punishment. Presumably by juristic interpretation, but perhaps by imperial legislation, someone was held to have written in something if the writing was that of someone in his power, whether as owner or *paterfamilias*.[182]

The *SC Libonianum* had elaborated on the *lex Cornelia*, but the first substantive development of the statute was to extend falsification from matters relating to wills to false witness. The *SCC Messalianum* of AD 20[183] and *Geminianum* of AD 29[184] laid down the principles. False witness, given directly or arranged to be given, whether through documents or oral evidence, fell under the penalty of the statute; such false witness might be from malice or for gain, and included conspiring to ensnare the innocent. As well as giving false evidence, withholding and withdrawing evidence was covered.[185] These two resolutions of the Senate brought about a considerable overlap between the *quaestio de falsis* and the *quaestio de sicariis et veneficis* in the stress on bringing about the death of the innocent. Giving conflicting, or even equivocating, evidence could be viewed as making the witness liable to the penalty for forgery; bad faith was not mentioned, but must have been presumed.[186] A related offence was the making of false accusations; there clearly was an overlap here with calumny and other procedural offences.[187] Fairly closely linked with procedural offences was the inclusion under *falsum* of the suborning, whether by money, threats or bribes, of judges or jurors.[188]

Then the Senate laid down that, to be valid and enforceable, wills and other formal documents must be sealed in a certain form.[189] Imperial extensions after Claudius' edict were to bring under the umbrella of *falsum* the selling of the same thing fraudulently to two separate people,[190] and also tutors and curators who came to a settlement with the fisc before having properly rendered their accounts.[191] It seems likely that the extension of the penalty of *falsum* to the introduction of a substituted child into a family was the product of specific legislation, not just interpretation; it seems too remote from the original sense of the statute to have been created by the jurists. The introduction of a supposititious child was not, however, a public crime, in that accusation was restricted to those with an interest.[192] The criminalization of false weights and measures might also have been deliberate widening of the *lex testamentaria*, although it could be an extension from the *lex nummaria*, or even from the jurisdiction of the Prefect of the Corn Supply.[193]

The wording of the statute (or that part of it) on wills seems to have been fairly comprehensive: it covered writing, attesting by seal, and reading aloud (*scribere, signare, recitare*) as methods of creating a will; getting rid of, concealing, carrying off and effacing (*amovere, celare, eripere, delere*) as methods of suppressing one; and also making erasures or insertions and breaking seals (*interlinere, subicere* and *resignare*) as methods of tampering.[194] 'Suppressing' was defined as deliberately not providing the tablets of a will (or codicils) in order to defraud the beneficiaries, but also as having them, and being able to produce them, but not taking the trouble to do so.[195] Also covered was causing such things to be done.[196] Livy's account of the Bacchanalian affair of 186 BC, where there were 'perjured witnesses, forged seals and wills and evidence' as well as sexual debauchery, and where capital punishment was imposed on those who had been contaminated 'by false testimony, forged seals, substitution of wills, or other frauds', makes clear that such doings had always been held to be seriously criminal.[197]

Seals, as an essential safeguard for a will, were important; someone who made or engraved a counterfeit seal was bound by the *lex Cornelia*.[198] It was an offence knowingly and dolosely to seal or arrange for the sealing of something other than a will (presumably as though it were a will).[199] To seal other documents than wills with forged wax also created liability to the penalty of the statute.[200] Making entries in, or removing entries from, account books, registers, wax tablets, etc., without sealing, caused such entries to be held forged, and making them was thus punishable under the *lex Cornelia*.[201] And it counted as forgery to give evidence contrary to a document fortified with one's own seal.[202]

The use in court of forged documents, dolosely[203] or even rashly, as in the case of the advocate who read out a false document when the governor was presiding over the court,[204] was punished with the penalty of the law. This was extended to the use of other attested or official material, or to its counterfeiting, such as issuing a false edict or false documents in the name of the praetor.[205] Anyone who used forged imperial enactments without authority was to be interdicted from fire and water;[206] presumably this meant using dubious records without checking their provenance, since the penalty is light for what might in some circumstances be construed as treason. Another text, set firmly in Marcian's discussion of the application of the penalty for *falsum*, says simply that a judge who neglects the imperial constitutions is to be punished.[207] The penalty for *falsum* covered the man who claimed a false *nomen* or *cognomen*; perhaps this was in an attempt to appear as the long-lost heir or to defraud the fisc, or it could have been a false claim to citizenship.[208] Equally serious were passing oneself off as a soldier, using usurped marks of rank, or using a forged diploma to get the benefit of the imperial post.[209]

Just as withholding evidence brought liability for *falsum*, the abstraction of genuine documents from before the court was the converse crime to the production there of false ones. The *lex Cornelia* itself may have dealt only with the removal of wills, since Paul contrasts that with the pilfering of other legal documents, which was not a crime of the *iudicia publica*; the removal of such other documents will have been dealt with only under *cognitio*.[210] In a text from the early post-classical period, it is made clear that, under *cognitio*, all dolose alterations, insertions and deletions into any kind of formally recognized document were penalized as forgery.[211] Further, the betrayal of the contents of a document, normally meaning a private document relevant to a lawsuit, was brought under the penalty for *falsum*.[212] In particular, this applied to the reading, and even the mere opening or unsealing, of the will of a living person.[213]

If something were held not to fall under *falsum*, nevertheless it could probably be successfully prosecuted as *stellionatus*.[214] *Stellionatus* was regarded as a residuary crime,[215] and that is why we find it so limited in the sources. Justinian, however, extended the concept of *falsum* to cover writing commentaries on the Digest, or abbreviating authorized legal texts obscurely.[216]

Under Constantine it became possible to interrogate even *honestiores*, such as decurions, under torture if they had drafted a will or other document which was being challenged as a forgery.[217] The penalties of the *lex Cornelia* were flexible. As with most other *quaestiones perpetuae* the formal penalty was interdiction from fire and water, but we find punishments ranging downwards from deportation (after confiscation of property) to an island for *honestiores* and capital punishment for *humiliores*.[218]

Miscellaneous offences

Someone whose business records had been made public could lay an accusation with the provincial governor against the one who had published. Marcus Aurelius and Lucius Verus confirmed that this was also within the sphere of office of the Urban Prefect, who could punish the wrongdoer.[219] This, along with the copying of a written document or accounts,[220] seems to be the closest the Romans came to the concept of intellectual property.

Certain offences against property rights do not fall neatly into the distinction between those offences, of which theft is the archetype, where the object of the wrongdoer is to make a lucrative gain, and those where there is malicious damage, such as incendiarism.[221] The cutting down of another's fruit trees at night was (as we have mentioned) an offence dating from the XII Tables; it was on the borderline between theft and damage, but a tougher remedy seemed appropriate such as forced labour for *humiliores*, and for *honestiores* removal from the decurionate or relegation, as alternatives to reparation.[222]

Violation of sepulture might include the stealing of building materials, a form of theft, or burying someone who had no right in the tomb, or even squatting in the tomb, matters not directly lucrative; it could also imply disturbing corpses, thus constituting an offence against the gods or good morals. The praetor in effect imposed a fine of HS 10,000, by granting a popular action for this sum if there was nobody with an interest; he stressed the need for *dolus*. The penalty when the circumstances were aggravated, bringing in criminal sanctions, was normally deportation for *honestiores* and the mines for *humiliores*, although this might be varied either way.[223] There was no great change in attitude between pagan and Christian concerning the desecration of tombs[224] and disturbance of funerals.[225]

The offence of removing or knocking down boundary markers, *de termino moto*, was somewhat similar; it too may have involved offending the gods. It was extended to cover misleading changes in the scenery, such as uprooting or planting trees, to disguise a property's limits.[226] It could be committed by a neighbour, a great man perhaps or his servant, trying to enlarge his property by stealth, or by someone by mishap or in ignorance taking what seemed usable stones; Hadrian in a rescript recommended relegation for the upper classes, a beating and two years forced labour for others, but no more than a beating where there had been no dolose intention.[227] The penalty was more severe than a fine, at least in the later Principate, although in Caesar's agrarian law there had been a fine of HS 5,000; under Nerva a slave might be capitally condemned if his owner chose not to pay the fine.[228]

IV

Violence against the Person

The treatment of crimes of violence, crimes against the person other than sexual offences, was relatively sparse in Roman law.[1] Murder was dealt with primarily under the *lex Cornelia de sicariis*; this was originally aimed more at repressing brigands and keeping the peace than at murder as a private matter. Poisoning – also dealt with under the *lex Cornelia*, whose full title was *de sicariis et veneficis*[2] – was and is an essentially domestic crime; it was often associated with magic and uncanny practices. Abortion, usually thought of by the Romans as brought about by drugs, was a related topic, but one where the perceived victim was not the unborn child but its *paterfamilias*, who was deprived of his lawful rights.[3] Parricide attracted a certain legal – as well, presumably, as sensational – interest. That we hear so little in the legal sources of common assault, wounding, etc.,[4] may be due to the existence of the delictual remedy of *iniuria*, and to the fact that assault on or injury to a slave, and sometimes also a child in power, would normally be pursued through the *lex Aquilia*[5] rather than the criminal courts. Finally we shall consider the Romans' rather unusual attitude to castration and circumcision.

Homicide[6]

It seems likely that for the Romans, as in our day, most murders were family affairs and, until well into the Principate, that these would therefore fall within the jurisdiction of the relevant *paterfamilias* or owner (or patron). Of course, when the *paterfamilias* was the murderer, someone technically outside the *familia* would need to intervene. Equally, status might alter cases. When the praetor Plautius Silvanus, for some unknown motive, killed his wife by throwing her out of the window, it was his father-in-law (probably still the woman's *paterfamilias*) who at once brought him before the emperor; Tiberius then remitted the facts, after investigation, to the Senate, who appointed a commission to judge the matter.[7] Domestic authority was only slowly eroded; most obviously, the exposure of unwanted infants long remained a proper exercise of *patria potestas*.[8] Until the late Republic, and perhaps even into the Empire, it is probable that, for an ordinary murder not within one household, the victim's family was able to use a private criminal action to obtain the surrender to them of the murderer[9] – or sometimes they may have been satisfied that the head of the perpetrator's household would take suitable steps to punish the offender by his domestic authority. This survival of domestic jurisdiction helps to explain why the focus of the crime in the *ordo iudiciorum publicorum* was on public order.

From an inscription we know that C. Claudius Pulcher, consul in 92 BC, had earlier been *iudex quaestionis veneficis*;[10] the title implies the existence before this date of a *quaestio perpetua*. There had been a perceived need for a series of special courts concerned with poisonings in the second century,[11] so the establishment of a permanent court may well have seemed expedient. *Sicarius* (*homicida* as a word for murderer was not much used in the legal sources until the time of Constantine[12]) meant a knife-man or gangster; the term indicates that the crime was seen more as an offence against public order than against the life or limb of the individual victim. A *quaestio de sicariis* to repress gangsters and hooligans was in existence in 142 BC, presided over by L. Hostilius Tubulus. It is not, however, clear whether this was a permanent or special court; that Tubulus could subsequently be successfully charged with taking money to give a judgment is odd for the president of a jury court, but may have fitted the remit of the special tribunal by which he himself was tried.[13] The *quaestio* of 138 BC we know to have been ad hoc. The references to L. Cassius' appearances as '*quaesitor*' do not prove the existence of a standing court, whether set up in 142 BC or somewhat later, but it is not improbable.[14] Sulla's *lex Cornelia* of 81 BC, and the *quaestio perpetua* (or *quaestiones*) it created, was entitled *de sicariis et veneficis* (or *inter sicarios et veneficos*). This suggests that Sulla was responsible for bringing together under one jurisdiction two specific kinds of killings.

We are told that the first chapter of Sulla's statute gave the court (specified carefully as the praetor, or judge of a *quaestio*, on whom the lot fell to preside over the jury court for murders committed within or within a mile of the City of Rome, with jurors, chosen by lot under the statute) capital jurisdiction over those who carried weapons, who carried them with the intention of killing or stealing, or who killed, or dolosely brought it about that such was done. Ulpian commented on these words of the statute: 'This law does not punish everyone who carries a weapon but only the man who bears a weapon for killing someone or committing a theft; it includes the man who kills someone, no matter of what status, so this statute appears to apply to a slave or a peregrine.'[15] The fifth chapter dealt with poisoning, that is with the possessing, making up and selling of a drug as well as its fatal administration.[16] Other chapters were concerned with giving or procuring false witness or, for a judge or juror, accepting a bribe for a verdict which brought about the death of someone.[17] Paul's version probably gives the statute as it was put into effect in the classical period: 'The *lex Cornelia* inflicts the penalty of deportation on anyone who kills a man or carries a weapon for theftuous purposes, and on anyone who possesses, sells, or prepares poison for the purpose of killing a man, or who gives false witness whereby someone dies or death is brought about. For all these crimes it is agreed that the penalty of death should be imposed on the better classes, but the lower classes are crucified or thrown to the beasts. A murderer is someone who kills a man with any sort of weapon, or brings about a death.'[18]

The surviving content of Sulla's statute appears a little strange, more concerned with the preparations than with the completed act of homicide; nevertheless, there is good reason to believe that furnishing the cause of death was included in chapters other than those which dealt specifically with killing by direct physical assault.[19] Its function in the area of preparatory crime may have been largely superseded by the legislation on *vis*. Nevertheless, this development would have taken time. Indeed, we hear of three courts handling murder cases in 66 BC,[20] and they can hardly all have been restricted to the political arena, or poisoning, especially as the operations of the *quaestio* were confined to the City and its immediate surroundings.[21] There was another Republican statute on murder, the *lex Clodia* of 59 BC – on the face of it a general law, although aimed at Cicero – which dealt with murder arising from abuse of office;[22] this presumably remained in force until Augustus' *lex Iulia de vi*.

Although public order was the background of the *lex Cornelia*, it did (or very soon came to) cover ordinary murder, not only murder on the public highway but also in private houses, as well as death inflicted in a brawl or arising from going about armed with murder in mind.[23] It extended to the killing of any man, no matter what his status.[24] In early law a slave could not be the victim of murder – it was merely a case of damage to property – but, at some stage, perhaps even in the *lex Cornelia*, it became possible for an owner (perhaps even a third party) to bring a criminal charge for the killing of a slave.[25] After the *lex Petronia* (of AD ?61) and some further resolutions of the Senate, it was a crime, even for the owner, to send a slave to the beasts without his having been condemned in court; it was also a crime to accept him.[26] Deliberate killing of one's own slave, and even cruel punishments or obscene physical abuse, were forbidden by Antoninus Pius.[27] Owners, nevertheless, had the right to punish their slaves, and the *SC Silanianum* (which will be explained shortly) was not repealed. Constantine repeated the prohibition on the deliberate killing of one's own slave, although not penalizing a death inadvertently following 'normal' punishment, but he did not explicitly call it murder.[28]

Self-evidently the statute covered murder by poisoning.[29] Making, selling or even possessing a murderous drug or potion brought liability under chapter five of the statute.[30] Drugs compounded for this purpose were distinguished from those which might have a medicinal use, but love potions and fertility drugs were, like abortifacients, considered dangerous, and if their use brought about a death, however inadvertently, such use was made punishable under a resolution of the Senate.[31] Abortion was seen primarily as a particular form of poisoning, performed by the pregnant woman either to thwart her husband or to conceal from him the result of an adultery. She was therefore deserving of exile, even although the child was part of her while in the womb, because she was depriving her husband of his potential right.[32] It would seem likely that there was no offence in itself in an unmarried woman having an abortion.

The *lex de sicariis* covered – Ulpian's language does not suggest an extension – abuse of office by the *quaesitor* of a jury court or other magistrate, whether actively through procuring false evidence or passively by taking a bribe, which put a man's life at risk; it also came to cover giving false evidence in order to bring about the capital conviction of someone.[33] There clearly was an overlap with *vis publica* but how it worked in practice is somewhat obscure. Other offences which could be classed as murder, or at least fall under the penalty of this *lex Cornelia*, were fire-setting,[34] preparing for armed robbery or armed seizure of property, instigating a sedition, and concealing a shipwreck, although all these would again more normally have fallen under *vis*.[35] Human sacrifice in the course of magic practices was also covered.[36] Suicide was not a crime, except in a soldier – and a suicidal tendency was a defect in a slave; indeed, in the Stoic view, suicide was often an honourable course.[37] The penalty of the statute was also extended to castration, which we shall deal with below.

Anyone, free or slave, male or female, could commit murder. An intention to kill was necessary, and it was this intention which made someone who ordered a killing a murderer;[38] an infant or a madman could not be liable since they could not form a murderous intention.[39] The motive was irrelevant; a mercy killing would have still counted as murder. An absence of premeditation might reduce the liability.[40] If a killer lacked intention to kill there should be acquittal from the charge of murder, but wounding with intent to kill might be sufficient to found homicide.[41] Hadrian wrote that if Epafroditus (a slave) had struck with a sword or other weapon, there was no doubt as to his murderous intention, but if he struck the blow with a key or a cooking-pot there need be no will to kill; 'in crimes it is the intention, not the issue, to which regard is paid'.[42] Guilty intention could be presumed from the deed, which need not be direct, for furnishing the cause of death was expressly provided for,[43] but gross carelessness did not amount to the *mens rea* for murder.[44]

The major exception to the requirement of a guilty intention was the case of the slaves of a murdered owner. According to Tacitus, ancient custom required that every slave residing under the same roof must be executed; this was put into effect, following a debate in the Senate, after the murder of the Urban Prefect, L. Pedanius Secundus, in AD 61, despite so strong a popular reaction of sympathy that troops had to be called in to enable the executions to go ahead.[45] However, the more normal, and somewhat more humane, rule seems to have been that of the *SC Silanianum*, probably of AD 10, confirmed by a *SC Claudianum*. It laid down that all the slaves in the house at the time of the suspicious death were to be tortured in order to find out the murderer, to discover if anyone had incited him, and to make it possible to punish for their failure in their duty all those slaves who had not prevented the murder – for which they were all liable to be put to death; if the slave-owner was killed on a journey, then the law applied to all who were with him.[46] Until this had been done the dead man's will was not to be opened, partly so that no manumissions made in it would come into effect and partly, one suspects, to make sure that the heir or heirs had not had a helping hand; premature opening might make the estate forfeit to the fisc, and incurred a fine.[47] Under Nero, the *SC Silanianum* was extended by a further resolution of the Senate (probably the *SC Pisonianum*) to cover specifically those slaves whose freedom had been granted or was known to have been granted in the will. A *SC Neronianum* extended the rule so that all the slaves of the surviving spouse would also be tortured.[48] Trajan enacted that freedmen too should be put to the question, but Antoninus Pius said that torture should not hastily be applied to one due his freedom under a trust, 'and the preferable view is that he should not be punished on account of having been under the same roof unless he was an accomplice in the crime'.[49] While the torture was technically interrogation, not punishment, the two concepts were not always clearly distinguished;[50] the whole purpose of the law was to compel slaves to guard their owners both from members of the household and outsiders at the risk of their own lives.[51]

Killing could be justified, as when killing someone who had deserted to the enemy.[52] Carrying arms for self-defence, even killing in self-defence, including defence of a member of one's family against a sexual assault, was justifiable homicide, although under Justinian and possibly earlier the Romans accepted the doctrine of minimum force – if and only if the killer could not have spared the man's life without risk to his own.[53] Certain other killings, such as by a *paterfamilias* of a *filia* caught in the act of adultery in the *pater's* house, might be viewed as justifiable homicide.[54] Justification rather strangely included allowing citizens to resist ravaging soldiers: 'Let no man spare a soldier who should be resisted with a weapon as a brigand – *ut latroni*'.[55] Vengeance, however, was murder from early in Roman law; vendettas seem never to have been approved. There might be mitigating circumstances short of justification, as when a husband killed his wife caught in adultery.[56]

A father's paternal power in theory gave him power of life and death over his son, but Ulpian wrote that he should rather accuse his son – of adultery in this case, it seems – before the Urban Prefect or the provincial governor.[57] In the Later Empire, while the head of a family retained some power to punish his dependents, the case had to be tried by the ordinary judges if the offence was such that it deserved a serious penalty.[58]

An accusation of murder, although open to any male citizen, was likely to be brought by the kin of the deceased. It was the victim's father who took the case to the consuls when Pontia was stabbed by her jealous lover, Octavius, after a night of pleasure.[59] Plots by either spouse against the other were to involve the interrogation under torture of all the slaves in the common household.[60] An accusation of murder could be brought by a woman when it concerned the death of her parents or her children, or of her (male or female) patron or the immediate patronal family, or of any other person against whom she need not give testimony against her will.[61] Similarly a pupil, although in general disabled by youth from bringing charges, could lay an accusation concerning the death of a parent or grandparent, with the approval of his or her tutors.[62] A person barred by his own condemnation from making accusations against others, and apparently also other infamous persons such as calumniators or actors, could still lay charges arising from the murder of their children, their parents or their patron.[63] Just as any free person, even when disabled by holding office or by poverty, could pursue an accusation relating to a wrong he himself had suffered, so this was interpreted to allow him to make a charge concerning the death of someone very closely related.[64]

The statutory penalty, according to Marcian, was deportation and forfeiture of all property; originally, presumably, it had been interdiction from fire and water, as with other *quaestiones perpetuae*. Marcian remarked, however, that in his day condemnation was normally followed by the aggravated death penalty for most murderers, with deportation for *honestiores*, defined by Modestinus as those who held an official position of honour.[65]

Parricide

Parricidium is an old word, and there has been much discussion of its meaning in early law.[66] However, the first reliable record of a parricide in the sense of a parent-killer is the conviction of Malleolus in 103 BC and his execution for the murder of his mother.[67] In the Republic domestic jurisdiction must often have been the forum for parricide.[68] Cicero defended Roscius Amerinus on this charge before the *quaestio de sicariis* in 80 BC, and he referred to a previous trial, not many years before, of two sons for the murder of their father – they were acquitted

– before a (pre-Sullan) jury court.[69] It seems likely that there was no specific statute concerned with parricide prior to the *lex Pompeia* of (70 BC or) 55 BC, but that it was earlier treated as an aggravated form of murder, justiciable before the assemblies or the *quaestio de sicariis*.[70] In the Principate parricide was, at least sometimes, heard *extra ordinem*.[71]

The *lex Pompeia* seems to have been concerned to define within what degree of relationship a murder became parricide: certainly parents and grandparents, brothers and sisters, and patrons, probably also uncles and aunts and first cousins; step-mothers and betrothed persons were brought within the scope of the law by interpretation.[72] The statute probably limited the strict sense of the word, associated perhaps with the horrific penalty of the sack (*culleus*), to the murder of ascendants,[73] but the term seems to have stayed in use for the killing of descendants (other than through the lawful exercise of *patria potestas*) and collaterals.[74] It has been argued,[75] but not entirely convincingly, that whereas premeditation was required to constitute murder, mere culpable killing within the family was here penalized; lunacy, however, was a valid defence. A man who killed his mother in a fit of madness was not to be punished, but he was, however, to be restrained, if necessary with chains.[76]

The penalty of the *lex Pompeia*, at least for the killing of anyone other than an ascendant, was as for the *lex Cornelia de sicariis* – the ordinary death penalty or *interdictio aquae et ignis* and forfeiture of all property, later deportation, and this seems to have remained the case.[77] The sack as a penalty had probably been introduced in the late third or early second century BC; it would seem to have been primarily an expiatory rite more than a punishment.[78] By the end of the classical period burning alive or being sent to the beasts had replaced it.[79] The return of the sack, and the introduction of the various animals to be enclosed with the convicted man, was probably an invention of the Christian Empire; there was clearly a desire to impose an extraordinary and aggravated penalty.[80] (In Germanic law parricide was classed as petty treason, because the murder was of someone to whom a special allegiance was owed.[81]) In cases of the murder of parents, accomplices seem to have been held liable to the same penalty as the principal, even although not related to the victim; Ulpian gave an example of a man knowingly lending money for the purchase of poison or for hiring killers.[82] Unusually, the suicide of someone charged with parricide led to the confiscation of his property, although the ordinary law of succession operated after a natural death.[83] There was no prescriptive period for an accusation of parricide.[84]

Vis as assault[85]

Vis was something of a catch-all crime. It is mentioned here because it could cover physical assault, but such assault seems necessarily to have been either political,[86] or for the sake of lust or gain; drunken quarrels were not, at least in classical law, subsumed under *vis* but rather *iniuria*. We are told, for instance, that anyone who forcibly violated a boy, a woman or a young girl was liable to the penalty of this statute[87] and that anyone who raped either a single or a married woman was punished by the extreme penalty, without the benefit of a five-year prescriptive period, and even if the woman's father was ready to forgive the rapist for the injury done to him (*sic*).[88] Abduction was covered too, of freeborn boys, and also of girls or women;[89] this will be treated further in the next chapter. Justinian was deeply concerned about abduction of freeborn women, especially if they were virgins or widows dedicated to God; he abrogated previous laws dealing with the offence[90] and legislated *ab initio*. He made a capital offence of all abduction, even of freedwomen and slaves, as well as of virgins (betrothed or not) and widows; the abduction of a married woman was, of course, adultery as well. For the abductor of women who were not freeborn, death was to be sufficient punishment, but where freeborn women were concerned, in addition to death all the property of the abductor, and of his accomplices in the actual abduction, was to be confiscated and handed over to the victim, to become her dowry if she chose to marry. Accomplices less closely concerned in the deed were merely to suffer death, by burning if slaves. Parents who showed tolerance or a willingness to overlook the abduction were to be punished with deportation. While Justinian seems less inclined than earlier emperors to presume fault in the woman, nevertheless he explained the severity of his penalties as partly due to providing that 'no woman, whether willing or unwilling, will have any scope for sinning, ... for if he does not beguile her with his odious arts, he cannot induce in her the desire to betray herself into so great a disgrace.' [91] Abduction falling under the *lex Fabia*, on the other hand, was primarily economic in motive, and has been dealt with in that context.[92]

Vis was an offence which had links with *rapina* and *metus*; for example, it covered armed assaults with intent to rob on villas,[93] or an attack on a man which did not amount to expelling him from his own property.[94] It was also *vis* to shut a man up, or besiege him, or even to interfere with a funeral.[95] Liability for *vis* under this statute was also imposed on the man who used *iniuria* – it is not clear whether an assault or a threat to reputation is meant – to extort a promise to give games or money.[96] More simply, the man who called a group together to flog or beat up someone, even if nobody was killed, was liable for *vis*.[97] If someone was killed the penalty was strengthened.[98]

Under Marcus Aurelius it became settled that an owner whose property had been seized was still not entitled to self-help; further, *vis* could be imputed even when people had not been physically injured.[99] More remotely, *vis* could be stretched to cover having another man's slave put to the torture, although this fell more suitably under *iniuria*, as a delict rather than as a crime of the *ordo*.[100]

Abuse of office, such as killing, torturing, flogging or imprisoning a citizen who was appealing to the people or the emperor, fell under *vis publica*.[101] Ulpian records that the rules about who could not give evidence at all, and who could not be forced to give evidence where someone related was involved, were listed under chapters 87 and 88 of the *lex Iulia de vi publica et privata*.[102] In the Later Empire, confining people in private prisons could even be seen as a crime akin to treason; Justinian, rather more aptly, laid down that those who established private prisons should themselves, whatever their rank, spend as many days in the public prison as they had imposed on others, and also lose any legal claim they might have been trying to win by such means.[103]

Iniuria or outrage[104]

Since we know of a *lex Cornelia de iniuriis*, Sulla perhaps established a *quaestio perpetua* for *iniuria*,[105] but this is not actually evidenced; Cloud suggests that *iniuria* as assault was originally heard before the *quaestio de sicariis*.[106] *Iniuria* was, of course, also a delict,[107] covering both assault and defamation;[108] these could include an element of financial loss, but the essence of the offence was the outrage suffered. It could therefore be committed against all human beings; it was even possible, in a limited way, to inflict it on slaves.[109] Idiots and infants could, it was deemed, suffer *iniuria*, but since there was no *iniuria* where the victim consented[110] this may have been relatively rare; they could not, however, commit it, since they could not form the necessary intention.[111] The boundary between the crime and the delict is not at all clear;[112] for example, a son in paternal power could exercise his own rights under the statute, while his father would have no remedy except under the praetorian action.[113] Gaius' description of *iniuria* suggests that the two procedures, criminal and delictual, existed side by side.[114]

Paul said: 'We suffer outrage (*iniuria*) either in the body or outwith the body; in the body through beating (*verberibus*) or sexual assault, outwith the body by jeering or defamation'.[115] On assault, the *lex Cornelia de iniuriis* provided not only for *verberatio* which involved injury, a beating-up, and *pulsatio*, which meant a relatively trivial blow or blows, but also for entering a man's house by force, rather than with the decent stealth of the burglar;[116] Ulpian described this as covering every physical affront, including a blow to the head with a sword.[117] The Mohock pranks of Nero and his companions, their night brawling, would probably have fallen under this head, despite the occasional seizure of property.[118] Indeed, it seems that the wanton killing (by someone other than the owner) of a slave might most properly be pursued under the *lex Cornelia de iniuriis*, and not as the praetorian delict,[119] nor even under the *lex Aquilia*, in any case where, because of the public consequences, not reparation but punishment was required.[120]

Iniuria was an offence against a person's honour,[121] his reputation, his dignity, or his physical integrity. In cases of defamation truth was a defence.[122] Writing, composing or publishing something to someone's disrepute incurred infamy, and a SC extended this to cover anonymous victims, while there was a reward for the man who informed on such offences; for (despite the general prohibition on informing) public good might come out of it.[123] The role of the Senate in providing, because of the difficulty of proof of malicious intention or individual detraction where the intended victim was not specified, for a criminal hearing in such a case, stresses that even this private crime had a public nature.[124] Imperial enactments extended defamation to the untruthful pronouncements of an astrologer.[125] An enactment of Valentinian and Valens, in the fourth century, ordered defamatory writings to be destroyed and their contents kept secret, on pain of capital punishment, as if the finder, by publication, became the author.[126] Earlier enactments on defamatory writings seem to be dealing with unsupported accusations, with calumny, rather than with an insult to someone's reputation as an offence against him.[127]

Attempts upon chastity might also be interpreted as outrage,[128] and so were such lesser acts as calling out lewd names, or a man's exposing his private parts.[129] Less use may have been made of *iniuria* in the criminal sense when the concepts of *stuprum* and adultery came to be enlarged; however, attempts upon the chastity of a slave continued to fall under this statute.[130] There is no doubt that sexual assaults of all kinds were treated as crimes, even when the ground of the charge was legally obscure; abduction particularly was, as we have seen, viewed very seriously.[131]

We find subsumed under *iniuria* a wide range of outrageous behaviour: the intentional treatment of a free man as a slave,[132] the deliberate covering of someone with filth or the intentional pollution of water supplies, and so on,[133] and the leading of a slave or a son into a cookshop, or gambling with him.[134] A related offence seems to be one found in the province of Arabia, described as '*skopelismos*', when the enemies of someone would place stones on his land to signify that a horrible death would descend upon whoever cultivated the land.[135] Perhaps the curious offence of the itinerants who carried and produced snakes to someone's fear and harm should be considered as much an offence against the person, a kind of assault, as a means of extorting money.[136] Someone who had claimed to be able to procure a judgment was condemned for *iniuria* by the governor, and on this account was beaten *fustibus.*[137] The Senate laid down that to carry an image of an emperor *'in iniuriam'* of another person was to be punished by imprisonment – *vincula publica.*[138]

As with the title on theft, the Digest title on outrage concludes with the remark that nowadays, *'nunc'*, it is normal to proceed by *cognitio.*[139] Sulla is alleged to have said that slaves could not be accused under the *lex*, because its statutory penalty was a fine,[140] although clearly they were punished in some way; this is a little odd because slaves do not anyway seem in Sullan times to have been justiciable before the public courts. By the third century, however, the penalties were flogging for slaves, a beating for *humiliores* (significantly described as free men of the humbler sort), and relegation or interdiction from their profession for others.[141] For more aggravated forms of insult the penalties might be heavier; slaves could be returned to their owners to be kept in chains for a while, or even be sent to the mines for really outrageous acts.[142] Paul tells us that the Senate, in the interests of public discipline, laid down deportation to an island for the composition of defamatory verses, while publicly singing a song (*psalterium*) designed to defame someone brought punishment *extra ordinem* on both composer and singer; however, relegation, though to an island, was sufficient for those who simply planned defamatory writings.[143]

Castration and circumcision

Castration received particular attention as an act of violence against the person, even the person of a slave, with whom, indeed, the greater part of its legal manifestations seem concerned. The *lex Aquilia* was likely to be irrelevant, if the slave was now of more value; the options offered for reparation were the *actio iniuriarum* or the fourfold penalty under the aedilician edict.[144] *Iniuria* was a possible remedy for a free man castrated against his will, but there is no record of its use on this ground; we hear of paramours caught in the act who were castrated by angry husbands,[145] but in such circumstances public opinion may have held that it served them right.

Domitian is recorded as having forbidden the practice,[146] and a Digest text (which ascribes this – probably – to AD 83) says more precisely that a resolution of the Senate fined an owner who handed his slave over for castration half his property.[147] Another resolution of the Senate brought under the penalty of the *lex Cornelia de sicariis* any person who castrated a man whether for lust or for gain.[148] It presumably covered the one who authorized the deed as much as the doctor or other who performed it; it remains slightly odd that this should fall within the ambit of a statute dealing primarily with murder. Hadrian legislated in a rescript on the matter. Those who made eunuchs were to be deported and their property confiscated, but the doctor who performed the operation was to suffer capital punishment; a slave who committed this crime was to be put to an aggravated death. As with murder under the *lex Cornelia*, sentence could be pronounced against an absent defender who (contumaciously) failed to appear in court. Victims, here presumably slaves in particular, had a right of audience by the provincial governor, but it was a capital offence to offer oneself for castration.[149] Forms of castration other than cutting were also covered by Hadrian's legislation.[150] It seems likely from a reference in Justin that a governor could dispense a doctor from the sanctions of the law if there were genuine medical need to perform such an operation as castration;[151] this argument is supported by the repeated stress on *libidinis aut promercii causa*. Paul stressed that if castration was performed for lust or for gain on an unwilling man, whether free or slave, the penalty for the person who brought this about was capital unless he was an *honestior*, who suffered what was still the formal penalty of the statute.[152] It may be significant that he makes no mention of a penalty for the willing victim, for mostly he would either be too young to be held responsible or a slave under a duty of obedience to his owner.

Hadrian was also concerned to suppress circumcision, essentially by extending the ban on castration; it was contrary to the Hellenistic way of life that he sought for the whole Roman commonwealth.[153] It was not a repressive consequence but a cause, along with the foundation of Aelia Capitolina as the new Jerusalem, of the Second Jewish Revolt of 132-5.[154] This ban was modified by Antoninus Pius, who allowed Jews to circumcise their own sons, although for persons of any other faith the penalty remained the same as that for castration.[155] We have an elaboration of this from Paul; in this version the penalty of perpetual relegation to an island, with confiscation of property, was restricted to Roman citizens who had themselves or their slaves circumcised according to the Jewish rite, while the doctor was put to death; non-citizens who were not Jews presumably met a harsher penalty. Jews who bought non-Jewish slaves and had them circumcised were to be either deported or put to death.[156] Under Constantine a Christian who was circumcised while the slave of a Jew could claim his freedom, and Constantius added capital punishment for the Jew; under Honorius and Theodosius the circumcision of a Christian by a Jew incurred confiscation of all property and perpetual exile.[157]

Constantine also repeated the ban on castration, under threat of capital punishment; he was clearly assuming that it was of a slave, for he laid down that, as well as the capital penalty, the slave and the place where the crime was committed, if the owner knew and did not lay a charge, should be confiscated.[158] Leo reformulated the ban as one on trading in eunuchs of 'Roman' race, whether they had been made so on

Roman or barbarian soil, punishing too the notary who drew up an instrument of such a sale and the person who accepted the tax on slave sales in such a case. Barbarian eunuchs, provided they had not been made so on Roman territory, could still safely be bought and sold.[159] Perhaps the stress had changed because in the Church there were extreme ascetics, who castrated themselves for the love of God and the avoidance of sin;[160] a Christian emperor would hardly wish to penalize such a man, and, of course, his action would be neither for lust nor for gain. Justinian legislated comprehensively.[161] Those who had been castrated were to be free and remain free – thus implying that it was the trading element which had survived, since he must be referring to slaves – and this was to apply to any future unfortunate; there were to be no more imports. He specifically excepted castration on medical grounds from penalty, but here too the slave was to become free, to stop any attempt at evasion of the law by this means. And he laid down the penalty of castration as itself fitting those who castrated others, with confiscation of all property and lifelong exile in Egypt. Women who committed the offence were also to lose all their property and be sent into lifelong exile; the same punishment was to be applied to those who furnished the means.

V

Sexual Offences

This chapter will look at incest, forbidden marriages, bigamy, adultery and *stuprum*, *lenocinium*, homosexuality, and abduction and rape. Incest was always a crime, based on traditional morals; in sacral law to offend against the chastity of a Vestal Virgin was so classed.[1] Apart from incestuous cases, certain other marriages were forbidden at various times; bigamy, in the technical sense, could only appear when marriage acquired official, public, recognition. Homosexual practices with a free man or boy were forbidden in the Republic, although Greek influence seems to have led to their being tolerated, at least with slaves or male prostitutes. After Augustus' legislation, which was the first to put extra-marital sex among ordinary crimes, adultery together with *stuprum* was the focus of juristic development; however, in the Republic offences against sexual morality had sometimes been tried before the public courts.[2] *Stuprum* was a wide enough concept to be seen also as an offence against the *lex Cornelia de iniuriis*, or as *vis publica*.

Incest[3]

Incest was a crime founded not on statute but on custom. It applied, as a matter of natural law, to blood relationships among slaves, despite their lack of legal capacity; thus, even if there was doubt about the relationship, a freedman could not marry his possible daughter 'since in contracting marriage natural law and a sense of honour must be observed'.[4] 'If anyone should marry a woman from those whom we forbid him to wed on moral grounds, he is said to commit incest.'[5] There does not appear in the pagan sources a violent religious revulsion against incest;[6] it was seriously immoral, but did not call forth the horror aroused by parricide. Incest was not regulated by Augustus' *lex Iulia de adulteriis coercendis*,[7] and indeed it sometimes specifically differed from adultery: for example it was possible to charge two people simultaneously with incest.[8] It seems to me, however, that the facts of incest constituted either *stuprum* or adultery and so might well be subsumed under these heads after the passing of the *lex Iulia* created a court for sexual offences. This would explain why juristic interest, otherwise strangely, concentrated on incestuous marriages. Presumably then, charges of incest were competent before the *quaestio de adulteriis*, or under *cognitio*.[9] A charge of incest combined with adultery was not excluded on the expiry of the five-year prescriptive period which applied to adultery.[10] In the Republic, slaves could only be tortured about their owners when there was a charge of incest;[11] after the *lex Iulia de adulteriis* they could be tortured about their owners' adultery, but only, it seems, concerning incest if this incest was also adulterous.[12] As with adultery, a charge of incest could be brought even when one of the parties had died.[13] In the Later Empire parties who had defended themselves against a charge of adultery (or, presumably, *stuprum*) by stressing their close relationship, but then subsequently married, were held to have proved the earlier accusation, and were to be punished as if they had been convicted.[14]

Incest was, naturally, linked with *conubium*, the right to marry, and much of the jurists' discussion of it was placed in the Digest title *de ritu nuptiarum* in the context of avoiding incest. Marriage was forbidden to those related more closely than the fourth degree: i.e. it was allowed between first cousins.[15] Claudius' relaxation in favour of the daughters of one's brother was an oddity;[16] we are told that his example was followed by two sycophants.[17] One wonders how frequently someone took advantage of this thin boundary between abuse and legality; it must have occurred sometimes in view of Papinian's comment on accusations against those who married a sister's daughter.[18] Perhaps permission had always to be specially sought from the emperor?[19] The relaxation was abolished in 342 by Constantius II;[20] nevertheless, Zeno thought it worth while to reiterate the prohibition on any marriage with a niece, in strong language.[21]

Relationships by marriage normally counted as though natural: that is to say, a man could marry neither his step-daughter nor her daughter, nor indeed his daughter-in-law or mother-in-law.[22] The rules were complicated by the existence of both agnatic – where there might be no tie of blood – and cognatic relationships. We are told that an adoptive son, even if subsequently emancipated, could still not marry the wife of his adoptive father because she counted as a step-mother; nor could an adoptive father in such a situation marry his former daughter-in-law.[23] To marry anyone who had been at any time in the line of either ascent or descent was always incestuous.[24] A grey area could appear in such a case as a divorced woman having a daughter by her second husband; could her first husband marry her child? While there was no tie of blood nor direct relationship, it was nevertheless held, by Julian among others, that such a marriage should be abstained from, implicitly on moral grounds.[25] There was clearly a flavour of incest about these vertical ties; where, however, the relationship was only lateral, it was the tie of blood which counted, and it would be lawful for someone with an adopted sister who was then emancipated to marry her when there was no longer an agnatic link between them.[26] In the Later Empire, presumably under Christian influence, we find a prohibition on marriage with a deceased wife's sister or a brother's widow,[27] and – unless with imperial permission – between first cousins.[28]

The crime was extended beyond marriage to concubinage,[29] and must also have applied to more casual relationships.[30] There was no crime of incest, it would appear, without sexual consummation.

No excuse was admitted for incest within first or second degrees of kinship – parents or siblings; knowledge of fact could here normally be presumed, and there was no place for ignorance of the law. The woman suffered the same penalty as the man where she was his stepdaughter, daughter-in-law or stepmother, and this regardless of whether the relationship was also adulterous.[31] We hear of one case where a mother is alleged to have conceived an unnatural passion for her son, thus driving him to suicide; she was exiled for ten years, to protect her younger son.[32] A woman would normally only suffer the penalty for incest where the relationship was forbidden by natural law (*ius gentium*); if the relationship was barred only by the *ius civile* she could hope to be immune from prosecution.[33] Ignorance of the law was not readily applicable to a man, though we are told that age as well as sex might excuse (but age was no defence to adultery);[34] it seems he might be permitted to escape through understandable confusion if he were to marry in error a sister's (as opposed to the – legalized – brother's) daughter, although not if he committed *stuprum* with her.[35] This was reinforced by the frequently-held view that married incest was less serious than adultery, the fact that a 'marriage' had taken place showing the parties' honourable if mistaken intentions;[36] provided they abstained from further sexual relations and divorced there might well be no penalty. Marcus Aurelius and Lucius Verus issued several rescripts on this point,[37] and Diocletian and Maximian also legislated to the same effect.[38]

The penalty was usually capital, whether literally[39] or in the form of deportation to an island,[40] but was sometimes milder, particularly for the woman,[41] even excluding the cases where pardon was granted. An incestuous marriage was no marriage; it was void.[42] This is why, when a 'wife' in an incestuous 'marriage' committed adultery, her 'husband' could only accuse her by the right of any third party.[43]

Some other forbidden marriages seem to have been treated criminally – for example, marriage between a tutor and his pupil;[44] others were not held criminal, at least in the Principate, although juristic interpretation classed as forbidden (under the *lex Iulia et Papia*) the marriage of a military officer or provincial official with a woman of the province,[45] or marriage between someone of senatorial rank and someone of freed or debased status. (Other freeborn men were able to marry freedwomen, but not women from a – slightly different – list of debased status.[46])

In the Later Empire marriage between a freedman and his female patron, or the daughter or (widowed or divorced) wife of his (male) patron, became criminal.[47] Marriage between Christian and Jew was also forbidden,[48] presumably on grounds of *mores* rather than religion since marriage with heretics was not so treated. Also forbidden, on pain of capital punishment, were marriages between Romans (here described as provincials) and barbarians.[49] Marriage between an adulterous couple was also made void, and penalized, but we shall look at this in the context of adultery. This, however, only applied where a woman had been convicted of the adulterous sexual act itself (and perhaps also of *stuprum*).[50]

The penalty in classical law for a forbidden marriage lay not precisely in its nullity – a question which is obscure – but in its exposure of the partners, as though they were not married, to the restrictions of the *lex Iulia de maritandis ordinibus* and the *lex Papia Poppaea*, in effect a pecuniary penalty. In the Christian Empire exemplary penalties were threatened, as for so many offences.[51]

Bigamy[52]

Bigamy was a crime not really possible in classical Roman law because of the legally indefinite nature of marriage; we do not hear of it even in the Republic when *manus* marriage must have made it legally practicable. The classical jurists did not accept the possibility of concurrent marriages.[53] The doctrine of *affectio maritalis* and the absence of any official recognition of the existence of a marriage meant that what happened was (normally) simply fraud by the man on the first wife. Even so, to be involved in two betrothals or two marriages simultaneously incurred infamy.[54] Valerian and Gallienus stressed that to have (more properly, purport to have) two wives made the man infamous, and could render him liable for *stuprum*.[55] Diocletian repeated that it made the man infamous, and added that the offence should be avenged by the competent judge, thus suggesting a criminal charge.[56] The legal texts of the Christian Empire continued to ignore the crime in the form most familiar to the modern world (and to Cicero) of a man maintaining two purportedly legitimate families unknown to each other; discussion focussed instead on the circumstances in which a woman who made a second marriage had committed adultery.[57]

Adultery and *stuprum*[58]

The Republican state of affairs

All through the Republic, and up to the time of Augustus' legislation, adultery and other sexual lapses seem primarily to have been dealt with as domestic matters. Sometimes sexual offences by both men and women were brought before the assemblies by magistrates, commonly the aediles; there seems usually to have been a heavy fine imposed on those who had offended against public morality.[59] The mention in the *Collatio* of previous laws which the *lex Iulia de adulteriis* abrogated[60] may refer to (non-domestic) masculine *stuprum*, as under the *lex Scantinia* (see below), or to laws passed on specific occasions; there is absolutely no record of any previous general law on sexual misdemeanour. Earlier – in the archaic period – we hear of punishment of a woman by her husband[61] or by her *paterfamilias* by right of his paternal power (or, presumably, by her immediate family if husband or father were unavailable);[62] in any case, and perhaps necessarily for the husband, it seems that the family or families would normally have provided a *consilium*.[63] As for the lover, public opinion might well have viewed him, when caught in the act, as justifiably killed or beaten up, or abused in some other way.[64] If the paramour's adultery had been notorious, he might have been visited with a censorial *nota*, or with praetorian infamy.[65] It is possible that an action for *iniuria* would have lain against him,[66] and likely that he would have been liable in damages.[67] Divorce was otherwise the remedy for a marriage broken by adultery; there were penal retentions of dowry by the husband in cases of divorce on moral grounds, and also, in time, recourse for the injured wife.[68]

The basis of Augustus' legislation

The reasons for Augustus' legislation, making *crimina publica* of adultery and *stuprum*, have been much debated. Augustus himself certainly expressed a moral aim.[69] However, it is also probable that he wished to restrict the potential exercise of domestic jurisdiction, perhaps because it had not been habitually exercised of late – although this is not certain – but more likely because he wished jurisdiction in all matters to go through the courts, which, ultimately, he controlled. This would also explain why he carefully restricted the father's or husband's *ius occidendi*. Whatever the reason, in 18 or 17 BC, some months after the *lex Iulia de maritandis ordinibus*, the *lex Iulia de adulteriis coercendis* was passed.[70] The Code title is *ad legem Iuliam de adulteriis et de stupro*; we are told that the statute used the terms indiscriminately.[71] There were at least nine sections in the statute,[72] which, as was usual, was extended by resolution of the Senate,[73] imperial legislation[74] and juristic interpretation.[75]

Jurisdiction

The *lex Iulia* set up a *quaestio perpetua* which, although probably entitled *de adulteriis*, seems to have been, or to have become, the forum for sexual offences in general. Despite the existence of the *quaestio*, even under Tiberius some trials – of those of senatorial rank – were before the Senate.[76] The court which the statute set up may well have been the longest-surviving of the *quaestiones perpetuae*; some have even thought that it lasted into the Severan age,[77] although it seems far more likely that procedure *extra ordinem* had completely superseded all the jury courts earlier in the second century. The non-existence of the *quaestio* seems implied in the possibility of the two alleged parties to an adultery being accused simultaneously by separate accusers (as long as the woman had not remarried);[78] there would have been a control for trials before one *quaestio*, even if it met as more than one session. On the other hand, it was a charge of adultery that was used as a model libel in the Digest title on accusations,[79] which may argue for its survival. At any rate, the establishment of the adultery law in the structure of the *quaestiones perpetuae* meant that men continued to describe adultery as a *crimen iudiciorum publicorum* and to talk of the *poena legis Iuliae*, and that its proceedings under *cognitio* were guided by the norms of the *ordo*.

Definitions

Adultery in the strict sense focussed on the woman; it comprised sexual relations between a 'respectable' married woman and a man not her husband. A man was just as much an adulterer as a woman was an adulteress, but he could not be so described for lack of fidelity to his own wife;[80] he could sleep with whom he pleased, as long as it was not with someone of the respectable classes.[81] His sexual relations with a female (or, presumably, male) slave might make him liable under the *lex Aquilia*, or for *iniuria*, or for the corruption of a slave, but they could not in the Principate bring him within the scope of the criminal law.[82] (Slave women could not, as a matter of law, commit adultery,[83] but male slaves naturally could.[84]) *Stuprum* covered sexual relations between a man and a girl or an unmarried or widowed woman of respectable status,[85] or homosexual relations with a respectable man or boy.[86]

There had to be a breach of morals; the words of the statute required that the deed be done 'knowingly and with malicious intent' to constitute adultery or *stuprum*.[87] A text, purportedly of Ulpian, argued that a husband had no moral right to accuse his wife when he was demanding of her a purity which he did not show himself;[88] it seems quite clear that such a 'clean hands' doctrine was never Roman law, though perhaps the judge might take it into account when weighing the value of the husband's evidence. A woman who, acting on a false report of her husband's death, married another man was innocent, unless she had already committed *stuprum* with the second man.[89] (The tone of the jurist is hostile to the woman, particularly in view of her complete legal freedom to divorce the first husband.) In the Later Empire, when a woman divorced her husband for other than the permitted reasons, an accusation of adultery seems expected, almost required, from her husband by the legislator.[90]

As with incest, consummation was probably required for there to be the offence of adultery; something less might be sufficient for *stuprum*, and perhaps could ground *iniuria*.[91] The particular offensiveness to the Romans of adultery lay in the possibility of introducing another man's child into the agnatic family.

Although the statute had not made clear the distinction between adultery and *stuprum*, it was found necessary to do so, at least when there was a question of the right of making an accusation, but such a distinction was probably not fully developed until the end of the classical period.[92] Whereas an accusation of *stuprum*, as of *lenocinium* and the other offences under the *lex Iulia*, was open to anyone, just like the other crimes of the *ordo iudiciorum publicorum*, there were special rules for adultery, giving priority to the husband, or father, of the alleged *adultera*, and also restricting accusations in certain circumstances. The public right of accusation of adultery was abolished by Constantine, who limited it to close kin of the woman concerned, nevertheless giving preference to the husband.[93] Most juristic interest seems to have been focussed on the *ius accusandi*, to which we shall shortly turn. Another distinction between the two was that there was no regulated *ius occidendi* in cases of *stuprum*, although the rights of a *paterfamilias* do not seem to have been formally curbed. Despite the *lex Iulia* one suspects that a *pater*'s powers remained considerable over a daughter in his power, at least in the country. The formalization of divorce, moreover, hitherto as vague in law as was marriage itself, seems likely to have been a consequence of the *lex Iulia de adulteriis*.

Ius occidendi

While in strict law any *paterfamilias* had rights of life and death over those in his power, it seems clear that, by the Empire, this power was normally only exercised in the acceptance or rejection of children at their birth, that punitive use of it probably required by convention a family *consilium*, and that otherwise its exercise was likely (at the least) to be frowned upon. The *lex Iulia*, in its second section, laid down that it was permitted to a *paterfamilias* (adoptive as well as natural) to kill with his own hand his daughter together with her lover (no matter what his status) taken in the act of adultery in his own house or that of his son-in-law;[94] he was also allowed to beat up the lover.[95] (The statute did not extend this right to a father who was still himself a *filius-familias*, to a *paterfamilias* who was not the actual father, or to the father of an emancipated daughter.[96]) The couple must be surprised in the act.[97] The father's entitlement to kill was limited to his own house or that of his son-in-law because of the particular outrage to family honour, and 'his own house' was interpreted strictly as where he actually lived.[98] If the father killed the lover but not his daughter he was liable for homicide.[99] Similarly, the couple must be killed together, on the spot, almost with one blow – *uno ictu et uno impetu*; however, if the daughter fled while he was killing the paramour, and the father took some hours to catch up with her, this was counted as being killed together.[100] In a case where she survived – by chance rather than intention – the serious injuries her father had inflicted, Marcus Aurelius and Commodus laid down that he was immune from prosecution.[101]

The statute allowed the husband who surprised his wife *in flagrante* to kill the paramour if, and only if, he was caught in the husband's own house, and if the paramour fell into the class of degraded persons.[102] The wife must then be divorced without delay,[103] presumably the three days mentioned elsewhere.[104] Any lover caught in the act, however, where the husband either did not wish or was not allowed to kill him, could, according to the fifth chapter of the *lex*, be held for not longer than 20 hours for evidentiary purposes, and this came to apply no matter where the couple were caught;[105] once let go, the paramour could not be put under further restraint, but if he escaped before the 20 hours had elapsed, he could be recovered.[106] In no circumstances was it lawful for a husband to kill his wife,[107] but if, after he had lawfully killed the paramour, he did not immediately dismiss her and bring an accusation of adultery, he would be liable for *lenocinium*.[108] However, when a husband had surprised his wife in adultery and killed either her or her lover, a plea in mitigation would be accepted,[109] and furthermore her slaves and his were exempt in these circumstances from the operation of the *SC Silanianum*.[110] Papinian was of the opinion that a freedman should not kill his patron whom he had surprised, even if the patron himself fell into the class of debased persons and so was theoretically unprotected by the law, but that in these circumstances a freedman must be allowed to accuse his patron of adultery.[111]

Accusations

Under the *lex Iulia* a husband was required to divorce a wife taken in the act of adultery[112] and to bring an accusation against her, and he must also divorce her if she were convicted of adultery on someone else's charge[113] – perhaps initiated before he had married her, or while he was abroad.

The *lex Iulia* gave priority in time to accusations by the injured husband or the woman's *paterfamilias*; this was known as the accusation by a husband's right – *iure mariti* – or a father's. For two months – sixty available days,[114] which went into suspense for the other alleged party to an adultery once the first party was charged – they and nobody else had the right to bring an accusation.[115] Thereafter, for four months – *menses utiles*[116] – anyone could exercise his citizen's right, a third party's right, to make a criminal charge.[117] This did not, however, bar the husband from bringing a charge in his own right, even after his former wife's acquittal, provided that he had not failed to take advantage of his prior right through negligence;[118] he could, of course, accuse as a third party during this time.[119] After the six available months, a married woman was immune from prosecution.[120] After five years all rights of accusation – against a woman no longer married or the man – lapsed.[121]

There was some debate about the respective rights of husband and father, but the husband was generally preferred, because of his 'more intimate anger and greater grief', although the father would be preferred, at the discretion of the court, to a negligent, dilatory or infamous husband, or one colluding with his wife.[122] The husband's right was protected regardless of whether he was *sui iuris* or in power;[123] moreover, a husband's right to accuse his former wife of adultery was exempt from the normal restriction on any citizen that he might bring only two criminal charges at any one time.[124] However, once the husband had begun his process, time did not run against the father, whether for accusing the same party as the husband or the other party.[125] If both husband and *pater* decided that they were not going to bring an accusation, the original view was that outsiders still could not make charges until after the sixty days were up, but Pomponius first held, and Ulpian agreed with him, that time at once began running for them; for one thing it would be improper to allow one who had stated he was content the continued possibility of a hearing.[126] When outsiders were competing to bring an accusation of adultery, it was up to the president of the court to decide on the proper accuser; Ulpian stated that this was explicitly provided in the statute.[127]

Certain persons could not accuse at all, as the statute expressly laid down. Ulpian says that this included persons under 25, unless pursuing an injury to their own marriage, but he then appears to add that a minor could also use a third party's (as well as a husband's) right to accuse his wife when it was on technical grounds, if, for example, the sixty days allowed the husband had elapsed.[128] An accused could object to the capacity of an accuser; he was not formally listed as accused until this had been dealt with but, once he was listed, he could not re-open the question.[129] Under the *lex Iulia*, in the pagan world, a husband who had not divorced his wife could not bring a charge of adultery;[130] in the Christian Empire it was his duty to stay married until his accusation was proved.[131]

Further, the general position of women was that they could only bring criminal accusations where their own interests were concerned; under this statute they were not seen as having an interest at all.[132] A wife could not accuse her husband of adultery, although she could divorce him; still less, therefore, could any woman other than the wife make such an accusation, since who could be more interested than the wife of an unfaithful husband? A woman may have been able to make an accusation of *stuprum* – rape or indecent assault – on herself. It is possible, however, that the competent charge would be under the *lex Cornelia iniuriarum* or the *lex Iulia de vi*;[133] the availability of these alternatives may have barred the charge of *stuprum*. (A mother, grand-mother, or sister would clearly have had no standing where adultery was concerned, but with *stuprum* matters may have been otherwise.) Adultery was therefore to some extent, but not totally – because the male partner was also criminal – an offence of the double standard.

A husband could accuse his wife of adultery committed not when his wife but in a previous marriage; the presumption was obviously that he had not known of her earlier affair when he married her. However, in such a case he naturally could not accuse with a husband's right, any more than he could if she had committed adultery while being his concubine before he married her, or if he had been party to what must be classed as a *matrimonium non iustum* (because the girl's *pater* had not then given his consent). Had she been married but repudiated by him and then later remarried, he was not entitled to accuse her, any more than, once he had married her, he could accuse her of an earlier *stuprum*.[134] This makes clear yet again that adultery was serious, in a way that *stuprum* was not, because of the risk of introducing a bastard into the agnatic family.

If the woman had married again after a divorce, the statute laid down that the paramour must first be convicted before she could be charged; where a widow was said to have committed adultery, the accuser had a free choice about which of the parties to accuse first.[135] The statute forbade the two parties to be charged simultaneously.[136] The conviction of a paramour did not, in theory, prejudice the woman.[137] Where the woman's remarriage took place only after an accusation had been made against her alleged paramour, his acquittal did not give her immunity from being charged; this was also true if she were again to cease to be married,[138] for the statute only protected a married woman as long as she was married. (This was unlike the case of incest, where it was permitted to accuse both parties simultaneously.[139]) The death – or *capitis deminutio* – of one of the parties was no bar to an accusation against the other.[140] The requirement of first convicting the paramour applied particularly in cases where it was alleged that an adulterous couple had married; this was explained as being necessary to prevent jealous first husbands breaking up harmonious second marriages.[141] On the other hand, a husband who repudiated his wife could charge her with adultery to prevent her marrying someone else;[142] such notification should prevent any marriage.[143] In a relationship where marriage was either illegal (as incestuous) or impossible, the woman's partner naturally did not have a husband's right to accuse, but she could be accused by him under a third party's right.[144]

Adultery in the strict sense also covered sexual infidelity by any female of the respectable classes in a relationship which was not *iustae nuptiae*: that is, she could commit adultery in a *matrimonium inius-tum*[145] – the equation of all marriages seems due to Constantine[146] – or even when only betrothed,[147] and (in classical law) in concubinage.[148] There is even a case in a rescript where a woman was raped before her marriage; her subsequent husband can only make a husband's accusation – against the rapist – if they were already engaged.[149] On similar lines, a captive woman who was raped was of course not guilty of adultery, but she does not seem readily to have had the benefit of the doubt if there was anything short of violence, for a concession allowed her husband to accuse her of adultery by a husband's right, even though, while she was a captive, she was not his wife but a slave and therefore incapable of marriage.[150] Even a woman who was a prostitute could be accused by her husband.[151] (While a woman who was below the law because she was a prostitute could not be liable to a charge of *stuprum*, nor could the man having sexual relations with her,[152] yet if she found a husband she then became liable for adultery, like any other wife.) But the desire to give a man his full rights as a husband did not extend to the curious case of the girl wife, formally given in marriage below the legal age of 12, who was held to have committed adultery – despite her youth – before she came of marriageable age; her husband was only allowed to accuse her, as though betrothed to her, by a third party's right – logical enough, but hardly humane.[153]

Interrogation of slaves and procedural rules

Adultery, and adultery alone, not incest, and a fortiori not *stuprum*, justified the interrogation of slaves against their owner or the person who had effective control of them, the wife or her *paterfamilias*.[154] This may have originally been limited to a charge made *iure mariti*.[155] With this in mind, it was forbidden to sell slaves after a divorce until the two-month priority period for accusations was past.[156] When it was the slave himself who was alleged to be guilty of adultery with his owner's wife, Antoninus Pius laid down that the husband should rather begin by accusing his wife than torturing his slave.[157] When it was a slave outside the family who was alleged to be the *adulter* and was put to the question, his owner, if he was found innocent, was to get double his price from the accuser, quite apart from any damages arising from calumny.[158] In the Later Empire the law was extended so that all slaves in the household at the time the adultery was alleged to have taken place, the wife's as well as the husband's, could be questioned.[159] This right to interrogate the slaves of the household was extended under Gratian to charges of murder or attempted murder by one spouse of the other.[160]

While normally an accuser must take an oath against calumny[161] – that his accusation was not in bad faith – there were exceptions. A husband could accuse without fear of calumny;[162] by the third century he had this concession even when making an accusation *iure extranei*.[163] A husband who only began proceedings but then stated that his suspicions were groundless was not penalized for *tergiversatio* and could resume his marriage.[164] A minor, one under 25, who was allowed only to bring a charge concerning his own marriage, was not readily to be charged with calumny, because of his youthful heedlessness[165] – the wife's feelings in both these cases were clearly not seen as important. But a father, although privileged as an accuser, was not immune from a charge of calumny.[166]

A husband who had once properly begun his accusation was not allowed to drop it without getting an annulment (*abolitio*) from the president of the jury court or from the governor; if he did so drop it he was barred, by the *SC Turpillianum* of AD 61 and the *lex Petronia*, from ever again bringing a charge of adultery, and perhaps of any other crime falling under the *lex Iulia*.[167] Similarly, a husband who began on an accusation, divorcing his wife, but who then remarried her, was viewed as falling under the penalty of *lenocinium*.[168] A husband was thus like any other resiling accuser in being required to obtain an annulment. When a certain father-in-law, where the husband was his son in paternal power, chose to abandon his accusation after a formal delation because he would benefit from his right to retain *propter mores* a share in the dowry (and if the wife were convicted not only would half her property be confiscated but he could not be sure of receiving a share in the remainder), he does not seem to have been at risk for *tergiversatio* – had he applied, properly, for an *abolitio* but his motive had become known? – but for fear of setting an appalling (*turpissimum*) precedent he was denied the action for the dowry.[169] Constantine clearly wished it to be easy for an accuser other than the husband to withdraw his accusation.[170]

It was specifically stated that it was illegal to compromise a charge of adultery or to prevaricate[171] – as of course with all other crimes. If *praevaricatio*, that is collusion, was proved, the time taken for that

prosecution was discounted in reckoning the *menses utiles* or the quin-
quennium available to a serious accuser.[172]

Procedural rules forbade a woman once charged being defended in
her absence,[173] and the charge remained valid if she left the province
after the accusation had been notified.[174] A man could send the necessary notification prior to an accusation through a procurator.[175] A man
absent – and this meant absent from Rome or absent from the province
which was the *forum delicti*[176] – on public business could not be charged
so long as he was working for the state, unless his absence was with
intent to evade accusation.[177] Such absence also justified a delay beyond
the normal limits in bringing an accusation; his being absent from
Rome on the service of the state prevented a man being charged in the
province where he was serving with an adultery committed at Rome.
Service in the Urban Cohorts or the *Vigiles*, however, was not reckoned
in this context, although it was for some others, as absence on public
business.[178] Unless his status was such that he must be accused at
Rome, such as someone of senatorial rank, a man serving officially in a
province could be accused of an adultery committed there.[179] In the
Later Empire, military service was not to be pleaded by a man accused
of adultery.[180] An accused widow was not allowed to plead her infant son
as grounds for adjournment; it was pointed out that her guilt, if proven,
was itself no proof of the boy's illegitimacy.[181] While preliminary questions might need to be settled,[182] these were firmly subordinated to the
criminal process under Theodosius.[183] The defence of *lenocinium*
against the husband was the only defence – apart from the five-year
prescriptive period – allowed after Diocletian's legislation.[184]

Penalties

The original *lex Iulia* seems to have imposed pecuniary penalties. The
male partner was fined half his patrimony, the female a third of hers,
with the loss of half her dowry; at some stage relegation – to separate
islands, it is stressed – was added.[185] The wife suffered financially in
that the husband was to retain a (larger) share of her dowry *propter
mores*; some even-handedness was later achieved when a wife recovered her dowry somewhat faster when she divorced her husband for
reasonable cause.[186] A woman convicted of adultery in the strict sense,
or caught in the act, was not allowed to remarry, in that her new
husband might be held guilty of *lenocinium*,[187] and the marriage be held
void[188] – or at the least it would incur the disadvantages of celibacy
under Augustus' legislation.[189] A man convicted of adultery was deprived of the ability to be a witness to formal acts of law.[190] Infamy was
thus also a consequence of conviction, and we are told that a convicted
paramour lost his power both to testate and to receive under a will.[191] If
a freedman, who had obtained the privilege of freeborn status through

the grant of the *ius anulorum*, committed adultery with the wife of his patron or with his female patron and was caught in the act, it was held that he was to be viewed as an ordinary freed slave, and could be treated as such.[192]

Abduction for sexual purposes may have incurred a capital penalty as early as the third century, although the incomplete act was treated more mildly.[193] Constantine introduced the death penalty as normal[194] although, rather oddly in view of the breach of trust, a tutor who debauched his pupil seems only to have been deported with confiscation of property.[195] The penalty of the sack for adultery[196] seems unlikely to have been normal.

Lenocinium[197]

Lenocinium was basically assistance with the commission of any other sexual offence, as laid down in the *lex Iulia* on adultery, which created it as a crime.[198] It covered, not only the complaisant husband – its main, and perhaps original, concern – but also the pimping father,[199] and outsiders acting as go-betweens;[200] it was not, however, normally committed by a brothel keeper,[201] since, until the Later Empire, prostitution was not illegal,[202] at least among the lower orders[203] – although it involved infamy. The husband who, in his own house, retained a wife caught in adultery and let the lover go was liable to the charge according to the words of the statute,[204] but only because he could not help knowing of the violation of his marriage. He must at once divorce his wife, and the formality for divorce described by Paul[205] is almost certainly the product of the *lex Iulia de adulteriis* and aimed particularly at the situation when he has killed the lover; the retention of the lover to provide evidence for the trial would originally have been publicity enough to explain the wife's departure. The divorce was, in classical law, a necessary step on the way to an accusation,[206] and the statute specifically forbade marriage with a *deprehensa* as well as a *condemnata*. Also held liable under this section of the *lex Iulia*, and condemned as though for adultery, was the man who married a woman previously convicted of adultery or, after juristic discussion, of *stuprum*, although there was no crime if she had been condemned under some other section of the statute.[207] One or two texts, presumably interpolated in the Christian Empire, seem to stretch this to a woman under accusation.[208] A husband acted properly who divorced a woman convicted of adultery; since he was forbidden to keep such a wife, she was held to have caused the divorce.[209] The husband's *lenocinium* did not absolve his wife, but this probably arose not from his complaisance but rather from his participation (as in a wife-swapping party?).[210] More particularly, pimping for her, taking anything, even once, for her to play the whore, was to be punished.[211] To bring a charge of adultery and then deliberately let it fall was *lenocinium*,[212] but an over-jealous husband could with-draw a charge with the permission of the court.[213]

Lenocinium commonly, but by no means always, involved the mak-ing of a profit from some third party's sexual offence – a husband's aim might be malicious rather than lucrative, and friends might be offering misplaced helpfulness. It is not clear whether demanding money with menaces (which might include the threat of rape, whether of man or woman) in return for silence counted as *lenocinium*,[214] but the crime certainly covered a man (including the husband) or woman taking money or some other thing to keep quiet about an adultery or *stu-prum*.[215] The husband who acquired anything at all from the adultery of his wife was liable;[216] so was the wife who took a bribe to keep quiet about her husband's adultery with another married woman.[217] Making available any sort of dwelling for sexual purposes was covered, includ-ing a friend's residence; further, the provision of somewhere out of doors or at a bathhouse grounded liability.[218] However, as already remarked, a father-in-law who abandoned an accusation of adultery against his daughter-in-law because he preferred to seek profit from the dowry does not seem to have been held liable for *lenocinium*, although he was to be denied his claim on the dowry.[219]

But clearly profit was not necessary to constitute the crime of *leno-cinium*. Deliberately not to act when prosecution of a public crime was a public duty was to be reprobated, and was in theory itself to be prosecuted.[220] A particularly nasty example was the husband who acted as *agent provocateur* deliberately to make his wife infamous; unfortu-nately (though logically) she was held guilty of adultery along with him.[221] A person, male or female, who made a house available for adultery or *stuprum* was not required to profit to be liable, but the deed must be done knowingly;[222] indeed the provision of somewhere to plan an adultery was sufficient.[223] As well as the helpful friend,[224] we find the complaisant husband who, because of some relationship or affection, retained the *adulter* in his *familia*.[225] A husband, however, who allowed his wife licence to err, knowing in his heart but not knowing irrefuta-bly,[226] was not liable for *lenocinium*, even though he was seen as despising his own marriage.[227] Nor, as we are told, if he put up with her misconduct through carelessness or his own fault, through patience or excessive credulity, was he liable for *lenocinium*, which seems only to have arisen when he patently must have known.[228] In this way the husband protected his wife by remaining married to her;[229] this was the consequence of the legislator's intention not to interfere, as well as of what seems to have been the preference of the senatorial class – among whom the jurists must be numbered – for washing their dirty linen in private.

Prostitution

Although prostitution, if in any way organized, fell technically under *lenocinium* in pagan Rome, it does not seem to have exposed *leno* and *lena* to any worse penalty than infamy.[230] A husband who found *in flagrante* in his own house a paramour who was a *leno*, an actor, a family freedman, or a slave, could lawfully kill him.[231] The rationale for this licence would seem to have been the social status of those normally involved; they were below the law, specifically the *lex Iulia de adulteriis*, which was primarily concerned to govern the conduct of respectable women, and also below the *lex Iulia de vi* which checked the abuse of official power. Where *lenocinium* was pursued with the statutory penalties (which included exile) this was because it was aggravated by the status of the parties.[232] Caligula imposed taxes on prostitutes, which Severus Alexander, although he had qualms about them, did not abolish.[233]

Some restrictions on prostitution may have been applied, at least by the later second century. Slaves who forcibly suffered indecency or foul abuse or obscenity were justified in seeking asylum at an imperial statue, and Septimius Severus is said to have extended general protection to slaves trying to avoid prostitution.[234] Probably, however, sexual assault was only a ground if it amounted to gross cruelty, and it seems likely that Severus, like Hadrian, had in mind primarily such circumstances as when a slave had been sold with a condition attached '*ne prostituatur*',[235] and that the generalization in the Digest is attributable to Justinian. In the *Historia Augusta* (therefore not very reliably) we are told that Severus Alexander wished to abolish male prostitution and that Philip did do so, and that Alexander also at one time ordered all female prostitutes to be enslaved and all male ones to be deported; the Emperor Tacitus went so far as to forbid all brothels within the City – 'but this could not last long'.[236] Diocletian, in a case where a freeborn girl appears to have been kidnapped and forced into prostitution, issued a rescript to her father laying down that he did not have to pay to redeem her;[237] this seems, however, to deal with a particular case rather than having general import.

In the Christian Empire Constantius issued an enactment concerning women – slaves – who had dedicated themselves to the Christian religion, which presumably means that they were classed by the Church in the category of holy virgins and widows. Their owners might wish to sell them into prostitution and so, to ensure their safety, they were not to be bought by anyone other than known Christians.[238] Theodosius and Valentinian allowed girls to appeal to the bishop against a father or owner who wished to force them into prostitution; such a man lost his rights over the girl, and any acquisitions made through her, and if he tried to claim them he was to be sent to the mines.[239] The same emperors purported to abolish the tax on prostitution, and they forbade pimps to practise under pain of flogging and expulsion from Constantinople.[240] Leo prohibited the trade of prostitution, even of slaves, and abolished the tax on its profits. *Lenones* were liable to condemnation to the mines or banishment (for the humble) and loss of office and confiscation of property (for the upper classes); a slave who had suffered this fate could thereafter be claimed from a convicted *leno* by anyone, including a cleric or a monk, without having to pay a price.[241] Individual prostitutes were not affected; it was the trade which was banned. Justinian too legislated on prostitution and pimps. He was scathing about procurers who went round the provinces luring girls to the city with promises of fine clothes. The trade of prostitution was to cease to exist and pimps were to be expelled from the city after a flogging; moreover, women were to be chaste.[242] There was no mention of the *lex Iulia*, although we know from the *Basilica*[243] that the connection was made.

Homosexual practices[244]

As has been common practice, the Roman law dealing with homosexuality was concerned only with men. At no stage did the legislator or the courts seem concerned with female homosexuality, although its existence was recognized by the satirists and presumably the medical writers;[245] it was not seen as a threat to the Roman male ego or to society at large.[246] For men, homosexual relations were only criminal in pagan Rome when they could be described as *stuprum*;[247] this implied the rape or seduction of a freeborn boy or man.[248] Sexual relations with male slaves and male whores were acceptable.[249] The Republican *lex Scantinia*, of uncertain date and content, was concerned with homosexual relations.[250] We have a number of moral stories from Valerius Maximus of the repression of homosexual practices in the Republic, in all cases aimed at preserving the reputation of freeborn young men.[251] In 227 BC an aedile prosecuted Scantinius, a plebeian tribune, for the seduction of his son; the other tribunes refused to intercede and Scantinius was condemned by the popular assembly. One of the *tresviri* had the noted veteran centurion, C. Cornelius, put in chains for *stuprum* with a freeborn young man; Cornelius claimed the young man was a whore but the tribunes refused to intercede, and Cornelius died in prison. In 105 BC Marius is said to have held that his own nephew, a military tribune, had been legitimately killed by a soldier who had been compelled into *stuprum*.[252] Caelius Rufus was indicted under the *lex Scantinia* in 50 BC, but countered with the same accusation against Appius the censor, who had arranged for the charge to be made.[253]

It seems likely that the Romans felt a need to legislate on male homosexual relationships earlier than on women's extra-marital relations, because women were domestic creatures, operating within structures which included father or husband, or at least male relatives, who could exercise a domestic jurisdiction. The homosexual aspect of *stuprum* was thus an established concept in the late Republic, although we know almost nothing about its enforcement. It does not seem to have been covered directly in Augustus' legislation, although, for example, *lenocinium* was extended to making available a house for *stuprum cum masculo*.[254] The *lex Scantinia* seems to have continued in force in the Empire since, under it, Domitian condemned several men from both senatorial and equestrian orders,[255] but we are not told what their punishment was. By the later Principate, and perhaps earlier, the rape of a freeborn male incurred capital punishment, while a (freeborn) man who willingly played a feminine role was fined half his property and deprived of the power to testate the rest.[256] Paul also distinguished between the completed act of *stuprum* on an abducted freeborn boy, which was capital, and the attempt, which incurred deportation to an island.[257]

The situation, however, changed in the Christian Empire, where the Judaic tradition of total hostility to homosexuality replaced the Greek;[258] condonation gave way to condemnation. The restrictions on castration *libidinis causa* were presumably also linked to homosexuality.[259] Constantius and Constans issued a law so modestly veiled in rhetorical outrage that one imagines that someone could read it and not guess its meaning:

> When a man 'marries' in the manner of a woman, a 'woman' about to renounce men, what does he wish, when sex has lost its significance; when the crime is one which it is not profitable to know; when Venus is changed into another form; when love is sought and not found? We order the statutes to arise, the laws to be armed with an avenging sword, that those infamous persons who are now, or who hereafter may be, guilty, may be subjected to exquisite punishment.[260]

In 390 death by being publicly burned alive was laid down for men who played a passive or feminine role.[261] Justinian in the Institutes stated that the *lex Iulia de adulteriis* punished with death not only adultery but also homosexual practices; he later repeated the prohibition, and perhaps the penalty.[262]

Rape and abduction

Abduction, that is seizure of a person with sexual intent (and perhaps rape, although this may never have been treated merely as a delict) gave the victim the action for *iniuria*, and if the victim was a woman, it also gave this remedy to her husband and father, even if she had not been unwilling. The offence was also classed under *vis*; there was no doubt that forcible *stuprum* committed on a male or female fell under this heading, incurring the death penalty, and moreover not limited by the five-year prescriptive period of the *lex Iulia de adulteriis*.[263] The penalty might be capital, but was in any case severe.[264] The victim of a rape, rape in the modern sense, was self-evidently not guilty of *stuprum* (or adultery).[265] Rape, sexual intercourse against the woman's will, is, however, surprisingly difficult to detect in the sources;[266] it seems to have been classed as the man's *stuprum* (presumably on the logical ground that, where it was committed on a woman, it could not be adultery since she was innocent of *dolus*).

In the Christian Empire from Constantine on, however, abduction was much more severely regarded; it became an independent crime. Perhaps rape or kidnapping to bring about marriage with a rich woman was becoming more common.[267] Constantine carefully dealt alike with the rape of an unwilling and the abduction of a willing girl; in the latter case, the consent of the girl, because of her frivolity and weak judgment, was to be no defence for the abductor, and indeed made her a party to the crime.

> If willing agreement is discovered in the girl, she shall be punished with the same severity as her ravisher, since impunity must not be granted even to those girls who are ravished against their will, when they could have kept themselves chaste at home up to the time of marriage, and when, if the doors were broken by the audacity of the ravisher, the girls could have obtained the aid of neighbours by their cries, and could have defended themselves by all their efforts. But We impose a lighter penalty on these [unwilling] girls, and We command that only the right of succession to their parents be denied them.[268]

Ravishers who had been convicted beyond doubt were denied the right to appeal, and their assistants were to suffer the same punishment or, if slaves, to be burned alive; nurses or chaperones who betrayed their charges were to have molten lead poured down their throats, and parents who connived at an abduction were to be deported; slaves who reported such a crime were to become Latins, Latins Roman citizens.[269] Constantius reduced the penalty imposed on ravishers to simple capital punishment, but slave accomplices were still to be burned.[270] Constantius also laid down that the rape of virgins and widows dedicated to God was to incur severe punishment; Jovian specified that it should be capital. Honorius and Theodosius restored the penalty of confiscation of all property, but reduced death to deportation.[271] Valentinian, Valens and Gratian laid down a five-year prescriptive period for making an accusation of an abduction-marriage; accusation was open to any citizen, not just the family, unlike the rule by then current on adultery.[272]

Justinian abolished those chapters of the *lex Iulia* which were concerned with the rape or abduction of virgins or widows – the old law continued in force as the legal base concerning the rape of married women, but the rape of holy women was, he asserted, even worse – and he imposed capital punishment without the right of appeal. Ravishers or abductors of slaves or freedwomen were relatively lightly treated; they did not lose their property as well as their lives. However, in the case of a rape or abduction of a freeborn woman, the ravisher was to suffer death and the victim was to receive all the man's property in reparation, with the property of accomplices also being confiscated for this purpose. Marriage with such a ravisher or abductor was forbidden, but the woman now had a substantial dowry to attract some other man, who must properly seek permission to marry her from her parents.[273] Thirty years later, Justinian reiterated the death penalty for ravishers, and their accomplices, and also for the conniving parents and other family members; the woman was to receive her ravisher's property. However, it was repeated that no ravished woman was to be permitted to marry her ravisher, and if her parents should consent to this they were to be deported.[274]

VI

Offences Against the State

This chapter is concerned with offences against the state in the secular sense; offences against the state religion, whether that of the Roman gods or Christianity, are dealt with separately, because they were not fully within the criminal law. It deals with treason and with sedition, often described as *vis*; then with those crimes against the state which could only be committed by persons holding (in a wide sense) or striving for office, such as extortion, embezzlement of public funds, and electoral corruption, including illegal associations; then it deals with counterfeiting coinage, and finally with offences against the public food supply.

Treason[1]

The Latin terms for treason are *perduellio* and *maiestas*, or more properly *crimen laesae* (or *inminutae*) *maiestatis*, diminishing the majesty of the *populus romanus* – or the emperor. *Perduellio* seems to be the older word; like the term *proditio*, it carried some etymological implication of an outside enemy's involvement. *Crimen inminutae maiestatis*, on the other hand, seems originally to have been a formulation to protect the sacrosanctity of the tribunes of the people, but it came to be more concerned with failure in duty to a superior; it was stronger than our *lèse-majesté*. This relative sense probably explains why, in the course of the Empire, *crimen laesae maiestatis* came to be the usual formal term, since there were, in general, few external enemies. *Maiestas* has indeed, been called 'the cloud of glory which overhung the people of the *respublica*; ... it shone about the person of Augustus and his successors in the Principate; it was the veil that covered the despotism of the Dominate; ...'.[2] But commonly, in the Digest as well as by modern romanists, the term *maiestas* is used to describe the crime rather than the glory.

Treason must in a sense be the oldest crime, in that it can be defined as an offence against society itself. Treason, *perduellio* in some form or other, was thus the crime with which the assembly trials of the Republic were primarily concerned.[3] As treason was developed in the second and first centuries BC, now specifically as *maiestas*, there came to be overlaps between it and *res repetundae*[4] and *vis*. Violence, *vis*, specifically included seditious or political violence; it expanded on both *de sicariis* and *de maiestate*. It was these wide categories that made reasonable the prosecution of related crimes before the one court, whereas too narrow a definition would have demanded successive charges before different *quaestiones* – which did, indeed, occasionally happen.[5] Treason, as explained in a simplified treatise of the late third century, covered taking up arms against the state, waging war or levying troops without authorization, leading armies into ambush, or desertion; moreover, it covered words as well as deeds.[6]

The first *quaestio perpetua* for treason seems to have been set up by the *lex Appuleia*,[7] probably of 103 BC, and it was concerned with *maiestas, maiestas populi romani diminuta*. Saturninus, the proposer of the *lex Appuleia*, 'intended the statute to protect popular leaders like himself who as *populares* embodied the *populus*, but to his optimate opponents the *populus* was the whole community directed by the Senate'.[8] The law appears to have created a standing jury court, for not only did it have an equestrian jury, like the other such courts of the period, but also the trial of the *popularis* Norbanus in the later 90s (between 96 and 91 BC) was before the Appuleian court, and it is unlikely that a special court would condemn both *optimates* and *populares*.[9] The *lex Varia* of 90 BC probably set up a special commission to deal with those responsible for causing the Social War; such behaviour fell within *maiestas*, at least as defined in the Digest, but the use by Cicero of the term *proditio* to describe the charge against M. Aemilius Scaurus under this statute seems to isolate it from the standing courts.[10] Sulla's revision of the *quaestio perpetua* for treason was simply part of his general consolidation; his law perhaps added regulations about provincial government, provisions which were to overlap with the *lex Iulia de repetundis*. (Could the new court have been intended to prosecute lesser men as well as senators, for what had primarily been understood as a magistrate's offence?) There remains uncertainty whether the *lex Iulia maiestatis* was Caesar's or Augustus', or indeed laws from each of them;[11] Caesar may have introduced formal interdiction from fire and water as a penalty and not just the consequence of voluntary exile, to replace the seldom-applied death penalty. The *lex Appuleia* and the *lex Varia* did not exclude comitial trials for treason, whether *perduellio* or *maiestas*, but, with the exception of the strange case of Rabirius, there are no recorded comitial prosecutions for *perduellio*, or indeed any other form of treason, after Sulla's *maiestas* law – unless we accept Dio's account of two tribunes jointly accusing a man of greeting Caesar as king as referring to a prosecution before an assembly.[12]

Treason is inevitably a wide-ranging offence; moreover, since it is an offence against the established order, its definition can change with the government. However, there are constants. To bear arms against the Roman people must always be treasonable, as must be (unauthorized) communications with an enemy, including flight to them, giving them a password, or aiding them dolosely in some other way,[13] such as selling them flint as a fire-striker, or explaining to the barbarians how to build ships.[14] To the Twelve Tables were ascribed the capital offences of stirring up an enemy,[15] or handing over a Roman citizen to the enemy. Other examples given of treasonable conduct are dolosely causing a Roman army to be ambushed or otherwise betrayed, bringing about the escape of the enemy, giving an enemy aid such as weapons or money, and taking part in the betrayal of a province or *civitas*.[16]

Some forms of treason could most readily be committed by those having a lawful authority. Cases of such misbehaviour by a provincial governor are evidenced for the Republic.[17] Killing hostages in bad faith without the command of the emperor was treasonable,[18] and this seems likely to have been the act of a general or governor. Such a man was also guilty if he failed to relinquish his province on the arrival of his successor.[19] Again, waging war, or even raising a levy or preparing an army, without the command of the emperor,[20] would not be an offence of the common man. Acting in such a way that allies became enemies, or maliciously ensuring that a foreign king failed to make submission, and also handing over hostages, money or cattle to an enemy against the interests of the *respublica*, seem all to be crimes that a commander would best be in a position to commit.[21] Lightly to surrender in the field or yield a camp could fall under the *lex Iulia* on treason; no less heinous was to abandon an army.[22]

A soldier is normally perceived as having a stronger duty of loyalty than a civilian; information bearing on this is to be found in the Digest title on military law. Scouts who betrayed information to the enemy were traitors and, like those on reconnaissance who absented themselves in the face of the enemy, or those who retreated from an entrenchment, they merited capital punishment.[23] Desertion to the enemy brought an aggravated death sentence (though this was not normally inflicted on soldiers), and even an attempt to desert was capital, although in time of peace the penalties might be less severe.[24] Laying hands on a superior officer was likewise a capital offence of a treasonable nature.[25] Moreover, the violation of imperial statues or likenesses was a much aggravated treason in a soldier.[26]

Then there was internal treason or sedition, committed by conspiring to kill any magistrate or other officer of the Roman people, or assembling a mob, armed or otherwise, against the interests of the state, or occupying temples or other places or inciting troops to sedition and mutiny.[27] A similar crime was to induce someone to take an oath to act against the state, or to connive at the escape of someone convicted of treason.[28] Other forms were to seek to make a king, or a magistracy not subject to *provocatio*, or to return from exile without having been recalled.[29]

Other crimes described as falling under the *lex Iulia maiestatis* were less obvious, and must have been due to later development. Among them was knowingly writing or dictating a falsehood onto the public records, which fell under the first chapter of the statute.[30] It became possible to accuse a judge of treason for giving a false judgment, although such an extension of the concept might be deprecated.[31] Another was for a private citizen deliberately and in bad faith to act as though he were holding office.[32] It was not lawful for a governor or other person to inscribe any name other than the emperor's on a public building, unless he himself had paid for it.[33] In the Later Empire we find even intercession on behalf of someone guilty of treason treated as itself treasonable,[34] whereas ancient custom laid down no more than that a traitor should not be mourned.[35]

Finally there were the crimes of *lèse-majesté*, crimes which could affect the honour of the emperor, or of his family. A sort of 'royalism' had existed from the time of Marius; the late Republican warlords had seen themselves as special. Nevertheless, Augustus and his immediate successors did not see themselves as gods,[36] and elements of sacrilege or blasphemy were not part of the crime until late in the Empire. Melting down rejected statues of an emperor must actually have led to someone's being accused and tried, for we are told that the Senate acquitted him.[37] And a jurist thought it worth saying that restoring statues which had fallen into disrepair was not treasonable, while an imperial rescript of Severus and Caracalla declared that it was not treasonable to hit an imperial statue with a chance-flung stone.[38] The same emperors in another rescript held that there was no *maiestas* in selling unconsecrated imperial likenesses; it would have been a different matter if they had been consecrated.[39] Later, when the emperor became divine, even using the imperial purple could be classed as treason.[40] Long before that, consulting astrologers as to the duration of the emperor's life or refusing to swear by his spirit (*anima*) were potentially treasonable.[41] Swearing rashly by the imperial genius could also lead to trouble; to swear thus and not to fulfil one's oath was to earn a flogging.[42] There is a very curious text on cursing the emperor:

> If anyone, ignorant of decency and unaware of shame, thinks fit to assail Our names with wicked and petulant cursing and, boiling with drunkenness, maliciously criticizes the times, We do not wish him to be liable to punishment nor to suffer any hard or rough treatment; for if he acted out of levity of mind it is to be despised, if out of madness it is most worthy of pity, while if it arose from suffering it should be forgiven. Therefore it should be brought to Our attention, complete with all the details, so that We may weigh men's words by reference to their persons and decide whether the offence should be passed over or duly followed up.[43]

The demand for all the details somehow does not seem conducive to dismissive treatment.

Treason, unsurprisingly, was one of the crimes where those normally barred from making accusations were permitted to lay charges: the infamous, soldiers, slaves and freedmen even against their owners and patrons, and women.[44] However, a jurist advised (and one can well believe there was need) that the judge should not be too eager to show reverence for the imperial majesty but should investigate the facts and the character of the accused, and not normally punish a slip of the tongue.[45] It was important to discover what resources, what accomplices, a person accused of treason had made use of.[46] Accusations of treason were also risky; accusers might themselves be subject to torture, to balance the fact that in the Later Empire anyone accused of treason might be put to the torture, no matter what his status.[47]

In the Republic death was the usual penalty for *perduellio*, but some accusations were so mixed up in politics that it is quite hard to isolate the legal element, and the penalty might be exile. Death, with confiscation of property, was the usual penalty for high treason in the Principate, although lesser penalties would normally be imposed for lesser offences. The property of a condemned man's freedmen should not be confiscated if he had children, according to Severus;[48] this presumably referred to that share of the freedmen's estate which could be claimed by the patron. If a man died under an accusation of treason, or at least of *perduellio* rather than some lesser offence under the statute, he was presumed guilty and his estate confiscated, unless his heirs could clear his name and thus succeed to his property.[49] The formal passing of sentence of death on the dead, and the imposition of a blood taint on his descendants, would seem to be innovations of the Later Empire,[50] although we find Marcus Aurelius cited as having introduced the charging of a dead man with treason.[51] *Damnatio memoriae* was, of course, voted as a political measure against unpopular emperors.

Sedition

While there was no clear boundary between the behaviour which might constitute treason and that incurring the lesser charge of sedition, nevertheless lesser charges might well be more suitable, and were normally brought as *vis*. *Vis* as a crime was relatively modern (obviously violence as such had normally been held wrongful), arising in the disturbed times of the 70s BC. Lintott has argued, cogently, that the first statute on *vis* was the *lex Lutatia*, and that it set up a permanent *quaestio* in 78 BC to deal with the consequences of Lepidus' insurrection. To this end, the *lex Lutatia* dealt specifically with, first, armed attack on the Senate or magistrates, second, with seizure of public places – compare the way modern revolutionaries take over radio and TV stations – and third, probably, with going armed in public, qualified most likely as *contra rem publicam*. In the context of the post-Sullan confusion, a fourth chapter could have forbidden usucapion of property seized during seditious events; a fifth may have made criminal the gathering together of a band of men to create a public disturbance. The *lex Plautia de vi*, perhaps of 70 BC and certainly between 78 and 63, since it was under this statute that we find Catiline accused in 63 BC,[52] then confirmed the range of offences covered by the *lex Lutatia*, and extended the jurisdiction of the *quaestio* to private offences or, more precisely, offences against private individuals that were *contra rem publicam*.[53] The stress on '*contra rem publicam*' explains why the penalty was to become banishment under the *lex Iulia*. In 56 BC the Senate extended the penalty of the law to illegal *sodalicia* or *collegia*, because of the violence so often involved in their activities.[54] Pompey's law of 52 BC was aimed specifically at Milo. To cope with private acts of violence in this period there were other courts, the *quaestiones de sicariis* and *de iniuriis*, or civil remedies such as the action *vi bonorum raptorum*,[55] which was considered in chapter 3.

The final statutory development was the *lex Iulia de vi*. Although fundamental to the jurists' development of the norms of *vis* throughout the classical period, including Diocletian's reign,[56] this statute raises many problems. Was it Julius Caesar or Augustus who was responsible? Were there two laws or only one?[57] What was the distinction between *vis publica* and *vis privata*? Were *rapina* and the interdicts *de vi* and *de vi armata* linked to the criminal law when the *lex Iulia* was passed, or only later?[58] Cloud has provided quite convincing answers for some of these questions.[59] He holds that there were indeed two *leges Iuliae de vi*, one the work of Caesar in his dictatorship and the other of Augustus, probably between 19 and 16 BC. Each statute built on its predecessor back to the *lex Lutatia*; there was no connection with the *leges iudiciorum* of Augustus. Each *lex Iulia* covered both of what were later to be defined as *vis publica* and *vis privata*, and these terms probably did not appear in the statutes. The distinction was probably made by the jurists in the early second century, since both Seneca and Quintilian talk simply of '*vis*'; when Pliny the Elder spoke of *vis privata* it was in the sense of a drug having special force – against spider bites.[60] The *Institutes* of Justinian, like the Theodosian Code, refer simply to the *lex Iulia de vi publica seu privata*.[61] The novelty of the Augustan law must have been that it brought abuse of office under *vis*; otherwise Livy could never have written that the only statute with a penalty to protect the citizen against arbitrary flogging was the *lex Porcia*.[62]

By late classical law at least the distinction drawn between *vis publica* and *vis privata* was that the former was committed by magistrates or officials, the latter by private persons.[63] Both were offences, usually grave offences, against public order. Anyone holding *imperium* or office who put to death, flogged or tortured a Roman citizen contrary to his right of appeal, or who ordered such things to be done, was liable for *vis*; it also included the abuse of the power to correct or enforce, i.e. the power of *coercitio*, such as the imprisonment of someone without right or authority. To impose a new tax (*vectigal*), presumably on a province, created liability for *vis*.[64] *Vis* covered conspiring to raise a riot or sedition, and keeping men, slave or free, under arms.[65] Like the law *de sicariis* it could be used to prevent or restrict the carrying of arms in public places.[66] *Vis* covered usurpation of jurisdiction, especially by private persons, and hiding or otherwise assisting someone lawfully exiled;[67] also guilty were those who assaulted persons with diplomatic immunity.[68]

Collegia

The repression of *collegia* is a topic that fits here, since, at least in the Empire, it was the risk of sedition which justified their close control, although in the Republic they were frequently associated with *ambitus* and electoral violence.[69] The Senate in its resolution of 56 BC, says Gruen,[70] 'was moving toward a rational means of curbing the illicit actions of organizations without infringing freedom of assembly'. To the same end the *lex Licinia* was passed in 55 BC to check bribery and intimidation, but probably it did not outlaw *sodalitates* – a narrower term than *collegia* – as such. This law certainly co-existed with the *lex Plautia de vi*, and may have had the same penalty of interdiction.[71] *Collegia* of all sorts, bodies with a common fund and a treasurer or manager, came to need specific permission, from Senate or emperor, with soldiers not being allowed to participate at all.[72] Burial clubs were tolerated, and even slaves might belong, but regular meetings were to be no more than monthly[73] – this is one reason why the Christians could hardly have formed legal *collegia*, since they needed to meet weekly for worship; Jews had an exemption. *Collegia* represented a threat to public order rather than a standing offence, but they could be repressed severely;[74] accusations were made before the Prefect of the City.[75]

In the Later Empire it might be seditious to attempt to protect the ordinary citizen by the exercise of patronage, or to make a clamour at a court hearing.[76] Treason was too strong a term to describe the independent behaviour of the *potentes*, even though they diminished the authority of the government; to charge them with an offence carrying only a fine, particularly since it was unlikely to be enforced, would not cause civil war or serious disloyalty. The boundary between the treatment of what we should call sedition and full-blown treason was fluid; for example, the penalty for the authors of a sedition or stirrers up of the populace might be, according to rank, crucifixion, the beasts, or deportation to an island.[77] Infamy might be a sufficient penalty for *vis privata*; the loss of one third of one's property was only suitable for *vis publica*.

Abuses by magistrates

Vis publica[78]

As we have seen above, some of the law on *vis* was certainly aimed specifically at the abuse of power by magistrates, an abuse which was only legally possible when directed against the good citizen; the infamous and other disreputable persons were not protected against arbitrary rough treatment.[79] We have mentioned ill-treating a citizen contrary to his right of appeal – *adversus provocationem*[80] – and binding or otherwise hindering an accused from making an appeal or presenting himself in Rome by a due date.[81]

Res repetundae[82]

Of the statutes dealing with extortion, it seems likely that the *lex Calpurnia* of 149 BC was aimed at the protection of Roman citizens in the provinces[83] but, at the latest by the time of the statute of the *tabula Bembina*, commonly called the *lex Acilia*,[84] the crime extended to cover extortion from provincials who were peregrine, and more particularly from Latins and *socii*.[85] There is no record of hostility to this *repetundae* law, which is one of the arguments against its being Gracchan; if it was part of his policies, it was not repealed in the aftermath of his death, and the *lex Servilia Caepionis* of 106 BC seems merely to have altered the make-up of the jury.[86] The *lex Servilia Glauciae*, probably of 104 BC, restored equestrian juries to the *repetundae* court and also divided the procedure there into two sessions – *comperendinatio*;[87] further, it seems to have extended liability from the actual extorters to those who received misappropriated monies.[88] It is not clear what changes were made by Sulla's *repetundae* law, other than restoring the jury to the Senate, but perhaps he introduced some stiffening of the penalty.[89] The *lex Iulia* of 59 BC (the year of Caesar's consulship) was a major restatement,[90] which widened the scope of the crime from pecuniary extortion to non-lucrative abuse of office,[91] although the extension to abuse of office in Rome (beyond the corruption of jurors) may well be due to juristic interpretation and development by resolutions of the Senate. Further, the *lex Iulia* laid down its own procedure.[92]

The offence known as *res repetundae* covered any improper exaction from those in the provinces made by anyone holding a magistracy or other office in the public service;[93] the normal element of gain is stressed by the prohibition on usucapion of things acquired contrary to the statute.[94] Originally only senators as governors in a province were liable, but by the *lex Iulia* this was extended to their entourage (*comites*);[95] a resolution of the Senate extended liability to their wives.[96] Much of the extortion envisaged was simply lucrative: in particular the acceptance of presents (the statute carefully excepted gains which were proper, presents from close relatives[97]), trading, including owning commercial vessels, buying slaves except as replacements, demanding forage (or allowances in lieu) except when actually on circuit, and other offences of this sort.[98] The principle of these prohibitions continued in the Later Empire.[99]

Among the abuses of official power, there was taking money to give or withhold a judgment, civil or criminal,[100] or, more widely, taking a bribe to do more or less than one's duty.[101] More specifically, we are told that the statute covered being bribed to give or withhold evidence, or making or not making an accusation, and that the penalty for this included being barred from giving evidence, making accusations or acting as judge.[102] The prohibition at the end of this fragment on *urbani magistratus* indulging in financial impropriety or accepting favours in any year to more than the value of 100 gold pieces would seem to be an interpolation from a later period, when 'urban' was no longer an adjective specific to the city of Rome. The *lex Iulia* itself forbade not merely bribery in matters that clearly fell within a governor's jurisdictional powers – providing judges or arbiters, imprisoning persons, and giving judicial sentence – but also in administrative affairs, such as the improper approval of public works – and these were defined as including the provision of a public grain supply as well as the maintenance of buildings.[103] So there was some overlap with *maiestas*, *peculatus* and *vis*.[104] In the Later Empire we find emperors imploring their subjects to charge corrupt officials with any sort of extortion (including sentence delivered or penalty imposed or remitted for a bribe) and bidding junior officials accuse their superiors if they were not to be liable themselves.[105]

The penalty of Caesar's law was almost certainly interdiction from fire and water, exile under pain of outlawry if the exile returned, since we know that Caesar formalized this as the new form of capital conviction where condemnation had taken place in the *quaestiones de vi* and *de maiestate*.[106] *Repetundae* could be viewed as a capital offence in the post-Sullan period,[107] but this may have been specifically linked with judicial corruption bringing about the death of an innocent man; this was in the Empire to be punished with the death sentence or deportation to an island.[108] The element of reparation, as in theft, which was predominant in the earlier statutes, seems – reasonably – to have survived; because it was a case of unjustified enrichment, the heirs of an accused remained liable within a year of his death.[109] At the end of the classical period, it appears that removal from office might sometimes be sufficient penalty.[110]

Peculatus and de residuis; sacrilege

There was almost certainly a Sullan *quaestio de peculatu*, for a *quaestio perpetua* functioned in the Ciceronian period;[111] moreover, it is mentioned together with the *quaestio de sicariis* and the *quaestio testamentaria nummaria*. It is possible that there may have been an earlier court, since Pompey may have been tried before such a *quaestio* in 86 BC;[112] however, the trial of Q. Caepio in 104 BC was by a special tribunal. The *lex Iulia* of Augustus superseded the earlier legislation. Under it, if not earlier, the misappropriation of monies remaining and sacrilege were classed with the embezzlement of public property for trial by the one court.

Peculation was the embezzlement of public monies,[113] and an offence originally committed only by senatorial magistrates. The *lex Iulia* forbade unlawful (hence the immunity of someone acting as an honest agent) acquisition – taking, diverting, converting – from 'any money dedicated to sacred or religious or public purposes', or making it possible for anyone else unauthorized so to acquire.[114] Debasement, and permitting the debasement, of public monies was also covered.[115] Public slaves working in the mint who, outside its premises, stamped for themselves coin with the public die, were held to have committed peculation rather than forgery or coining; strangely, this was also the case if they stole legitimately stamped coin.[116] The explanation may be that before it went into circulation it was viewed as still being a commodity, since stealing gold or silver from imperial mines was counted as aggravated theft.[117] Stealing booty captured from an enemy was classed as peculation, but the penalty was that of manifest (i.e. aggravated) theft.[118] Claiming money from a private person by falsely holding oneself out as a creditor of the fisc could be held to be peculation,[119] because thus the debt appeared to be discharged; on the other hand, there was naturally no crime in claiming money that was due, even if the debtor also owed money to the fisc, because this did not affect the status of his fiscal debt.[120]

Peculation was also possible from a municipality's property, at least from the times of Trajan and Hadrian.[121] When the liability imposed by the statute was extended to cover removing or tampering with the tablets on which a law or an official map was inscribed, this presumably applied in the provinces; however, the extension of liability to any deletion or addition to public records fits equally well with Rome.[122] Even allowing the unauthorized transcription or inspection of public records could, by a resolution of the Senate, amount to peculation.[123]

A distinction was drawn between the theft of public property, which was peculation, and the misappropriation of public money with which the wrongdoer had been entrusted and which had not all been expended on the intended purpose – monies remaining.[124] This money might have been received for a particular transaction, such as a lease, a purchase, or the provision of foodstuffs, or anything else that constituted proper public expenditure.[125] It was because of this correct initial receipt that a temple caretaker could not be held liable for peculation or sacrilege,[126] although he might be responsible *de residuis*.

The wrongful taking of money, or other things, dedicated to sacred or religious purposes was sacrilege, but it was viewed as an offence of dishonesty not blasphemy.[127] It was not an offence which had its own *quaestio*, but those who committed it were charged before the *quaestio peculatus* and incurred the penalty of the *lex Iulia peculatus*, when not dealt with *extra ordinem*, which is why it is mentioned here. Sacrilege in the Later Empire was no longer a form of public theft but rather an offence against religion,[128] or against the imperial wisdom – it was akin to sacrilege to doubt the worthiness of imperial judges chosen by the emperor.[129]

The penalty of the *lex Iulia* on peculation as originally passed was interdiction from fire and water; as with *res repetundae*, there was *litis aestimatio* at the end of a successful prosecution.[130] The punishment inflicted in the Empire was normally deportation, with forfeiture of property;[131] for embezzlement of monies remaining there was a fine of one third of what was (civilly) owed.[132] For embezzlement of public monies or monies remaining, as for *res repetundae*, the heirs might be liable under criminal proceedings,[133] because it was in effect a case of unjustified enrichment. Sacrilege was punished in accordance with the degree of the offence, as imperial enactments laid down;[134] where a band had broken into a temple at night this could mean the aggravated death penalty, but where the circumstances were less serious, such as abstracting something by day, condemnation to the mines, or deportation for the upper classes, might suffice.[135] For peculation, and probably the other two offences, there was a prescriptive period of five years.[136]

Ambitus[137]

This was essentially a crime of the Republic,[138] for obvious reasons, although one that is in that period sometimes difficult to isolate from the political battles waged through the courts.[139] Elections continued, however, to be seriously contested even after they were transferred under Tiberius from the assemblies to the Senate.[140] Later, municipal corruption, including contests for local priesthoods,[141] became the main target;[142] later still the crime consisted of buying office or promotion within the bureaucracy.[143] In theory, improper behaviour, particularly in elections, by the senatorial class could have been punished by the censors,[144] but factional loyalties were often too strong.

Various passages of Livy purport to relate to electoral corruption as a statutory offence as early as 432 or 358 BC, and then under a *lex*

Cornelia Baebia in 181 BC;[145] the *lex Cornelia Fulvia*, a consular statute, was passed in 159 BC.[146] It is hardly possible that this, rather than some lost law,[147] created the *quaestio de ambitu* before which Marius was tried in 115 BC;[148] that court, or at least its jury, seems likely to have been composed under the rules of the *tabula Bembina*. The existence of a Sullan *lex Cornelia* on *ambitus* remains unproven, but inherently likely.[149] His *lex Cornelia de magistratibus*, specifically on the *cursus honorum*,[150] may suggest that there was hardly any need for this, but he may have wished to reform this *quaestio*, like the others, in the interests of systematic justice. There followed the *lex Calpurnia* of 67 BC,[151] a modification of a bill originally proposed by the tribune C. Cornelius; this probably covered the *divisores* who acted for the candidates, since there is evidence from Cicero that non-senatorial offenders might be liable.[152] A *senatusconsultum* seems to have amended the statute[153] before the *lex Tullia* of 63 BC sharpened the penalties and defined the offence more clearly.[154]

The *lex Licinia de sodaliciis* of 55 BC was aimed particularly at the formation or adaptation of organized groups for corrupt political purposes; the violent events in the months surrounding the murder of Clodius show the particular need.[155] It criminalized the organizers, not the ordinary members, although they might, of course, become liable for *vis*. Moreover, Crassus (along with his consular colleague Pompey, who seems to have redefined eligibility to serve on the juries[156]) tried to reduce the risk of bribed *iudices* by laying down a more random system of selection, less open to the parties' manipulations.[157] It is not quite clear whether the *lex Licinia* existed beside the *lex Tullia* or replaced it; the latter is more likely, since it was under this statute that Vatinius was charged. The *lex Pompeia* of 52 BC may have set up a *quaestio extraordinaria*, as was the case with Pompey's *lex de vi*; however, since it was in use in 51 BC for the trial of Messalla, who had nothing to do with the events of 53 and 52, it may rather have reformed the *quaestio perpetua de ambitu*.[158] The *lex Pompeia* introduced the same summary procedure as for *vis*, with the witnesses produced on the first days, and on the final day two hours being allowed to the prosecutor for his speech and three to the defence:[159] other features were no *laudationes*, a limited number of advocates, arrangements to postpone the final selection of *iudices*, as described by Asconius,[160] and an overall limit of five days for a trial. If the *lex Pompeia* reformed the procedure in two of the *quaestiones perpetuae*, it explains why later writers could think that the procedural changes were applied to all the *iudicia publica*.[161] Finally there was the *lex Iulia de ambitu* of 18 BC, which had only a brief life.

Being corrupted does not seem in this context to have been criminal, any more than the formation of a party as such. *Divisores* or active accomplices were directly liable in the *lex Tullia*, which laid down that giving banquets, as well as cash, should fall under the scope of *ambi-*

tus;[162] so did giving gladiatorial shows within two years of candidacy,[163] as with Vatinius[164] (though it was possible to get round this by giving games in memory of someone *ex testamento*[165]) or the distribution of (free) seats for other candidates' games.[166] There was, moreover, a limit, which we do not know, on the size of a candidate's escort.[167] The right of assembly was not denied,[168] but unofficial assemblies were always suspect. For reasons, presumably, of convenience, *ambitus* could overlap with other crimes. To introduce a new tax was, by a resolution of the Senate, to be punished with the penalty of *ambitus*, that is, when it did not fall under *vis*.[169] And something that was deemed an attempt at judicial corruption – as when either accused or accuser entered the house of a judge – was classed by the *lex Iulia iudiciaria* as electoral corruption, punished with a fine of 100 *aurei*; in some other contexts bribery of a judge fell under *falsum*.[170]

The penalties were suited to the crime, in that they were primarily directed at the convicted person's honourable status. The *lex Cornelia Fulvia* imposed ten years' disqualification from *honores*,[171] which was made perpetual by the *lex Calpurnia* of 67 BC. The latter expelled the offender from the Senate and also imposed a fine, although it did not require departure from Rome,[172] unlike the *lex Tullia* of 63 BC. Under this, the condemned man was banished (relegated) for ten years;[173] stiffer sanctions were also imposed on non-senatorial offenders, and fabricated excuses from appearance at a trial were penalized.[174] The *lex Licinia de sodaliciis* seems to have imposed interdiction from fire and water.[175] Someone convicted could recover his full rights if he successfully prosecuted another man for the same offence; this was the 'reward' of the *lex Cornelia* or the *lex Calpurnia*.[176] Dio explained further that under the *lex Pompeia* the offender needed successfully to prosecute two men on the same or lesser charges as himself, or one man on a greater, to receive a pardon.[177] For municipal *ambitus*, the penalty came to be a fine of 100 *aurei* and infamy, which involved removal from the decurionate; this extension was laid down by a resolution of the Senate.[178]

Forgery: the counterfeiting of money

Since the introduction of their own coinage was a remarkably late phenomenon at Rome, not occurring until well into the third century BC,[179] it is not surprising that the first legislation on counterfeiting seems to be the *lex Cornelia nummaria* of Sulla.[180] The statute was passed because the debasing of the *denarius*, which had made its relation to the *as* quite uncertain, was causing much concern. The edict of Marius Gratidianus in 86 or 85 BC[181] was aimed at curbing this abuse. The Cornelian statute brought before a standing jury court, known as *de falsis* (sharing a court with Sulla's *lex testamentaria* on the forging of wills[182]) the unauthorized coining of silver, and also the buying and selling of base coinage disguised as silver.[183] Gold coinage did not yet exist at Rome,[184] and copper and bronze (or other base metal – but I use the term 'copper' because it is most familiar to us) coins were not at that time being issued by the *aerarium* (whereas municipalities, like allies, were free to issue coinage of this sort); copper therefore was not the concern of the *lex*, any more than gold. The purpose of Sulla's legislation seems essentially economic: to maintain the value of serious money, and to punish those who made illegal profits. It appears to have remained throughout the Roman period the basis of offences involving silver coinage.[185]

Copper coinage resumed with the Principate, but it does not seem to have been the subject of protective legislation, perhaps because forgery of such coins was not likely to be worth the costs involved, perhaps because it was a senatorial rather than imperial responsibility, remaining attached to the *aerarium*. However, under Constantine, the counterfeiting of copper was criminalized; the explanation given was the need to keep the mints fully occupied.[186] Mishandling copper coins seems to have been treated more severely than striking them.[187]

Whether wisely or not,[188] the Romans came to see the counterfeiting of gold coinage as a serious offence against the state.[189] This had an economic aspect, but the stress was on the treasonable nature of tampering with coinage bearing the imperial portrait; Suetonius even tells (unsubstantiated) stories of accusations of treason for carrying a coin stamped with Tiberius' image into a privy or brothel.[190] Constantine legislated against speculators who tried to sell the new gold *solidus* at a higher rate if the portrait of the emperor on it were larger than average; he must have wanted to hold up confidence in the new coinage, but such profiteering also affected the emperor's majesty.[191] He does not, however, appear directly to have held coining equivalent to treason.[192] Constantius added a reward for informers whose delations led to a conviction for counterfeiting gold coins, and stiffened the penalty.[193] Under Theodosius II counterfeiters were held liable for treason.[194]

How far the offence of counterfeiting money was defined in the *lex Cornelia* and how far developed by interpretation is difficult to say; perhaps because coins in precious metals were an imperial monopoly, there do not seem to be any resolutions of the Senate developing this aspect of *falsum*. In the *Sententiae* of Paul there is a list, perhaps original, of the ways by which coins could be diminished in value – counterfeiting, washing (with *aqua regia*), melting, shaving, clipping, adulterating. However, to define as *falsum* the refusal to accept lawful coins stamped with the portrait of the emperor must be a development of the Principate.[195] The same is obviously true of the case of those who struck coins that would have been false if completed, but were not; this may refer to a change of heart, however motivated, by a coiner, or it may refer to those who struck commemorative medals, etc.[196] *Falsum*, or the penalty of the crime of *falsum*, was extended to those who did not forbid such practices when they had the power to do so.[197]

The aggravation of the offence in the case of employees of the mints seems reasonable for a breach of trust, so it is strange that using official dies, clearly fraudulently, outside the mint was classed not as coining but as *peculatus*, the theft of public money.[198] (Similarly, stealing gold or silver from the imperial mines was punished only by exile or condemnation to the mines, depending on rank, while someone who hid the thief was liable for manifest theft and made infamous; melting down such illicit gold brought a penalty of fourfold its value.[199]) However, Constantine was sterner with those who abused their position to produce false copper coinage – it must be copper or the language would be fiercer, and their position must have enabled them to forge copper at a profit; the owner of the premises used was also held liable.[200] In the mid-fourth century, certain *flaturarii* were to be capitally punished for washing off the silver coating of the debased coins which had replaced the *denarius*.[201]

The original penalties of the *lex Cornelia* (for tampering with silver coins) were, presumably, exile for free men and death for slaves, but by the later Principate these had become deportation to an island for *honestiores*, the mines or crucifixion for *humiliores*, and unspecified death for slaves,[202] aggravated, in the case of tampering with gold coins, to condemnation to the beasts for free men and *summum supplicium* (burning or crucifixion) for slaves, while in certain circumstances burning might be appropriate even for free men.[203] From the crimes listed in the general amnesties of the later third century, it seems likely that death was in fact not the norm, even for coining gold, but only imposed at the discretion of the judge, since counterfeiting was not, until the reign of Theodosius II, listed among the crimes to which an amnesty did not apply, and it was then specifically linked to treason.[204] Forging copper coins does not seem to have been capital, except for slaves, but it earned perpetual exile, with loss of property for the decurial classes, confiscation and forced labour in perpetuity for humbler men.[205] Modified forms of exile and confiscation applied to owners of property used for such coining, but their age, sex and status could reduce the penalties.[206] Melting down base coinage could, somewhat oddly, be capital, with Constantius viewing it as sacrilege; in his edict the offence was linked with trafficking in coin, in the literal sense of transporting it. He seems to have been anxious to preserve the integrity of official coinage, and not to let its value be driven down by competition.[207]

Offences against the *annona*

Although the free or subsidized corn supply was only issued to a relatively small proportion of the Roman population,[208] it had enormous psychological and social importance in revealing the state's care, creating the emperor's grateful *clientela*. The jurisdiction of the Prefect of the Grain Supply, and in the provinces the governor, was therefore privileged.[209] A slave was permitted to accuse his owner of defrauding the *annona*, and it was one of the charges that a woman, like a soldier or someone infamous, could make even where she had no personal interest.[210] The *annona*, in roughly the form it lasted throughout the Empire, had been the creation of Augustus, and it was not something for which (for good political reasons) he saw a *quaestio perpetua* as a suitable forum, unlike most of the offences we have considered. They, apart from adultery, all had a Republican tradition, but the corn supply[211] needed to be protected by *cognitio* reflecting the direct authority of the emperor and his delegates.

Augustus' *lex Iulia* therefore laid down a penalty for anyone who did anything prejudicial to the corn supply, or who tried, with a partner, to raise the price.[212] This latter point stresses the importance of the unsubsidized proportion of Rome's supplies, because, at the time of the *lex Iulia*, it cannot possibly have been meant to refer to machinations within the civil service.[213] The statute also penalized the malicious delay of a grain ship, or of its master, with a fine.[214] Commodity hoarders and those who used false measures were also punished according to the degree of their offence.[215] In the later Principate we find the *divi fratres* condemning pressure to make decurions sell corn cheaper than the grain supply's current rate, and also forbidding them to lay down a price for grain 'which is imported'.[216] The former may have been viewed as being likely to arouse expectations which could not be satisfied, and might therefore lead to riots; the latter would disturb the market.

Other Offences: Against Good Morals or Public Discipline

The preceding chapters have been mainly concerned with offences of the *ordo*, the offences dealt with under the system of *quaestiones perpetuae*. This chapter is concerned with a range of miscellaneous offences, frequently but by no means always less serious, although a few of them do seem to have been, if only temporarily, the subject of *quaestiones perpetuae*.[1] They are mostly offences against public order in some form.

Offences against *bonos mores*

At one end of their spectrum these offences were matters which incurred not so much a conventional criminal penalty as infamy[2] or some loss of normal rights. For example, the effect of Augustus' marriage legislation was to penalize the unmarried and the childless for their failure in their duty to society.[3]

Cruelty was not something to which the Romans seem to have been very sensitive; limiting an owner's rights over a slave was only slowly accepted as socially desirable and a matter for legal intervention. However, in the second century measures against cruelty were taken; Hadrian relegated a woman for five years because of her appalling treatment, for trivial reasons, of her slave girls. Antoninus Pius too was concerned with the abuse of owners' powers, while careful to stress the rights of ownership.[4] Severus gave authority to the Urban Prefect to hear slaves' appeals against cruel treatment, including starvation and sexual abuse, and against enforced prostitution.[5] In fact, it seems to have been consideration for slaves that led to the return of the right of asylum, which Tiberius had abolished because it had been much abused, especially in the provinces.[6]

Offences concerning expenditure and income

Sumptuary laws were issued in the Republic by the Senate, by the censors, or in legislative form; they mostly seem to have been concerned with meals.[7] The tradition continued into the Empire, and it seems that both Augustus and Tiberius issued such edicts, for example forbidding the use of solid gold as tableware, and silk clothes for men.[8] Emperors also, rather oddly, imposed restrictions on what could be sold in bars and taverns.[9] These restrictions were all of the Julio-Claudian dynasty; by the second century moderation seems to have come back into fashion. A related topic, but very differently motivated, was the control of prices attempted by Diocletian in his Edict; the sanctions were fierce – capital for both buyer and seller[10] – but they probably soon fell out of use, since they were not preserved in the Codes.

Usury was reprobated; it was one of the matters dealt with by the aediles in the Republic.[11] There was a *lex Marcia* governing moneylenders, even before Julius Caesar's legislation. Rates of interest were controlled, the maximum permitted in the Empire being 12%; compound interest was always forbidden.[12] While the main 'penalty' was the debtor's right to set off excess interest against the principal, multiple restitution was sometimes imposed on the avaricious moneylender.[13]

Taxes were payable on, among other things, prostitution, the urine collected from the public latrines, access to public utilities (at least in the provinces), inheritances, and the sale of slaves;[14] in the Later Roman Empire we learn of the *siliquae*, a sort of early VAT, and a couple of years later the Emperor Valentinian was referring to the black economy.[15] Taxes – *portoria* – were originally payable on bringing goods into the City;[16] later they were exigible at the frontiers of the Empire,[17] and had become primarily an imposition on barbarians. We hear of tax avoidance and evasion, and even more of the related problem of informers to the fisc;[18] smuggling clearly could be risky since the ship was forfeit to the fisc, or the skipper capitally punished where the owner was innocent.[19] Nevertheless, compared to what we hear of direct tax evasion there is more than a little on illegal exactions.[20]

Dubious persons: gamblers, actors, philosophers, etc.

Then there were those whose way of life was loose, gamblers, and actors of all kinds, and also charioteers and gladiators.[21] Gambling, except in the private family circle, was forbidden in the Republic. Under the Praetor's Edict there was no remedy for gambling losses or for being beaten up as a result of gambling, although the Praetor might penalize, by a fine or imprisonment, the use of force to make someone gamble or to oblige him to continue.[22] Sulla was perhaps responsible for a statute restricting gambling; it has been suggested that it was actually a chapter in his sumptuary law.[23] A resolution of the Senate forbidding playing games for money, except for certain manly sports, was quoted by the jurist Paul.[24] Both investigative functions and jurisdiction were, and continued to be until well into the Principate, exercised by the aediles.[25] Gambling undoubtedly continued, and probably was not normally very severely repressed.[26] Justinian deplored gambling, in part at least because it led to blasphemy, but he seems to have permitted the equivalent of tombola at the parish fête where no meaningful losses would be suffered, although the clergy were strictly forbidden to indulge or even to watch.[27] Interestingly, our sources reveal no trace of organized gambling.

Actors, along with gladiators and pimps, were disqualified from public office and from various public functions.[28] They were not protected by the *lex Iulia de vi* against flogging or being locked up at the whim of a magistrate.[29] They might be banished arbitrarily from Rome or Italy.[30] They were also among those classes of person whom an indignant husband could lawfully kill if he surprised him *in flagrante* with his wife.[31] An actress or a madam was not liable to the penalties for adultery – she was below the law – as evidenced by a resolution of the Senate which imposed liability on those who specifically tried to evade the penalties by turning to such a way of life.[32]

Rhetoricians, philosophers and astrologers formed another loosely linked element in society – sometimes overlapping with cults[33] – which suffered intermittent repression because of activities seen as contrary to public discipline; while many of the sources for this are literary, almost all cite legal authority. Rhetoricians became respectable sooner than the others, but to begin with they were (Greek) foreigners teaching honest Romans foreign ways; in consequence they were repressed when they scandalized too many persons of influence.[34] Philosophers too were originally foreign, again Greek, and men whose ideologies were often askew from the Roman norm, and therefore potentially dangerous. As late as 92 BC the censors passed an edict against rhetoricians, whose teachings were 'novel and not in accordance with the customs of our ancestors'.[35]

Philosophers of the upper classes, such as Paetus Thrasea, were in the forefront of the opposition to 'bad' emperors; there were dangerous political connotations in the term.[36] As well as Arulenus Rusticus and Herennius Senecio, many others also perished under Domitian as a result of this charge of philosophizing, and all the philosophers that were left at Rome were banished once more.[37] Christians could be considered as philosophers; Lucian and Philostratus both saw the parallel.[38] Origen, for example, lived like a philosopher.[39] Philosophy, particularly Stoic philosophy, and astrology were linked disciplines, concerned with questions of free will and man's innate capacities, and the consequences of these questions. Many were interested in this subject (as Republican leaders such as Cato and Cicero had been) including emperors, perhaps most notably Hadrian, but such questions could be dangerous, even treasonable. It is hardly surprising that this was a grey area, in which people were punished for what they might do rather than for what they had done; suspicion might be enough to secure conviction.[40] A further parallel with Christianity was that abstention from practice restored innocence of guilt.[41] As with astrologers, whom we now consider, such bans on undesirables, though recurrent, were not permanent.

Astrologers not only understood the stars but could predict the future from them; when this involved the future of the imperial house, the threat of treason could not be far away. And below the serious astrologers, who were also often what we would call astronomers,[42] were the soothsayers and magicians, presumably mostly charlatans[43] and associated with spells and potions.[44] In 33 BC the expulsion of astrologers and charlatans was carried out by Agrippa as aedile with *cura urbis*, and an edict was issued against them in AD 11.[45] Under Tiberius, around AD 17, a resolution of the Senate was passed expelling *mathematici* and *magi* from Italy, and some were executed.[46] A legal source of the early fourth century talks of the same episode: it tells us that such men were interdicted from fire and water, and their property confiscated; if they were not citizens they were put to death.[47] Later emperors, Nero, Vitellius, Vespasian, Domitian, issued similar bans, accompanied by various penalties, according to the measure of the offence.[48] Capital, or severe, penalties were inflicted on those who touched the imperial safety, but lighter ones on those who merely sought to discover their own fates. Soothsayers were counted in with astrologers, although punishable in their own right, since they often upset public peace and due order by the exercise of their arts. We hear of adverse judgments by the Emperor Antoninus Pius, in a rescript addressed to a governor of Lyon, and of a rescript of Marcus Aurelius relegating a soothsayer.[49] Diocletian spoke of the 'damnable art of mathematics'; and he was disturbed by those preaching vain and superstitious doctrines. The ringleaders were to be burned; other active participants to be put to death and their property confiscated, though persons of the better sort might be sent to the mines instead of being executed.[50] The *Pauli Sententiae* (in a passage not taken into the Digest) tell us that soothsayers should be expelled, after a beating, from the cities in which they were operating, so that they could not corrupt public morals or create public disorder. Those who persisted were liable to be put in chains and deported or relegated; those who were preaching a new or unsettling religion were to be deported, if classed as *honestiores*, otherwise put to death. To predict the future of the imperial house incurred a capital penalty, whether done by astrologers, diviners or soothsayers – clearly differing categories.[51] Equally severely treated was a slave who consulted an astrologer or soothsayer about his owner.[52] We are also told that the magicians themselves should be burned, and their accomplices crucified or sent to the beasts. It was forbidden to possess books on magic and, if any such were found, they were to be burned and their owner deported to an island, or put to death if of the humbler sort.[53]

In the Later Roman Empire things were rather different. Astrologers remained for a while a manifestation of those skilled in interpreting the will, the intentions, of the gods; they were a foreign form of the native augurs or *haruspices*, priests whose very function was to foresee.[54] In the Christian Empire, they were in principle seen as outside the divine order, and so they were prohibited, with certain concessions for ignorant rusticity.[55] Constantine at one stage tried to forbid soothsayers altogether.[56] His successors, particularly Constantius, seem so outraged as to be presumed credulous.[57] Sometimes the offence was treason, at others heresy,[58] sometimes creating public disorder.[59] It may reflect the return of a more disciplined society that Justinian was not concerned enough to legislate in this area.

Offences concerned with status

It was a crime for a *dediticius* to live near Rome, or for a runaway to seek to escape to the barbarians;[60] it was also a crime for a slave to live as though a freedman, when ordered not to.[61] Fraudulent self-sale involved a penalty, the penalty of truly becoming a slave,[62] as did living with a slave in defiance of the *SC Claudianum* of AD 52.[63] Ingratitude in a freedman or freedwoman could lead to revocation of the manumission.[64] Then there was usurpation of liberty,[65] and usurpation of freeborn status. The *lex Visellia* gave a criminal action, which did not exclude a patron's claim for services due, against freedmen who, without having received the privilege of the equestrian gold ring from the emperor, sought office or dignity, in particularly the decurionate, a duty reserved to the freeborn.[66] In all these cases there was no true penalty but rather an act which restored *ipso facto* the real state of affairs.

Usurpation of citizenship was an offence of wider, more than private, importance in the Republic. The *lex Licinia Mucia* of 95 BC set up what seems to have been a standing jury court;[67] its function was to expel Italians, including Latins, from Rome, and to challenge the status of alleged Roman citizens. Its ungenerous and ill-timed investigations were one of the major causes of the Social War. Thirty years later the *lex Papia de peregrinis* of 65 BC ordered all non-Italians to be banished from Rome;[68] this was most likely simply an obstacle thrown in the way of Crassus' political manoeuvrings. The two statutes were, however, thought of together, and may have remained the basis of what seems to have continued to be an offence well into the first century of the Empire.[69] The *tria nomina* – *nomen, cognomen* and *praenomen* – were the mark of the citizen, but a free man was not forbidden to change his name, unless for fraudulent purposes.[70] As the Empire developed, and status became more complex than the traditional freeborn, freed and slave, there came to be an offence of usurpation of rank, whether social or administrative, whether for the use of the public *cursus* or for some other purpose, such as extortion.[71]

Escaping from custody or from a place of exile was also an offence in itself, a further failure to accept society's rules. This applied to prisoners on remand, even if they should be acquitted of the charge for which they had been thrown into jail.[72] The sureties of those who had received bail might be liable to a criminal penalty if they connived at their principal's non-appearance.[73]

Offences against religion

Pagan repression

In dealing with offences against religion, we must distinguish two main periods, the pagan and the Christian. However, this is an oversimplification, since the treatment of certain groups, most notably the Jews, did not vary greatly with the change in the religion of the Roman state. Nevertheless it is simpler to look first at religious crimes in the Republic and early Empire, and only then at crimes of religion as seen by Christians. Further, there were two sorts of offences against religion: those with implications for public order, which were the concern of the secular authorities, and the more technical which fell under sacral law under the general jurisdiction of the *pontifex maximus*.[74] The latter were in no way viewed as part of the criminal law, and even the former were more a matter of public discipline than law.[75]

The Roman state religion (like most polytheisms) was tolerant of people's private worship and, normally, of other public worship. The Romans needed, for the health of their society, the Roman gods worshipped in the traditional way in the temples of Rome but, beyond that, religious practice was normally a matter of indifference. The Romans were not guardians of their gods; both Cicero and Tiberius tell us that the gods can avenge themselves.[76] However, toleration was not always the case. There is no doubt that there was intermittent repression of foreign cults. Perhaps best known, and certainly most dramatically told, is the Bacchanalian affair of 186 BC, which was dealt with by an extraordinary *quaestio*.[77] Another form of worship which the Romans were not prepared to permit, probably because it seems to have involved human sacrifice,[78] was druidism. Augustus forbade citizens (in Gaul, it is implied) to participate in the rites of the druids, and Tiberius forbade their priests to officiate; Claudius formally abolished druidism.[79] The cult of Isis, although not as such forbidden, aroused sufficient hostility for the Senate to order the destruction of the newly-built temple at Rome in 50 BC.[80] Augustus, in 28 BC, forbade Egyptian rites within the *pomerium*; in 21 BC the 'Egyptians' were in disfavour again, and

Agrippa forbade their rites even in the suburbs within a mile of the City.[81] There was further trouble around AD 18.[82]

There are some surviving legal texts on the suppression of other cults and uncanny practices, such as Marcus' decree of relegation against those who frightened frivolous minds through superstition, or the text from Paul's *Sententiae* on those who introduce new sects and religions unknown to reason, disturbing men's minds.[83] Further, while it was accepted jurisprudence that nobody ought to be criminally liable for his thoughts,[84] words were undoubtedly sufficient to constitute an *actus reus*,[85] and thus preaching could be covered.

The best known references to a religion rejected, or supposedly so, by the Roman authorities are to Christianity.[86] The first anti-Christian episode was the Neronian persecution, linked by Tacitus with the Great Fire of AD 64. Suetonius simply listed Nero's severe treatment of the Christians along with his more general reforms, such as the abolition of public banquets, restrictions on food served in bars, and the (temporary) banishment of the pantomimes and their fan clubs.[87] Tacitus admitted that the Christians were made scapegoats for the Fire, but held that this was highly suitable, if one must have scapegoats, because of their '*odio humani generis*'; he makes it clear that Nero was merely trying to confuse the issue and retain his own popularity with the mob.[88] Tertullian, Lactantius and Eusebius, of the Christian writers, all saw Nero as the first persecutor and Domitian as the second.[89] Under Domitian, Flavius Clemens, the consul, and his wife, Flavia Domitilla, a lady of senatorial rank and almost certainly closely related to the Emperor, were charged, along with various other persons, with 'atheism' – failure to worship the ancestral gods. Some converts were put to death and others suffered confiscation of their property; Domitilla was merely banished.[90] It has been argued that this was for Christianity, but it was more probably Judaism; however, Pope Clement I, a contemporary, records that the Church in Rome suffered under Domitian, but he gives no details. Under Trajan we know from the famous correspondence with Pliny[91] that there could be heavy sanctions imposed on Christians, yet at the same time they were not to be sought out. Septimius Severus is said to have forbidden conversion to both Judaism and Christianity in 202;[92] there probably was some decree against proselytism by the Jews, and certainly Christian martyrdoms are recorded during his reign.[93]

Nevertheless, there is no reason to believe that Christianity as such was illegal, any more than the cult of Isis, in the first two and a half centuries of our era. Overall, the period between Domitian (at the end of the first century) and Decius (in the mid-third century) appears in the Christian writers as a time of general peace and growth for the Church, with some localized troubles.[94] During that period the Romans treated the cults of Isis and Christ with equal indifference, and repressed them with equal brutality when it seemed expedient for public discipline. Well-behaved cults, like that of Mithras, were left alone; abominable ones, like druidism, were suppressed. By the mid-third century Christianity had grown into a significant body, with its members spread throughout society, and some holding positions of importance; the risk of disloyalty could be, and was, seen as real in a period of economic break-down and military threat from the Goths. An edict was issued by Decius in 250 or 251 demanding that all Rome's subjects sacrifice to the Roman gods; the Jews were exempt, so it is probably fair to hold that this was a measure de facto aimed at Christians. Later persecutions followed, briefly under Valerian, and then the Great Persecution under Diocletian and Galerius. These ended with Constantine's Edict of Toleration; Christianity thereafter was not merely licit but also normally held in imperial favour, until its formal recognition as the religion of the Empire under Gratian, Valentinian and Theodosius.[95]

The Jews

The trouble with the Egyptians in AD 18 had also included the expulsion of the Jews. Four thousand, who were freedmen, were sent off to repress brigandage in the notoriously unhealthy island of Sardinia; the remainder, apart from those who were citizens, were to leave Italy (or perhaps just Rome) unless they apostatized within a given time.[96] This was clearly not a permanent expulsion, for the Jews were in trouble again under Claudius.[97] The Jews, however, were a special case; they were not liked, but they were normally tolerated because it was clear that they lived in accordance with long-standing tradition, *mos maiorum* of their own[98] – unlike the Christians who rejected the past, claiming a new covenant. Nevertheless proselytism was often, though not always, forbidden.[99] A harsher attitude was taken as a result of the Jewish revolts in Hadrian's reign. Conversion to Judaism, marked by circumcision, led to perpetual relegation for the convert, or the owner of converting slaves, and death for the doctor; Jews who circumcised slaves they bought who were not of Jewish origin were to be deported or executed.[100] But Jews were in some ways privileged, as in the exemption from Decius' requirement to sacrifice to the Roman gods, and the recognition of their Sabbath.

In the Christian Empire, there was some persecution, particularly when Jews took steps against their members who had apostatized,[101] or blasphemed the Christian religion.[102] Severe penalties were imposed when they circumcised those outside their own race, particularly if these were Christian slaves.[103] Converts to Judaism from Christianity were punished by confiscation of their property.[104] Marriage between Christian and Jew was forbidden, doubtless for fear that the children would follow the Jewish faith.[105] A certain degree of public hostility to Jews is taken almost for granted, but is deplored.[106] However, compared with heretics and other non-orthodox believers, Jews continued to be privileged in such matters as immunity from public burdens, and recognition of the Sabbath.[107]

Christian repression

For a time the first Christian emperors continued to hold the office of *pontifex maximus*.[108] It took a while before the traditional pagan cults were forbidden; the Altar of Victory was finally moved from the Senate House in 382. Until then the official worship of the Roman state had remained paganism; thereafter it was Christianity. Rights of sanctuary became linked with churches.[109] The offences that one finds in the legal sources were seen as offences against the true religion rather than against the well-being of the state. However, as with blasphemy, severe penalties were sometimes threatened for those persisting in error;[110] God was not left to avenge his own injuries. Pagan temples were removed from any legal protection based on respect for religion, but in general their destruction was not ordered,[111] although they were sometimes closed;[112] their revenues were often cut off.[113] In particular, the sacrifices required by most pagan rites were attacked; they were described in such terms as mad, superstitious,[114] profane and sacrilegious, and making them often carried the death penalty, unlike other acts of worship.[115] Apostasy (from Christianity to paganism) was not very severely treated, but penalized by fines, inability to make or take under a will, or forfeiture of rank.[116]

Penalties were also to be imposed on those who did not accept the new religion in its authorized form; this clearly meant heretics far more often than pagans.[117] Heretics aroused more passionate feelings than pagans. In certain provinces, such as in Africa with the Donatists, there may have been a real danger from a political movement linked with a religious one. Heresy continued to be treated severely on occasion.[118] Nevertheless, a survey of the Codes shows that in general the penalties for heresy, as for apostasy, were essentially financial, similar to those of Augustus' marriage legislation, in that heretics were not entitled to take what they otherwise would have been able lawfully to receive, in particular inheritances. Alternatively they might be viewed as suffering from infamy.[119] These were not strictly criminal sanctions, but the juridical consequences of following a course of life – as was also true, say, of actors. One or two particular heresies, such as the Manichees, were perhaps genuinely criminalized, but even so, their treatment seems to have been closer to the traditional model: only when they made a nuisance of themselves, by proselytizing etc., were serious sanctions imposed.[120]

Procedural offences

The procedural offences were calumny,[121] *praevaricatio, tergiversatio*,[122] and also, of course, perjury and judicial corruption.[123] They were not themselves offences of the *ordo iudiciorum publicorum*, although originally they could only be committed in relation to charges concerning these crimes.[124] The *lex Remnia* seems to have dealt only with calumny; the *lex Iulia iudiciorum publicorum* presumably had something to say about all of them, but we find the *SC Turpillianum* of 61 treated as the basic source.

'Rashness in accusers is revealed in three ways and subject to three penalties: they may calumniate, prevaricate, or tergiversate. Calumny is the bringing of false charges, prevarication the concealment of genuine ones, while tergiversation means the complete abandonment of a completed accusation.'[125] Because of the private nature of the Roman system of criminal prosecution, its methods were much more subject to abuse than with a public prosecuting or police service. The early (in the context of the *iudicia publica*) decision to encourage accusers – *delatores* – by granting them a reward, usually from the property of the accused, meant that accusations might often be made merely from the hope of gain.[126] Another fault was that, in the absence of a public prosecution service, friends might be content to cover up an offence – particularly adultery – and there was a higher probability of acquaintances bringing accusations and then regretting (from whatever motive) the likely consequences. The system had therefore to provide a mechanism for a charge to be abandoned. There was, besides, an automatic annulment (*abolitio*) when the accuser died or was otherwise prevented from making his accusation;[127] similarly a tutor was able to withdraw an accusation made on behalf of a pupil now dead.[128] The death of the accused also normally annulled any accusation, with the exception of treason or a crime demanding reparation, such as extortion.[129] There were also occasional general amnesties, although these did not apply to the most serious crimes, and seem to have allowed renewal of the accusation within a set time.[130] Days of public thanksgiving were suitable for such announcements.[131]

Calumny was governed by the *lex Remnia* of some time before 80 BC.[132] Malicious or frivolous accusations were the most obvious danger in a system relying on private prosecution. (Indeed the oath against calumny has entered, by way of the canon law, into many modern systems of procedure.) In an attempt to prevent rash or vexatious accusations all indictments had to be signed.[133] Failing to make good one's accusation did not of itself incur liability for calumny but, after an acquittal, it was the same court's duty to investigate the accuser's intention and honesty, and to punish an accusation which had failed, not because of reasonable mistake, or even rashness, but because its

ground was malice.[134] It was classed as calumny to set up a man of straw
to make an accusation – unless of course the accusation was proved –
and the man of straw was punished for accepting a commission to put
a third party in fear.[135] Any form of purported evidence brought '*in
fraudem*' of someone was grounds for calumny.[136] However, in certain
cases, when accusers were pursuing their own wrongs, they might be
immune from liability for calumny or tergiversation;[137] examples were
a husband bringing an accusation of adultery[138] or a parent pursuing
the death of a child.[139]

Certain accusations, while not calumnious in the sense of being
malicious, were forbidden on grounds of good morals, and punished.[140]
This applied particularly to accusations attempted to be made by slaves
against their owners, where normally they were to be executed before
their charge was heard, except in cases of treason (and offences against
the *annona*); the same applied to freed persons and their patrons.[141] A
dubious case in AD 24, which clearly aroused public disapproval, was
the accusation by a son of his father.[142] Informers, *delatores*, those who
laid criminal charges, appear in Tacitus as an almost unmitigated pest.
Yet without a public prosecution service, and without any police force,
some encouragement to the citizen to lay charges must surely have been
necessary for the suppression of crime. But the easiest targets for
accusations had comparatively little public acceptance as criminal:
those men and women who failed to comply with the positive requirements of Augustus' marriage legislation, or who were guilty under his
lex Iulia on adultery. Later, the problem arose, on rather similar
grounds, with delations to the fisc, particularly in relation to the law of
succession.[143] Thus informers generally came to be classed as calumniators; in other words, to make an accusation, except where one had an
interest of some sort, was viewed as in itself malicious.[144] Thereafter we
find penalties imposed for denunciations, including and perhaps especially to the fisc, whether in person or through an agent, by men or by
women, slave or free – however, this naturally did not apply to the
slaves actually employed by the fisc.[145]

To prevaricate, it was necessary to collude with the accused, to
weaken the evidence against him and accept his spurious defences.[146]
This was often an offence of the professional prosecutor, guilty of taking
money, rather than an act of misjudged friendship.[147] If, following the
acquittal of an accused person, someone wished to renew the charge,
this could only be done by proving that his accuser had prevaricated.[148]
Bribery, or attempted bribery, to avoid the bringing of a charge might
make the recipient liable for prevarication, and thus bring him under
the *SC Turpillianum*.[149]

It was also punishable if, without proof of collusion but in excess of
the time allowed for the action, a prosecutor, after going through the
initial formalities, including providing sureties, failed to pursue his

charge or, worse, to appear in court.[150] While it was quite in order (indeed, sometimes natural) to discover that one had made a mistake in bringing an accusation, it was an offence, tergiversation, simply to drop the accusation;[151] permission must be formally sought from the court for an annulment of the charge, and several charges must be severally released.[152] An *abolitio* was the judicial cancellation of a properly made accusation, its annulment. Only the emperor could give leave to renew an annulled charge;[153] presumably good reason had to be shown. It was necessary to obtain such an annulment to escape liability for calumny or tergiversation, although seeking an annulment did not necessarily disprove such liability; an annulment was proper, although not necessary, even in the case of those accusers not at risk of calumny because the charge concerned their own loss.[154] An application for annulment must be made to the same judge, the same court, as the original accusation.[155]

In classical law, an accuser could not obtain an annulment without the consent of the accused, perhaps because the latter would wish to clear his name publicly.[156] Later, it was only if the accused had suffered harm because of the accusation, such as being imprisoned, flogged or tortured, that his consent was necessary for the granting of an annulment, as it was if an annulment was sought more than 30 days after the accused had been taken into custody; further, the flogging or torture of free potential witnesses barred an annulment.[157] An owner whose slave had been unjustly tortured because of a calumnious charge was able to claim twice the slave's value from the accuser.[158] Once a charge had been abandoned – not simply postponed – it could not be renewed by the same accuser;[159] this applied even to a charge of adultery brought by a husband's right.[160] Even after a conviction, if the condemned man appealed, an accuser who wished to withdraw the accusation must seek an annulment, because the appeal had re-activated the issue.[161] A general amnesty did not necessarily relieve the accuser of responsibility for carrying through his accusation;[162] nor did amnesties apply to slaves, who were normally to be held in chains until brought to trial.[163]

If an annulment was not sought when the charge was not pursued, the accuser was liable under the *SC Turpillianum* even if, on the face of it, the accusation could have been barred by prescription. A woman who had laid an accusation from which she was barred by reason of her sex, since the charge did not concern her, was held by Papinian not to have fallen under the resolution of the Senate; but, on the other hand, Papinian also held that someone who had (presumably in ignorance of the law) brought accusations of adultery simultaneously against the woman and the man[164] must obtain annulments of each if he were to avoid liability. Marcian argues, somewhat unconvincingly, that the solution lies in the relative failure of an accusation which is barred by time or statute – akin to being met by a dilatory defence – while a disability of sex or nonage is absolute – a peremptory defence; thus only women and minors are exempt from liability if they fail to seek an annulment.[165] But women and minors were not absolutely barred; they could bring charges where their own wrongs were concerned, and the same was true of the infamous or soldiers whose accusations were otherwise ineffective.[166] It seems rather more likely that Papinian's distinction was not based on logic but on the convention of womanly weakness, which might excuse her ignorance of the law. This surely must be the explanation for the non-liability of a woman who had been pursuing a forgery which affected herself.[167]

There was some discussion by the jurists of what facts constituted dropping an accusation, and therefore needed an annulment of the charge. It seems to have been constituted by discussing a compromise – which itself might be forbidden by statute or morality[168] – with the accused, or simply by a genuine change of intention, as well as failing to make use of the time allowed; once an informer (*nuntiator*) had submitted a written statement he must stand by it.[169]

There were certain cases where the *SC Turpillianum* was not applicable, such as the charge of a suspect tutor, and an allegation that someone had incurred liability under this very resolution of the Senate.[170] Charges of swindling (*stellionatus*), of pillaging an inheritance, or of theft or *iniuria*, could be dropped without incurring liability under the *SC Turpillianum*, but the judge might still impose punishment at his discretion.[171] A mere threat to bring a prosecution did not ground liability.[172] After a general amnesty an accusation, if it had not come to trial, could be resumed.[173] Similarly, a husband could renew an accusation by a husband's right, within a period of 30 *dies utiles*, after some public holiday had led to a general amnesty on charges.[174]

Perjury was an offence under the *SC Turpillianum*, as well – often – as under the courts themselves established for murder or forgery. Promising to produce a given result from a case which was pending before a judge was in itself unlawful.[175] So too was overfamiliarity with a judge, whether through friendship or patronage.[176] Corruption in a judge, however, might sometimes be punished only with removal from office, or temporary exile.[177]

Punishment for all the offences falling under the *SC Turpillianum* was at the discretion of the court, a penalty *extra ordinem* according to the degree of the offence, but a tariff seems to have operated, based on imperial enactments.[178] One text mentions a fine of five pounds of gold;[179] a conviction also made the guilty person infamous, barring him from prosecuting again, except in his own cause.[180] In some cases, particularly in late law, the calumnious accuser was threatened with the penalty to the risk of which he had put the accused.[181] We are also told of exile or relegation to an island, or degradation, as penalties, and that a calumnious action for *iniuria* – a charge which had to be brought in person – was to be punished *extra ordinem*.[182]

Administrative offences

A prison governor who was bribed to hold someone in custody without the usual chains was criminally liable; so too if he knowingly permitted poison or a weapon to be brought into the prison; if, however, this occurred without his knowledge he was, logically enough, to be punished for negligence.[183] Magistrates who had accepted someone into custody were to be liable to a fine if they released him without cause.[184] On the other hand, they were not to treat their prisoners inhumanely – 'put [them] in manacles made of iron that cleave to the bones' – nor to let them perish from the torments of prison.[185]

Soldiers in charge of prisoners were punished for escapes, after an investigation. The penalty could be death, but might be a flogging with or without reduction of rank or transfer of service; there might even be no further penalty.[186] However, if there had been a bribe the punishment was death.[187] If a prisoner succeeded in committing suicide, the guard was held at fault, but if the guard himself killed the prisoner, he was liable for homicide.[188] Under Constantine, the provincial governor (*iudex*) was held liable if any prisoner perished from starvation, or other means, and the governor was himself at risk of his life if he did not impose capital punishment on the guilty warder; later, we find the *commentariensis* being responsible for the safe custody of prisoners.[189]

It was illegal to operate a private prison, an offence deserving an aggravated death penalty; to do so was *lèse-majesté*, and provincial governors who permitted great men to do so were themselves guilty of treason.[190] Justinian also forbade private prisons, whether in town or country, and ordered that persons, however high their rank, who shut people up should spend as many days in the public prison as any of their prisoners had done in the private prison; if the governor failed to see to this, he was at risk both of his property and of his personal safety.[191]

One of the most notable features of the later Empire was the growth in offences of officialdom.[192] Partly this may reflect the growth of officialdom itself, but partly it seems the result of the decline in public morality.[193] These offences will not be treated at any length here because, properly speaking, they are administrative rather than criminal. A dramatic example was Constantine's edict to all provincials, positively imploring them to accuse corrupt officials;[194] an alarming one the leave granted to offer armed resistance to ravaging soldiers.[195] Penalties, usually pecuniary but sometimes including exile, were threatened against magistrates or judges who failed to do their duty.[196] More severe punishment was likely to be imposed in cases of maladministration or abuse of power.[197] The office staff of a provincial governor or other judge were frequently held liable for failure to observe proper procedure.[198] And beyond this, there seems sometimes to have been actual corruption, as in the offices of the Urban Prefect and the Prefect of the *annona*,[199] or by those seeking undeserved promotion.[200]

Finally, there are traces of what we should probably call planning offences. What was the crime of the contractors and local magistrates who were failing to maintain the roads of Italy? Whatever it was, it resulted in fines and infamy, and bankruptcies, after prosecution by the former praetor Corbulo.[201] Within the City burials were forbidden from earliest times.[202] There were building regulations, although we do not know much about the sanctions for their breach.[203] Demolition in particular was regulated, again probably from as early as the XII Tables. The *SC Hosidianum* and the *SC Volusianum*, of AD 44 and 56, forbade selling for demolition as well as demolition itself; knocking down one's own property in order to rebuild was excepted.[204] Interdicts will often have been sufficient in this sphere, but even they were sanctioned by the Praetor's *imperium*.

Notes

I. The Framework of Criminal Procedure

1. Livy 28.10; cf. Livy 29.36, which records that the trials were still going on in 204 BC.

2. Livy 43.2.

3. Cicero *Brutus* 27.106; II *Verr.* 3.84.195; 4.25.56; *de off.* 2.21.75; Richardson (1987).

4. Gruen (1974), 247, on the importance of system and permanency; (1968a), 258-64, on Sulla's work.

5. As Cloud says (1994), 530, the legislation that set up the *quaestiones* 'formed the basis for jurisprudential treatment of the crimes they handled, and continued to be influential wherever Roman law was influential'.

6. Cicero *pro Sestio* 44.95; *in Vat.* 17.40-1; *pro Milone* 15.40; *ad Q. fr.* 2.3.1-2 and 2.5.4; Gruen (1974), 298, argues that, despite the speeches to three *contiones*, the timing of the trial suggests that it was under the *lex Plautia*. The accusation of 43 BC mentioned in Dio 44.10.1 was thought by Jones (1972), 5, to be before the people. The last certain comitial trial was that of C. Rabirius in 63 BC.

7. Gruen (1974), 248-9.

8. Gruen (1974), 234-6.

9. Greenidge (1901) 417; see also Thomas (1963); Jones (1972); Santalucia (1989).

10. The main period of political conflict was, anyway, from Caius Gracchus to Sulla, but there were later changes, the *lex Aurelia* (70 BC), the *lex Vatinia* (59 BC), the *lex Fufia iudiciaria* (58 BC) and the *lex Pompeia* (55 BC).

11. *Inst.* 4.18; see also Robinson (1991-2).

12. Bauman (1980) 107.

13. *FIRA* i p. 84 is the edition I have used; its identification as the *lex Acilia repetundarum* now seems very doubtful, and it is better referred to simply as the *lex repetundarum* of the *tabula Bembina* – see Mattingly (1969, 1970 & 1975a) and Crawford, forthcoming.

14. *Lex Cornelia de falsis*: Cicero II *Verr.* 1.42.108; *de nat. deorum* 3.30.74; Ps. Asconius Stangl 248; Suet. *Aug.* 33. See chapters III & VI.

15. *Lex Cornelia de sicariis et veneficiis*: Cicero *pro Cluentio* 7.21; 54.148; 55.151; *de inv.* 2.20; *pro Rab. Post.* 7.16; Seneca *controv.* 3.9; Suet. *Caesar* 11. See chapter IV.

16. *Lex Cornelia de iniuriis*. See chapter IV.

17. *Lex Cornelia de maiestate*: Cicero *in Pis.* 21.50; *pro Cluentio* 35.97; II *Verr.* 1.5.12; *ad fam.* 3.11.2; Asconius *in Corn.* 59 (Stangl 48-9); *Auct. ad Her.* 2.12.17; Tac. *Annals* 1.72. See chapter VI.

Notes to pages 3-4

18. *Lex Cornelia de repetundis:* Cicero *pro Rab. Post.* 4.9; 5.11; *pro Cluentio* 37.104. See chapter VI.

19. Probable *lex Cornelia de peculatu:* Cicero *pro Cluentio* 53.147; *de nat. deorum* 3.30.74; I *Verr.* 13.39; II *Verr.* 3.36.83; *pro Murena* 20.42; Plut. *Pompey* 4; Vell. Pat. 2.56. See chapter VI.

20. The *lex Cornelia de ambitu* rests on the reference in *Schol. Bob. pro Sulla* Stangl 78; this speaks of a penalty previous to the *lex Calpurnia* of a ten-year ban on holding office: 'Nam superioribus temporibus damnati lege Cornelia hoc genus poenae ferebant ... .' Fascione (1984), 47, holds that this refers to the *lex Cornelia Fulvia* of 159. See chapter VI.

21. *Coll.* 4.2.2, Paul; cf. Plut. *comp. Lys. & Sulla* 3, who says Sulla 'continued to introduce marriage and sumptuary laws for the citizens, while he himself was living in lewdness and adultery'. Pomponius alleges that Sulla established a *quaestio perpetua de parricidiis* – D 1.2.2.32, *enchiridion* – but the complete lack of other mention strongly suggests that Pomponius was confused; Cicero's defence of Roscius Amerinus on a charge of parricide in 80 BC was before the *quaestio de sicariis.*

22. Cicero *Phil.* 2.23.56; D 11.5.2.1-3, Paul 19 *ad ed.* & Marcian 5 *reg.*

23. *Lex [Acilia] Calpurnia de ambitu:* Dio 36.21; 37.25; Asconius *in Corn.* 60 (Stangl 49); *in toga cand.* 89 (Stangl 69); Cicero *pro Murena* 23.46; 32.67.

24. *Lex Tullia de ambitu:* Cicero *pro Murena* 2.3; 3.5; 22.45; 41.89; *in Vat.* 15.37; *pro Plancio* 34.83; *pro Sestio* 64.133; Dio 37.29.

25. *Lex Licinia de sodaliciis:* Cicero *pro Plancio* 3.8; Dio 39.37.

26. As Mommsen says (1899), 867: later authors claimed that this statute put an end to *ambitus*, and rightly, in that three years later the Republic itself came to an end. Greenidge (1901), 391-92, doubted whether it was a permanent court, but *Vell. Pat.* 2.47 certainly implies it was.

27. *Lex Papia de peregrinis:* Cicero *pro Balbo* 21.48; 14.32; 23.52; *pro Arch.* 2.3; *de off.* 3.11.47. Earlier there was the *lex Licinia Mucia* – Asconius *in Corn.* 67-8 (Stangl 54); Val. Max. 3.4.5; Dio 37.9.5.

28. Sall. *Cat.* 31; Cicero *ad fam.* 8.8.1; *pro Cael.* 29.70; *pro Milone* 13.35; Asconius *in Milon.* 55 (Stangl 46). See chapters III, IV and VI.

29. Cicero *pro Rab. Post.* 3.8. See chapter III.

30. *Lex Pompeia*, probably of 55 BC, although 70 BC is also possible; this concerned the penalty for parricide. See chapter IV.

31. Cicero *pro Rosc. Am.* 4-5.11; cf. *ad Q.fr.* 1.2.2.5.

32. There was a *lex Iulia de pecuniis repetundis* (59 or 46 BC): Cicero *pro Sestio.* 64.135; *pro Rab. Post.* 4.8; *ad fam.* 8.8.2, probably a *lex Iulia de maiestate* (46 BC): Cicero *Phil.* 1.9.23, perhaps a *lex Iulia de vi* (?46 BC).

33. This is sometimes thought to be part of the *lex peculatus et de sacrilegiis*, but Justinian clearly thought they were separate – *Inst.* 4.18.9, 11.

34. D 48.12.2.2, Ulpian 9 *de off. proconsulis*; 48.12.1, Marcian 2 *inst.* See further chapter VI.

35. Whose number he may have raised from six to eight, but see Cloud (1994), 497.

36. Cicero *pro Cluentio* 53.147-54.148; 34.94; *pro Rab. Post.* 4.9; *de nat. deorum* 3.30.74; Asconius *in Corn.* 59 (Stangl 48-9).

37. Cicero I *Verr.* 8.21; *pro Mur.* 20.42; *Coll.* 1.3.1, Ulpian.

38. Cicero *ad Q. fr.* 3.1.7.24; 3.3.3; *pro Plancio* 17.43; 42.104, with Alfius presiding over both *maiestas* and *sodalicia* in 54 BC.

39. Cicero *pro Caelio* 13.32; *pro Sestio* 47.101; 54.116; *ad Q. fr.* 2.3.6; cf. Asconius *in Milon*. 54-5 (Stangl 45-6), showing two presidents for *vis* in 52 BC.

40. *ILS* 45 = *CIL* VI 1283; *ILS* 47 = *CIL* VI 1311; Cicero *pro Cluentio* 29.79; *Brutus* 76.264; Suet. *Caesar* 11.

41. Cicero *pro Balbo* 23.52; *pro Cluentio* 53.147; 20.55 & 33.89; 29.79; *in Vat.* 14.34; *pro Rosc. Am.* 4.11; *Coll.* 1.3.1, Ulpian; *ILS* 45 = *CIL* VI 1283.

42. *Schol. Bob. in Vat.* Stangl 150; cf. *Coll.* 1.2.3, Paul.

43. Cicero *pro Cluentio* 33.91. Cf. D 48.8.1.1, Marcian 14 *inst*.

44. Cicero *pro Cluentio* 20.55; 33.91; 53.147 (if Voconius Naso was not a praetor); II *Verr.* 1.61.157-8; Suet. *Caesar* 11.

45. Cicero *pro Cluentio* 28.76.

46. Suet. *Aug.* 32; cf. Cicero *Phil.* 1.8.19-9.23; Suet. *Caesar* 41-2; Dio 43.25.

47. *Tabula Bembina* vv. 13 & 16-17; there is no reason to suppose changes to these qualifications. See also D 4.8.41, Callistratus 1 *edicti monitorii*.

48. *VF* 197-98, citing the *lex Iulia iudiciorum publicorum*.

49. Under the *tabula Bembina*, 50 jurors were chosen from a panel of 450.

50. *Tabula Bembina* vv. 23-6; the obscure *lex Vatinia* of 59 BC also dealt with the rejection of jurors.

51. Cicero *pro Cluentio* 27.74, but I *Verr.* 10.30 suggests that a Sullan jury could be even smaller – the *lex Aurelia* was passed after this trial.

52. Cicero *pro Cluentio* 43.121.

53. Cicero *ad fam.* 8.8.5; *ad Att.* 8.16.2.

54. Cicero *in Pis.* 40.96.

55. Cicero *pro Flacco* 2.4; *ad Att.* 4.16.9 refers to 70 votes; Asconius *in Scaurian.* 28 (Stangl 29). But only 50 are mentioned in *ad Att.* 4.15.4, and there seem to have been 56 for Clodius' trial (*ad Att.* 1.16.5 & 10) – but this was a *quaestio extraordinaria*.

56. *Inst.* 4.18.1. A woman, like a minor, a slave, a peregrine and someone infamous, could do so only in a very limited number of cases; see Robinson (1981 & 1985).

57. D 3.3.42.1, Paul, 8 *ad ed*.

58. This was known as the *divinatio*; the most famous is that which allowed Cicero, rather than Q. Caecilius Niger, to prosecute Verres.

59. *Tabula Bembina* vv. 36-8; Cicero *ad fam.* 8.8.3. The *lex Remmia de calumniatoribus* (80 BC) concerned procedure in the *quaestiones*; see also chapter VII. This oath, which has descended into modern systems through the canon law, was taken by the prosecutor to attest his good faith.

60. Cicero received 110 days, to allow for travelling to Sicily in order to find witnesses and obtain documentary evidence against Verres.

61. Asconius *in Corn*. 59 (Stangl 48-9); Cicero *ad Q. fr.* 2.13.2.

62. Unless the penalty was not applicable to a slave, as, for example, with *iniuria* – D 48.2.12.4, Venuleius Saturninus 2 *iud. publ*.

63. D 48.1.5, Ulpian 8 *disp*.; but Caelius describes to Cicero, *ad fam.* 8.12, his own bringing of a counter-accusation under the *lex Scantinia*. CTh 9.1.12 (374/5); cf. CJ 9.1.19; CTh 9.1.19 (423).

64. Dio 54.3.

65. The *lex Ursonensis*, c. 102, gave a chief accuser four hours and his assistant two for their speeches; the defence was to have twice as long as the prosecution.

66. D 22.5.1.2, Arcadius *de testibus*; Val. Max. 8.1.10.

67. Asconius *in Milon*. 53, 55 & 56 (Stangl 45-6).

68. *Tabula Bembina* vv. 51-4; Cicero *pro Cluentio* 28.76.

69. Gellius *NA* 3.3.15, perhaps in 204 BC; Val. Max. 6.1.10 of ?318 BC; see also Sall. *Cat*. 52 & 58.

70. Cicero *in Vat*. 14.33.

71. *Auct. ad Her.* 2.28.45; Cicero *pro Sulla* 22.63-4; *ad Att.* 6.1.23; *Phil.* 2.23.56; Caesar *BC* 3.1; Suet. *Caesar* 41; Dio 43.27; 45.47.

72. And, as we know from the Cyrene edicts, shortly before the turn of the era Augustus, through the *SC Calvisianum*, was creating something analogous to the standing jury courts in at least some provinces for the better administration of justice there – *FIRA* i #68 V, pp. 409ff.

73. Tac. *Annals* 1.72: an iudicia maiestatis redderentur, exercendas leges esse respondit – despite Tacitus' attempt to make this sound sinister.

74. Seneca *Apoc*. 14.1; Tac. *Annals* 14.41.

75. Quintilian *inst*. 3.10.1; 11.3.130. For example, he talks sometimes of a husband's right to kill his adulterous wife, a non-existent right since such killing was specifically forbidden in the *lex Iulia*.

76. Pliny *Ep*. 4.29 may be talking of a civil *iudex selectus* – Solimena (1905) thought so, as did Pulciano (1913) – but Nepos' reappearance as praetor in *Ep*. 5.9 does suggest a criminal court, since he is a praetor 'qui legibus quaerit' and he is issuing an edict for *accusatores* and *reos*. The cases that came before the emperor when Pliny was acting as assessor (*Ep*. 6.31.6 & 8) could otherwise have been heard by *cognitio*, not necessarily before a *quaestio*. *Ep*. 7.6.8ff. is very unlikely to refer to a *quaestio* trial since the accuser demands a particular judge.

77. Sherwin-White (1966), 336; perhaps he envisaged a combined court for plebeian offenders under extortion, *ambitus*, and *peculatus* etc.

78. See Garnsey (1967) on the survival of the *quaestio de adulteriis*; Brasiello (1962) thought that the jury courts continued beside, although less used than, *cognitio* until the time of Diocletian. Papinian's remark on the continued liability for unjustified enrichment of the heirs of those condemned for embezzlement of public monies probably – in view of his inclusion of *res repetundae* – refers to *cognitio*.

79. D 48.2.3pr, Paul 3 *de adulteriis*.

80. D 48.5.18.6, Ulpian 2 *ad l. Iuliam de adulteriis* – as long as the woman had not remarried.

81. Dio 76.16.

82. D 48.1.8, Paul, *de iudiciis publicis*: ordo exercendorum publicorum capitalium in usu esse desiit, durante tamen poena legum cum extra ordinem crimina probantur. My own inclination is to think that the *quaestiones* disappeared earlier rather than later.

83. See Talbert (1984), ch. 16; also Bleicken (1962); de Marini Avonzo (1977); Arcaria (1992).

84. E.g. the Bacchanalian affair or the Catiline conspiracy; cf. the treatment of Salvidienus Rufus – Suet. *Aug*. 66; Dio 48.33.

85. Ovid *Tristia* 2.131-2: Nec mea decreto damnasti facta senatus, Nec mea selecto iudice iussa fuga est; Tac. *Annals* 3.68; 13.10 & 32; Pliny *Ep*. 2.11.4; 4.9.17. Judicial as well as other proceedings were governed by Augustus' *lex Iulia de senatu habendo* of 9 BC.

86. D 1.21.1pr, Papinian 1 *quaest*., perhaps supports this.

87. Further, Tiberius said he was entrusting to the Senate the investigation of Germanicus' death, *super leges* – Tac. *Annals* 3.12.7.

88. Suet. *Tib*. 30; Tac. *Annals* 3.49-51; 4.15; 14.28 & 40.

89. Tac. *Annals* 2.42 & 67; Dio 52.43.

90. But not exclusively. Apart from equestrians, who might have political importance, we hear of trials of astrologers in AD 17 (following the dating in *Coll.* 15.2.1) in Tac. *Annals* 2.32 – when the consuls had one of them put to death *more maiorum* outside the Esquiline Gate; of slaves in *Annals* 14.42-5; of provincials in *Annals* 15.20.

91. See Bleicken (1962), 40-3.

92. Tac. *Annals* 4.9; Pliny *Ep.* 2.11.4; 4.9.17.

93. 'Nella prima età imperiale, la differenza tra *cognitio senatus e iudicium publicum* non deve esser cercata nelle disposizioni della procedura, che anche per la prima erano spesso tratte dalla legislazione comiziale sulle *quaestiones*, ma nel diverso spirito animatore ... dalla nuova realtà giuridica' – Avonzo (1977), 82.

94. Pliny *Ep.* 2.11; 4.9; 6.2.

95. Tac. *Annals* 1.74; 3.10; 4.66; 6.7; *dial. de or.* 21.2. Accusator and *delator* are technical terms; an *index* is a low-class informer in the really pejorative sense. The Senate presumably had discretion as to whom it heard, such as women (Tac. *Annals* 2.67; cf. Dio 58.11, where Tiberius read out Apicata's accusation after her suicide; Pliny *Ep.* 9.13.21) or children (Tac. *Annals* 4.28); slaves were not likely to be admitted (Tac. *Annals* 13.10).

96. Tac. *Annals* 13.10; Pliny *Ep.* 5.20.

97. Dio 57.21, and 59.23; 60.15; Tac. *Annals* 13.44.

98. In the case of Caecilius Classicus, there was unjustified enrichment to be recovered from the heirs (Pliny *Ep.* 3.9.6).

99. Tac. *Annals* 3.10.

100. Tac. *Annals* 1.74; 2.30.

101. Tac. *Annals* 3.24-5; Quintilian *inst.* 3.10.1.

102. Tac. *Annals* 2.28; 3.22; 5.3.

103. Tac. *Annals* 2.74; 13.42.

104. Pliny *Ep.* 3.9.

105. It could also still use the simplified procedure of the *SC Calvisianum*, see Pliny *Ep.* 2.11; 5.20.

106. Tac. *Annals* 3.51; cf. Suet. *Tib.* 75.

107. Suet. *Nero* 10.2.

108. Tac. *Annals* 3.70; Suet. *Nero* 39.2; D 49.2.1.2, Ulpian 1 *de appell.*

109. D 48.8.3.4, Marcian 14 *inst.*; 48.8.6, Ven. Sat. 1 *de off. proconsulis*; on the *SC Libonianum* see Albanese (1976) and Robinson (1992b).

110. See D 48.10.15pr, Callistratus 1 *quaest.*; 48.10.32.1, Modestinus 1 *de poenis.* Robinson (1996).

111. Suet. *Aug.* 33.1-2. He does not seem to have had a formal power in AD 8 when Ovid (*Tristia* 2.131-2) wrote: 'nec mea decreto damnasti facta senatus, nec mea selecto iudice iussa fuga est', for surely Ovid would have mentioned such a formal imperial jurisdiction ordering his exile. For Trajan's personal jurisdiction, see Pliny *Ep.* 6.31.

112. Bauman (1982a).

113. Tac. *dial. de or.* 7.1; *Annals* 4.15.

114. Suet. *Aug.* 51; Pliny *Ep.* 6.31.3; 7.6.8. Sherwin-White's point (1966), 409-10, that only under *cognitio* could an accuser make multiple charges does not really explain the emperor's acceptance of jurisdiction.

115. *Inst.* 2.17.8(7); see also Archi (1957).

116. CJ 9.51.1 (Caracalla); *ILS* 1423 = *CIL* VI 1634 (an equestrian); 1455 = *CIL* X 6662. Cf. Crook (1955); Kunkel (1968a).

117. D 47.7.7, Callistratus 5 *de cogn.*: Marcus Aurelius on *vis*; see chapter IV.

118. D 14.5.8, Paul 1 *decret.*

119. See Gualandi (1963), and Appendix I to the stereotype CJ, ed. P. Krueger.

120. Harries (1993b) 1-6; cf. Millar (1977) 240ff.; 537ff.; CJ 9.24.3 (393) does, however, refer to their issue.

121. Honoré (1981), 137.

122. D 47.11.3, Ulpian 3 *de adulteriis*; 47.11.9 & 10, Ulpian 9 *de off. proconsulis*, deal with specific provincial crimes.

123. D 47.2.93, Ulpian 38 *ad ed.*

124. See chapter III.

125. Robinson (1990-2).

126. D 47.11.6pr, Ulpian 8 *de off. proconsulis.*

127. D 47.12 – but in Republican times this had been a matter for sacral not secular law.

128. D 47.20.

129. D 47.19.

130. De Robertis (1954); Garnsey (1970), 103-53; Rilinger (1988), 137-41.

131. Tac. *Annals* 6.10-11.

132. D 1.12.1pr, 4, Ulpian *de off. p. u.* Magistrates in the municipalities thus became subordinate, losing much of their power to punish even slaves – D 2.1.12, Ulpian 18 *ad ed.*

133. D 1.15.3.1, 4, Paul *de off. p. v.*; cf. 1.2.2.33, Pomponius *enchiridion.*

134. D 48.12.1, Marcian 2 *inst.*, allows a slave to accuse his owner; 48.12.3.1, Papirius Justus 1 *de const.*, allows the right to a woman although she had no personal interest.

135. SHA *Sept. Sev.* 4; *Coll.* 14.3.2, taken from Ulpian 9 *de off. proconsulis.* Seneca *clem.* 2.1 and Pliny *Ep.* 7.6.10 do not seem adequate evidence of an earlier jurisdiction.

136. D 1.11.1, Arc. Charis. *de off. p. p.*; CJ 4.65.4 (222); 8.40.13 (Gordian); PS 5.12.6.

137. D 1.21.1, Papinian 1 *quaest.*; 49.3.1pr, Ulpian 1 *de appell.*

138. D 49.2.1.4, Ulpian 1 *de appell.*; 49.3.1.1, Ulpian 1 *de appell.*

139. Villers (1956); Jones (1960), 51-65; Garnsey (1966).

140. D 49.2.1.2, Ulpian 1 *de appell.*

141. D 28.3.6.9, Ulpian 10 *ad Sab.*; 49.1.16, Modestinus 6 *diff.*; PS 5.35.2; cf. CTh 11.36.1 (314/15), 4 (339), 31 (392).

142. Appeal against arrest sprang from the nature of the Republican appeal to tribunician intercession, which could veto any act by a magistrate; appeal against sentence was a development of the understanding of due process.

143. D 2.8.9, Gaius 5 *ad ed prov.*

144. CJ 4.19-21 are titles which preserve imperial rescripts issued on evidentiary matters throughout the third century, as well as later enactments; cf. CTh 9.19.2 = CJ 9.22.22 (326).

145. D 1.16.11, Venuleius Saturninus, 2 *de off. proconsulis.*

146. D 49.15.7.2, Proculus 8 *ep.*, states that citizens of *civitates foederatae* could be charged and punished if condemned in Roman courts.

147. And Gaul south of the Loire (the future Languedoc) was now a diocese, with seven to eleven provinces. See *Notitia Dignitatum* pp. 170-1, or the map at Talbert (1985), 176.

148. CTh 9.22.1 (317, or more probably 343); 1.6.9 = CJ 9.29.2 (385); 10.21.3 = CJ 11.9.4 (424).

149. *Inst.* 4.18; Bauman (1980), 233, talks of 'Justinian's improved methodology' in arranging the texts in the titles of his code compared with the Theodosian.

150. CTh 2.1.12 (423); 9.1.13 (376); Cass. *Variae* 4.22; cf. Sid. Ap. *Ep.* 1.7.9. And see Coster (1935).

151. NovJ 62.1 (537); cf. NovMarcian 5 (455), where the emperor gave a decision on the validity of a will in the presence of the Senate.

152. That is *illustris*; the others were *spectabilis* and *clarissimus*, while the equestrian class had disappeared, although the ranks of *perfectissimus* and *egregius* remained as its shadow.

153. D 1.9.11, Paul 41 *ad ed.*; CTh 9.1.1 = CJ 3.24.1 (317); cf. CJ 12.1.15 (Theodosius & Valentinian); 12.2.1 (450); 3.24.3 (Zeno); NovJ 62.2. *Potentiores* had in general to appear in person to answer criminal charges, although they could use procurators in civil cases – CTh 9.1.17 = CJ 9.2.15 (390).

154. Sometimes they did; CTh 8.15.1 (Constantine); Amm. Marc. 18.1 on Julian; CTh 11.39.8 = CJ 1.3.7 (381).

155. CTh 11.30.16 = CJ 7.62.19 (331); Cass. *Variae* 6.3.

156. D 1.11.1, Arc. Charisius *de off. p. p.*; CJ 1.19.5 (365); NovTh 13 (439); CJ 7.63.5 (529).

157. Mommsen (1899), 289f.; cf. Cass. *Variae* 6.6; 6.7; 6.8; etc.

158. CTh 1.6.7 = CJ 1.28.3 (376). On the Urban Prefect in the Later Empire, see Chastagnol (1960). And the Prefect of the Night Watch continued to have jurisdiction, although the *vigiles* themselves had been disbanded – CTh 1.2.1 (314); CJ 1.43.1 (385/89).

159. Cass. *Variae* 6.15; cf. CTh 11.30.36 (374). See Sinnigen (1959).

160. CTh 9.2.2 = CJ 9.3.1 (365) or CTh 1.10.4 = CJ 1.28.3 (391).

161. Justinian reorganized the system – see Jones (1964), 482ff. – but the principles remained the same; his main achievement was to limit appeals to the highest courts.

162. CTh 1.29.2 = CJ 1.55.1 (365), 7 = CJ 1.55.5 (392); 9.2.5 = CJ 1.55.7 (409); NovJ 15 (535); cf. CTh 2.1.8.2 (395).

163. *Sirm.* 1; CTh 1.27.1 (318), 2 = CJ 1.4.8 (408); CJ 1.4.33 (534); NovJ 86; cf. for Jews CTh 2.1.10 = CJ 1.9.8 (398). See Jaeger (1960).

164. CTh 16.2.12 (355), 41 (412/11); NovJ 123.8; but cf. CTh 9.40.16 = CJ 1.4.6 (398). Mommsen (1899), 290ff.

165. CTh 9.35.4 = CJ 1.12.3 (431), although not very helpful for slaves – CTh 9.35.5 = CJ 1.12.4 (432); and it was restricted to those who did not raise a clamour or tumult – CJ 1.12.5 (451), 7-8 (undated).

166. CTh 9.3.1 = CJ 9.4.1 (320); cf. 9.37.1 (319)

167. CTh 9.1.5 (326), 8 (366), 19 = CJ 9.2.17pr (423).

168. CTh 9.1.14 = CJ 9.2.13 (383); 9.1.19 = CJ 9.2.17 (423). See chapter VII.

169. CTh 1.16.9 (364), 13 (377).

170. CTh 9.1.7 (338), 18 (396); CTh 9.3.6 = CJ 9.4.5 (380); CJ 9.4.6 (529).

171. CTh 9.2.2 (365), 3 = CJ 9.3.2 (380).

172. CTh 9.3.1 = CJ 9.4.1 (320), 3 = CJ 9.4.3 (340), 7 = CJ 1.4.9 (409).

173. CTh 9.35.2 = CJ 9.41.16 (376), where as well as treason those charged with *quae nefanda dictu* – magic? or homosexuality? – were not exempt; 9.35.6 = CJ 9.41.17 (399) did not grant the privilege to ordinary decurions; 9.37.4 (409) = CJ 9.42.3.3, dated 369. At one period at least, the use of torture in Lent was forbidden – CTh 9.35.4 = CJ 12.1.10 (380), 5 (389).

174. CTh 9.5.1 = CJ 9.8.3 (Constantine); CTh 9.35.1 = CJ 9.8.4 (369), 3 = CJ 12.1.10 (377).

175. CTh 9.40.4 = CJ 9.47.18 (346); 11.36.1 (314/15), 7 = CJ 7.65.2 (344), 31 (392); cf. CTh 9.19.2 = CJ 9.22.22 (326/20).

176. See Coleman (1990); it would not have been out of order then to pour molten lead down a convicted person's throat – CTh 9.24.1.1 (Constantine) – but only, at least in the first century AD, if the convict was not a citizen.

177. Aurelius Victor 41.4; CTh 9.40.8 (365). Constantine also limited penal tattooing – CTh 9.40.2 = CJ 9.47.17; see Jones (1987).

178. CTh 9.40.3 (319), 5, 7 (both 364), 9 = CJ 9.47.19 (368/70). See also Millar (1984).

179. CTh 9.40.1 = CJ 9.47.16 (314), 13 = CJ 9.47.20 (382/90).

180. For example, we find the sack (see CTh 9.15.1 = CJ 9.17.1 or *Inst.* 4.18.6 on parricide) as the penalty for adultery – CTh 11.36.4 (339) – and even if this was an aberration, adultery had become a capital crime – CTh 9.40.1 = CJ 9.47.16 (314); 9.38.2 (354/3). CTh 11.8.1 (397) = CJ 10.20.1.1 (dated 400) threatens death for the super-exaction of taxes; cf. CTh 11.7.20 (412).

181. CTh 9.42.2 (356); 9.42.8.3 (380); 9.42.23 (421); 9.14.3 = CJ 9.8.5 (397).

182. CTh 9.40.18 = CJ 9.47.22 (399), and see CTh 9.42 = CJ 9.49 passim.

183. CTh 1.2.7 (356); 9.10.4.1 = CJ 9.12.8.3 (390); cf. 9.40.12 (378/7).

184. CJ 9.47.15 (Diocletian and Maximian).

185. CTh 9.41.1 = CJ 9.48.1 (425).

186. CTh 9.40.22 = CJ 9.47.23 (414), 23 = CJ 9.47.24 (416); CJ 9.47.26 (529).

187. CTh 9.40.24 = CJ 9.47.25 (419).

188. CTh 9.11.1 (388); CJ 9.5.1 (486), 2 (529); see Robinson (1968).

189. CTh 16.10.4 = CJ 1.11.1 (354); CJ 1.11.9 (?Justinian); CTh 16.9.1 = CJ 1.10.1 [& 2 (Justinian)] (339); CTh 9.7.5 = CJ 1.9.6 (388); CTh 16.5.1 = CJ 1.5.1 (326); NovTh 3 (438); CJ 1.5.20 (530).

190. CTh 9.17.2.2 = CJ 9.19.3 (349); 9.40.8 (365); 9.3.5 = CJ 9.4.4 (371), 7 = CJ 1.4.9 (407); 9.42.11 (393); CTh 1.6.11.2 (423). See also chapter VII.

191. CTh 9.1.4 (325); 1.16.7 (331); 14.17.6 (370); 9.27.6 = CJ 9.27.4 (386); 9.14.2 = CJ 3.27.1 (391); 9.28.1 = CJ 9.28.1 (392, but ascribed to 415 in CJ); NovJ 8 (535). See Blockley (1969); Noethlichs (1981); Rosen (1990).

192. CTh 9.42.7 = CJ 9.49.7 (369); 9.1.15 (385); 9.40.15 (392).

193. CTh 6.29.1 = CJ 12.22.1 (355), 8 = CJ 9.22.4 (395).

194. CTh 9.26 passim; see also John Lydus *de magistratibus*.

195. CTh 9.11.1 (388); CTh 9.21.9 = CJ 9.24.3 (389/92 but in CJ ascribed to 326).

196. CTh 13.5.5.1 (326/9); 6.10.1 = CJ 12.7.1 (380).

197. *FIRA* i #94, vv. 12-14; CJ 9.39.2.3 (451); cf. CTh 10.10.2 (319/2.) against informers generally.

198. CTh 9.24.1.2 (320/26). CTh 15.8.2 = CJ 11.41.6 (428); NovTh 18 (439); CJ 11.41(40).7 (Leo).

199. Ammianus 28.6; MacMullen (1986).

200. Suet. *Tib.* 44 records the emperor's personal revenge, and on fairly humble persons.

201. D 50.17.155.2, Paul 65 *ad ed.*; 48.19.42, Hermogenianus 1 *epit.*

202. D 48.19.5pr, 2, Ulpian 7 *de off. proconsulis.*

203. MacMullen (1988).

II. Criminal Liability

1. D 48.13.7(6), Ulpian 7 *de off. proconsulis*; 48.19.16.1-8, Claudius Saturninus *de poenis pag*. Gaudemet (1962); Lebigre (1967); Garnsey (1970); Rilinger (1988).

2. Livy 39.18.6 of 185 BC; *per*. 48 of 152 BC; Tac. *Annals* 2.50 of *c*. AD 17.

3. Reidinger (1958); cf. Beard (1980).

4. For the importance, even in early times, of a 'just cause' for the exercise of the power of putting to death, see Yaron (1962).

5. Robinson (1981).

6. D 48.2.5, Ulpian 3 *de adulteriis*; 1.12.1.5, Ulpian *de off. p. u.*

7. D 48.8.2, Ulpian 1 *de adulteriis*.

8. CTh 9.12.1 = CJ 9.14.1 (319) & 2 (326/9).

9. CTh 9.13.1 = CJ 9.15.1 (365/73).

10. D 38.16.1.3, Ulpian 12 *ad Sab.*; 48.1.3, Ulpian 35 *ad Sab.*; 48.4.11, Ulpian 8 *disp.*; CTh 9.14.3 = CJ 9.8.5 (397); Volterra (1949).

11. D 48.2.20, Modestinus 2 *de poenis*; cf. G 4.112; D 31.76.9, Papinian 7 *resp.*; 48.19.20, Paul 18 *ad Plautium*; Tac. *Annals* 4.20.

12. D 9.2.5.2, Ulpian 18 *ad ed.*; 48.8.12, Modestinus 8 *reg.*

13. XII T. 8.9 & 14; D 29.5.14, Maecian 11 *pub. iud.*; 21.1.23.2, Ulpian 1 *ad ed. aed. cur.* citing Pomponius; 47.12.3.1, Ulpian 25 *ad ed.*; 48.5.14.8, Ulpian 2 *de adulteriis*; 48.6.3.1, Marcian 14 *inst.*; 48.10.22pr, Paul *ad SC Libonianum*; CJ 9.47.7 (Severus Alexander); CTh 9.24.4.1 = CJ 9.24.1.6 (320/26).

14. D 48.18.10pr, Arcadius Charisius *de test.*; 29.5.1.33, Ulpian 50 *ad ed.*

15. Tac. *Annals* 5.9. Generally, see Thomas (1977).

16. D 21.1.23.2, Ulpian 1 *ad ed. aed. cur.* citing Pomponius; 29.5.3.11, Ulpian 50 *ad ed.*; 48.4.7.3, Modestinus 12 *pand.*; CTh 9.4.1 = CJ 9.7.1 (393).

17. D 1.18.13.1, Ulpian 7 *de off. proconsulis*; 1.18.14, Macer 2 *iud. pub.*

18. SHA *Hadrian* 12.5.

19. D 48.2.12pr, Venuleius Saturninus 2 *iud. pub*; 48.2.8, Macer 2 *pub. iud.*

20. D 48.4.3, Marcian 14 *inst.*; h.t.7.3, Modestinus 12 *pand.*; 1.3.29, Paul *ad legem Cinciam*; 21.1.23.2, Ulpian 1 *ad ed. aed. cur*; CJ 9.16.1 (215); 9.22.20 (294); CTh 9.4.1 = CJ 9.7.1 (393).

21. D 48.19.11.2, Marcian 2 *pub. iud.*; CJ 9.16.4(5) (290); NovVal 19.2 (445).

22. XII T. 8.24b; 8.10 & 24a; cf. 8.25 = D 50.16.236pr, Gaius 4 *ad XII T.*

23. D 3.2.11.4, Ulpian 6 *ad ed.*; 41.3.36.1-37pr, Gaius 2 *rer. cott.* & 2 *inst.*

24. *Coll.* 1.11.3-4, Ulpian; cf. D 48.19.5.2, Ulpian 7 *de off. proconsulis*; *Coll.* 1.6.1-4, Ulpian; cf. D 48.8.1.3, Marcian 14 *inst*; 48.8.3.2, Marcian 14 *inst*. Cf. 50.16.226, Paul 1 *manual*: magna neglegentia culpa est; magna culpa dolus est.

25. D 39.4.16.5, Marcian *de delatoribus*, quoting Hadrian; *Coll.* 1.12.1, Modestinus; CJ 9.16.1 (215). See Perrin (1966); Peppe (1984); Dixon (1984); Robinson (1985).

26. D 2.1.7.4, Ulpian 3 *ad ed.*; 22.6.9pr, Paul *de iuris et facti ignorantia*; cf. CTh 9.14.3.2 = CJ 9.8.5.3 (397).

27. D 48.5.39.2, Papinian 36 *quaest*. And see chapter V.

28. D 48.10.15.4-5, Callistratus 1 *quaest.*; 48.16.1.10, Marcian ad *SC Turpillianum*.

29. CTh 9.21.4.1 = CJ 9.24.1.6-7 (320/6).

30. D 4.4.37.1, Tryphoninus 3 *disp.*

31. Cicero II *Verr.* 2.41.100; *in Pis.* 15.34-5; D 48.19.4, Marcian 13 *inst.*;

48.19.8.7, Ulpian 9 *de off. proconsulis*; 48.19.28.13, Callistratus 6 *de cogn.*, citing Hadrian.

32. D 4.3.15.1, Ulpian 11 *ad ed.*; cf. Lord Thurlow's 'Did you ever expect a corporation to have a conscience, when it has no soul to be damned nor arse to be kicked?' – cited in the *ODQ*.

33. D 9.1.passim; *Inst.* 4.9.

34. See Thomas (1962a); Genin (1968); Impallomeni (1982).

35. D 50.16.53.2, Paul 59 *ad ed.*; compare Queen Elizabeth I's reluctance to seek to make a window on men's souls (referred to by Beckingsale (1963), 80).

36. D 48.19.16pr, Claudius Saturninus *de poenis pag.*; the argument as to whether he is identical with Venuleius Saturninus is here irrelevant.

37. Hence Cicero (*pro Milone* 7.19) remarked that because the deed was not completed, it should not be punished.

38. D 2.2.1.2, Ulpian 3 *ad ed.*: quid enim offuit conatus cum iniuria nullum habuerit effectum?

39. D 48.10.22.4, Paul *ad SC Libonianum*; 48.19.38.6, Paul 5 *sent.*

40. D 48.10.6pr, Africanus 3 *quaest.*

41. D 47.10.15.10, Ulpian 77 *ad ed.*

42. For example, in Scots law the giving of a non-noxious substance to a pregnant woman with intent to abort was an offence but to give an abortifacient to a non-pregnant woman was not (this was certainly true before the 1967 Act), though putting a hand in an empty pocket is an attempt at stealing – see Thomas (1962a).

43. G 3.198; cf. D 47.2.46.8, Ulpian 42 *ad Sab.*

44. *Inst.* 4.1.8: ne ex huiusmodi impunitate et in alium servum qui possit corrumpi tale facinus a quibusdam perpetretur; cf. CJ 6.2.20 (530).

45. D 48.10.19pr, Paul 5 *sent.*

46. D 48.8.3pr-1, Marcian 14 *inst.*; 48.19.16.8, Claudius Saturninus *de poenis pag.*

47. PS 2.31.33.

48. D 48.10.1.5, Marcian 14 *inst.*; 48.19.38.7, Paul 5 *sent.*

49. CTh 9.26.1 (397); CJ 1.11.7.1 (451).

50. For a view on attempted crimes rather different from Daube's, see *Ancient Roman Statutes* p. 27, at footnote 1a.

51. D 49.16.3.11, Modestinus 4 *de poenis*: 'qui volens transfugere adprehensus est', which implies some act to arrest him in.

52. D 48.19.16.8, Claudius Saturninus *de poenis pag.*; 47.10.15.17, Ulpian 77 *ad ed.*; 48.8.14, Callistratus 6 *de cogn.*; PS 5.23.3.

53. D 47.11.1.2, Paul 5 *sent.*

54. Although specific conspiracies were recognized – D 48.19.16pr, Claudius Saturninus *de poenis pag.*; CTh 9.14.3pr = CJ 9.8.5pr (397).

55. See Chevailler (1953); Longo (1958); MacCormack (1983).

56. D 50.16.53.2, Paul 59 *ad ed.*

57. E.g. Cicero II *Verr.* 5.55.143; *pro Cluentio* 60.125; D 42.8.10.2, Ulpian 73 *ad ed.*; 48.9.6, Ulpian 8 *de off. proconsulis*; CJ 9.13.1.3a (533).

58. By counsel; by command; by consent; by provocation; by praise; by concealment; by silence; by a share in the profits; by defence of the evil done.

59. Even if not the same illegal act; for example in later law, one spouse could not be held guilty of theft of the other's property, and those in the same power could not commit theft against each other or against their father or owner – D 47.2.36.1, Ulpian 41 *ad Sab.*; 25.2.1, Paul 7 *ad Sab.* & 7, Ulpian 36 *ad Sab.* Similarly, if two slaves of different owners ran off together with what they had stolen, neither owner could sue his own slave, but each could raise a noxal action against the other for the complicity of the other's slave – D 47.2.36.3, Ulpian 41 *ad Sab.*

60. D 47.2.50.2, Ulpian 37 *ad ed.*, citing Pedius; 47.9.3.3, Ulpian 56 *ad ed.*; 50.16.53.2, Paul 59 *ad ed.*; CTh 9.16.3 = CJ 9.8.4.1 (317/24).

61. D 47.2.91(90).1, Javolenus 9 *ex post. Labeonis*; Thomas (1977) pp. 17f. argues that 47.2.23, Ulpian 41 *ad Sab.*, was essentially denying that a child could be in the full sense an accomplice.

62. D 48.9.2, Scaevola 4 *reg.*; CTh 9.29.2 = CJ 9.39.1.1 (383/91, dated in CJ to 374).

63. D 47.2.48.1, Ulpian 42 *ad Sab.*; 50.17.50, Paul 39 *ad ed.*; 50.17.109, Paul 5 *ad ed.*; cf. 50.17.47, Ulpian 30 *ad ed.*; 48.10.9.1, Ulpian 8 *de off. proconsulis.*

64. D 29.5.1pr, Ulpian 50 *ad ed.*; see the title passim.

65. CTh 9.14.3.1 = CJ 9.8.5.2 (397).

66. D 9.2.27.21, Ulpian 18 *ad ed.*; 47.2.50.4, Ulpian 37 *ad ed.*

67. D 47.2.50.1, Ulpian 37 *ad ed.*, citing Celsus.

68. D 47.2.36pr, Ulpian 41 *ad Sab.*

69. D 47.2.50.3, Ulpian 37 *ad ed.*

70. D 50.17.152.2, Ulpian 69 *ad ed.*; 43.16.1.14, Ulpian 69 *ad ed.*

71. D 2.10.1.1, Ulpian 7 *ad ed.*

72. D 9.4.2pr, Ulpian 18 *ad ed.*

73. D 9.4.3, Ulpian 3 *ad ed.*

74. D 9.4.2pr, Ulpian 18 *ad ed.* The strict liability of *nautae, caupones* and *stabularii* for their employees' thefts was delictual not criminal – 47.5.1, Ulpian 38 *ad ed.*

75. D 50.17.167.1, Paul 49 *ad ed.*

76. D 47.2.48.1, Ulpian 42 *ad Sab.*; 47.16.2, Paul *de poenis pag.*; 29.5.3.12, Ulpian 50 *ad ed.*

77. D 47.16.1, Marcian 2 *pub. iud.*; 48.5.15(14)pr, Scaevola 4 *reg.*

78. CTh 9.21.2.4-5 (318/21) & 9.21.4.1 (320/6), together = CJ 9.24.1.4 & 6-7 (321); CTh 16.5.21 (392); 9.39.2 (451).

79. D 47.10.15.8, Ulpian 77 *ad ed.*; 48.9.7, Ulpian 29 *ad ed.*; 48.19.16pr, at end, Claudius Saturninus *de poenis pag.*; CTh 9.29.1 = CJ 9.29.1pr (374); 9.14.3pr & 6 (397).

80. D 48.8.1.1, Marcian 14 *inst.*: who is the principal, the one who bribes the magistrate? or the magistrate? cf. 48.4.10, Hermogenianus 6 *iuris epit.*

81. CTh 9.16.8 (370/3); cf. CJ 9.18.8 (365).

82. D 43.24.15.2, Ulpian 71 *ad ed.*, citing Labeo; 47.2.21.9, Paul 40 *ad Sab.*; 48.8.17, Paul 5 *sent.*

83. CTh 16.5.34 (398) & 53 (398/412) & 65 (428).

84. *Coll.* 7.3.2-3, Ulpian; D 48.8.9, Ulpian 37 *ad ed.*; 9.2.45.4, Paul 10 *ad Sab.*; CJ 9.16.2 (243) & 3 (265); cf. Cicero *pro Milone* 4.10-11.

85. D 48.8.1.4, Marcian 14 *inst.*; PS 5.23.8.

86. CTh 9.14.2 = CJ 3.27.1 (391).

87. See Daube (1956) pp. 585ff. for the rhetoricians' arguments.

88. CTh 9.17.1 =CJ 9.19.2 (340) condemns a slave to the mines for demolishing a tomb without the knowledge of his owner, but merely relegates him if he was obeying orders – this raises a further problem in that a slave technically could not be 'relegated' – D 48.2.12.4, Venuleius Saturninus 2 *iud. pub.*, but he could be ordered to stay in a particular place; CTh 9.10.4pr = CJ 9.12.8pr (390). Cf. Tac. *Annals* 3.17; 11.36.

89. D 48.10.5, Julian 86 *dig.*

90. D 50.17.4, Ulpian 6 *ad Sab.*: Someone is not regarded as being willing if he obeys the command of a father or owner.

91. D 9.2.37pr, Javolenus 14 *ex Cassio*; cf. 3.2.11.4-12, Ulpian 6 *ad ed.* & Paul 5 *ad ed.*

92. D 44.7.20, Alfenus 2 *dig.*; 50.17.157pr, Ulpian 71 *ad ed.*

93. Daube (1956) p. 583; Tac. *Annals* 11.36 and Dio 60.22 on Mnester's unsuccessful plea of necessity; cf. D 19.2.13.7, Ulpian 32 *ad ed.*, citing Labeo, on the duty of resistance as far as was possible to a pillaging army.

94. D 48.8.1.5, Marcian 14 *inst.*, citing Antoninus Pius; 48.5.39(38).8, Papinian 36 *quaest.*, citing Marcus Aurelius and Commodus, and Pius.

95. D 29.5.3.3, Ulpian 50 *ad ed.*

96. D 47.16.2, Paul *de poenis pag.*

97. D 48.3.12pr, Callistratus 5 *de cogn.*, citing Hadrian; 48.19.11.2, Macer 2 *pub. iud.*; 49.16.6.7, Arrius Menander 3 *de re militari.* See Watson (1970a). Cf. Gratian *Decretum* C.15 qu.1 c.7.

98. D 9.2.9.4, Ulpian 18 *ad ed.*; the *campus* is to be taken as the Campus Martius, and the javelin throwing as the proper practices of young citizens preparing for military service.

99. Mommsen (1899) and Wolodkiewicz (1985) both point out that Rabirius was charged 37 years after the killing of Saturninus, and that Cicero (*pro Rab. Post.* 9.25) did not argue that this was illegal but only unbecoming; but the charge was *perduellio*, a crime that was never prescribed. It is generally accepted in the textbooks that the praetor required an action for *iniuria* to be raised within one year of the outrage, but a positive statement to this effect comes only from Diocletian – CJ 9.35.5 (290).

100. D 48.5.12.4, Papinian *de adulteriis*; 48.16.1.10, Marcian ad *SC Turpillianum*; and see chapter V.

101. D 48.13.9(7), Venuleius Saturninus 2 *iud. pub.*

102. D 29.5.13, Venuleius Saturninus 2 *pub. iud; sui heredes* were not liable anyway. (A freedman had five years from his manumission in which to claim *ingenuitas* – 40.14.2.2, Venuleius Saturninus 1 *de off. proconsulis.*)

103. D 29.5.13 Venuleius Saturninus 2 *pub. iud*; 48.10.19.1, Paul 5 *sent.*

104. CTh 16.5.40.5 = CJ 1.5.4.4 (407); and see chapter VI.

105. CJ 9.22.12 (293); like Thomas, I shall refer to it as vicennial, since that is the technical term of Scots law.

106. Volterra (1929) 57; Amelotti (1958) pp. 160ff.; Thomas (1962b) refutes them, and reverts to the traditional view of Mommsen (1899) 488-9. I follow Thomas in his interpretation of CJ 9.22.17 (294) and CTh 9.19.2pr (320/6), and this seems confirmed by Justinian's preservation of CJ 9.22.22 (320).

107. D 48.17.3, Marcian 2 *pub. iud.*, citing (implicitly) Severus and Antoninus); 49.14.1.3, Callistratus 1 *de iure fisci*, citing 'Titus'; cf. CJ 4.61.2 (Severus and Antoninus). See 7.33.1 (Severus and Antoninus) for the first mention of *longi temporis praescriptio.*

108. Wolodkiewicz (1985), however, thinks that the vicennial term was introduced by Diocletian, under the influence of Hermogenianus.

III. Theft and Related Offences

1. Gaudemet (1964).

2. On noxal liability, see e.g. Buckland (1963), 599ff.; Kaser (1971), 630ff.; Nicholas (1962), 223f.

3. See chapter I.

4. D 47.8; this will be dealt with later.

5. D 47.19; see also 47.4. This too will receive separate treatment.

6. D 47.3. *Tignum iunctum* seems to receive no criminal treatment; it is distinguished from theft because, by the doctrine of *accessio*, the materials had directly or indirectly acceded to the land.

7. D 47.7.2, Gaius 1 *ad legem XII tab.*; see Morgese (1983). The deed could also give grounds for an Aquilian action, if there was no lucrative motive, and indeed Ulpian, citing Pedius, stresses that it is the stealth rather than any taking away which is meant here, an interpretation reinforced by Paul: D 47.7.7pr-1, Ulpian 38 *ad ed.*; 47.7.8.1-2, Paul 39 *ad ed.*; see also Niederländer (1950).

8. PS 5.20.6.

9. D 47.5; 47.6; 47.14; 47.16; 47.17; 47.18, cf. 47.11.7, Ulpian 9 *de off. proconsulis.* Of these, I shall not deal with *nautae, caupones, stabularii*, because its particularity was to impose a strict and often vicarious liability for reasons of social and commercial expediency, nor with the limited liability of an owner for his *familia* because it is by definition outwith the scope of the ordinary criminal law.

10. Ulpian 37 & 38 *ad ed.*, at D 47.2.50,52,53,93 & 47.5.1 & 47.6.1,3; Paul *de poenis paganorum*, at 47.2.90 & 47.16.2; Macer *libri publicorum iudiciorum*, at 47.2.64 & 47.14.2. See, for a treatment in English, Jolowicz (1940), xii-xv.

11. CJ 6.2; the whole title consists of rescripts from Severus and Caracalla through to Diocletian, and of legislation by Justinian himself.

12. A slave who was a manifest thief was to be hurled from the Tarpeian Rock – XII T. 8.12, but it could be argued that the manifest element made it aggravated – like thieving by night. On domestic theft, theft within the *familia*, see D 48.19.11.1, Marcian 2 *de pub. iud.* and 47.2.90, Paul *de poenis pag.*

13. D 47.1.3, Ulpian 2 *de off. proconsulis*; 47.2.93(92), Ulpian 38 *ad ed.* Cf. CJ 9.37.1, AD 395, where such formality seems sometimes unnecessary, but CTh 2.1.8.1 (395).

14. D 47.2.57(56).1, Julian 22 *dig.*; see Balzarini (1969a). The text says 'Qui furem deducit ad praefectum vigilibus ...' which begs any question of proof. Cf. 1.15.3.1, Paul *de off. p. v.*, and 1.18.13pr, Ulpian 7 *de off. proconsulis.*

15. Whereas I presume it was given to the owner of the fruiting trees, since he would surely prefer compensation, if it was available.

16. Balzarini (1969a) again.

17. CJ 9.31.1pr (378), discussed by Balzarini (1969a), 275f.

18. G.3.189-92.

19. D 47.2.52.21, Ulpian 37 *ad ed.*; 47.2.67.4, Paul 7 *ad Plautium*; 13.7.36pr, Ulpian 11 *ad ed.*; 17.2.45, 51pr, Ulpian 30 *ad Sab.*

20. Sometimes called *furtum possessionis* – D 47.2.15.1, Paul 5 *ad Sab.*; 47.2.19.5, Ulpian 40 *ad Sab.*; 47.2.60, Julian 3 *ex Minicio.*

21. D 47.2.52.20, Ulpian 37 *ad ed.*; CJ 4.34.3 (239).

22. D 47.2.43pr-1, Ulpian 41 *ad Sab.*; 47.2.81.6, Papinian 12 *quaest.*

23. CJ 6.2.7 (228).

24. Gellius *NA* 11.18.19.

25. Or the *statuliber* who takes something from the estate before the entry of the heir – D 47.4 passim; CJ 9.32 passim.

26. D 48.19.16.4, Claud. Sat. *de poenis pag.*; cf. Robinson (1973); Gnoli (1974).

27. CTh 9.30.2 (364), 3 (365), 5 (399).

28. D 48.19.16.7, Claud. Sat. *de poenis pag.*; *Coll.* 11.8.2, Ulpian.

29. *Coll.* 11.3 = PS 5.18.1. The sheep are found only in *Coll*. The penalty for theft given here was, depending on the status of the thief, either twofold or threefold restitution, or a beating and a year of forced labour or, for a slave, being returned to his owner in chains.

30. This 'or four' must surely be a gloss inserted in the context of a tightening-up of the law.

31. D 47.14.3pr, Callistratus 6 *de cogn*.

32. This would explain the contradiction between this sentence and s.1, in which the taking of a single domestic animal incurs the lighter penalty, involves the lesser offence. See also Berger (1944).

33. D 47.14.3.2, Callistratus 6 *de cogn*.

34. D 47.14.1.1-2, Ulpian 8 *de off. proconsulis*.

35. PS 5.18.2 = *Coll.* 11.2.1.

36. Berger (1944), 35-7.

37. D 47.14.1.1, Ulpian 8 *de off. proconsulis*; cf. *Coll.* 11.8.1, Ulpian, ibid., where there is a single horse; in PS 5.18.4 = *Coll.* 11.5.1 there is also a single straying horse, but no mention of an uninhabited area.

38. D 47.14.1pr, Ulpian 8 *de off. proconsulis*. *Coll.* 11.7.1-2 gives a fuller version. In *Coll.* 11.7.5 Ulpian reported that in the same rescript Hadrian had emphatically stated that the penalty for rustling was not everywhere the same. A similar ruling, also for Baetica, about putting rustlers to the sword is ascribed to Antoninus Pius in *Coll.* 11.6.1, Paul *de poenis paganorum*.

39. D 47.14.2, Macer 1 *pub. iud*.

40. PS 5.18.2 = *Coll.* 11.2.1.

41. D 47.14.1.3, Ulpian 8 *de off. proconsulis*; *Coll.* 11.8.4, Ulpian, mentions the sending of rustlers to the beasts specifically by the courts at Rome, presumably on practical grounds – such shows were not available all that often in the provinces.

42. D 47.14.3.3, Callistratus 6 *de cogn*.

43. D 47.14.1.4, Ulpian 8 *de off. proconsulis*.

44. PS 5.18.3 = *Coll.* 11.4; *Coll.* 11.6.2, taken from Paul's *de poenis pag.*, gives a double or quadruple penalty (as with non-manifest and manifest theft).

45. Cf. Seneca *ep.* 56.2; Tertullian *de pers.* 13; *apol.* 44.

46. See van Hoof (1988).

47. D 47.18.1.1, Ulpian 8 *de off. proconsulis*, mentions *honestiores*.

48. PS 5.3.3; this might be done with a mob or gang, cf. the version in D 48.6.11pr, Paul 5 *sent*.

49. D 1.15.3.2, Paul *de off. p. v*.

50. D 47.18.1.2, Ulpian 8 *de off. proconsulis*.

51. D 47.18.2, Paul *de off. p. v.*; 1.15.3.1, idem; cf. 12.4.15, Pomponius 22 *ad Sab*.

52. D 47.11.7, Ulpian 9 *de off. proconsulis*; *directarii* in PS 5.4.8 seem more like *effractores*, for they were punished with exile, the mines, or forced labour.

53. D 47.17.1, Ulpian 8 *de off. proconsulis*; 47.17.3, Paul *de poenis militum*; PS 5.3.5; cf. Robinson (1992a).

54. D 1.15.3.5, Paul *de off. p. v*.

55. Which, certainly for the compilers and probably for the late classical jurists, usually seems to mean from the class of municipal councillors, the *ordo*; in the period when the *quaestiones perpetuae* flourished it is more likely to mean from the equestrian (or even senatorial) order.

56. D 47.18.1.1, Ulpian 8 *de off. proconsulis*.

57. PS 5.3.3.

58. D 47.18.1.1, Ulpian 8 *de off. proconsulis.*

59. D 47.18.1.2, Ulpian 8 *de off. proconsulis*, where the equestrian criminal was banished by Marcus Aurelius for five years from his home province, and also from Rome and Italy.

60. D 47.18.2, Paul *de off. p. v.*; the beating was to be with *fustes*. It seems possible that the proprietor's right, which went back to the Twelve Tables, to kill a thief who came by night or who defended himself by day, persisted – *Coll.* 7.3.2-3, Ulpian.

61. D 47.17.1, Ulpian 8 *de off. proconsulis.*

62. D 47.17.2, Marcian 2 *iud. pub.*

63. D 47.17.3, Paul *de poenis militum.*

64. PS 5.3.5.

65. E.g. Hume (1829³), ch. 2.

66. D 47.16.1, Marcian 2 *pub. iud.*; 1.18.13pr, Ulpian 7 *de off. proconsulis*, uses the same words.

67. PS 5.3.4.

68. D 47.9.3.3, Ulpian 56 *ad ed.*

69. D 47.16.1, Marcian 2 *pub. iud.*

70. D 47.16.2, Paul *de poenis pag.* The Watson edition has 'For their offence is not equal to that of those who harbour brigands with whom they have no connection'.

71. CJ 9.39.1 (374).

72. CJ 9.39.2 (451).

73. See Coroï (1915); Balzarini (1969b); Longo (1970); Vacca (1972).

74. Children and freedmen could lay a complaint of forcible dispossession against their parent or patron 'not in order to bring a charge of *vis* against them, but to recover possession' – D 48.2.11.1, Macer 2 *de pub. iud.* Even in the Later Empire the frequency of the concurrence of civil and criminal remedies was carefully pointed out – CJ 9.31.1 (378).

75. *Inst.* 2.6.2. But D 41.3.33.2, Julian 44 *dig.*, citing the *lex Plautia* and the *lex Iulia*, allows usucapion after a landowner, thinking that armed men were approaching, took flight, because although he was reckoned as forcibly dispossessed, the land was not actually taken by force; cf. Cicero *pro Caecina.*

76. Lintott (1968) ch. viii, especially 110ff. Gruen (1974), 225-7 does not think that 'contra rem publicam' was necessarily in the *lex Plautia*; it could simply have extended the remit of the *quaestio* to deal with private violence. Cf. for other trials *Schol. Bob. pro Sulla* (Stangl 84); Cicero *pro Sulla* 19.54-21.60; *pro Milone* 13.35; *ad fam.* 8.8.1; *pro Caelio* 29.70; *de har. resp.* 7.15; *ad Att.* 2.24; *pro Sestio* 39.84; Asconius *in Milon.* 55 (Stangl 46) re Saufeius; Quintilian *inst.* 9.3.56.

77. CTh 9.10. Longo (1970), 531, sees juristic development of the norms all through the classical period and in Diocletian's chancery; then, under Constantine, there was an attempt to include in *vis* any aspect of violent behaviour; Justinian tried to go back to distinct categories of offence.

78. PS 5.26.1, 3. This is the view held by Vacca (1972), 87, citing her article of 1965-8. I shall deal with the abuse of power in chapter VI. See also D 50.17.152pr, Ulpian 69 *ad ed.*

79. D 48.6 and 48.7.

80. D 48.6.1; 48.6.3.3; 48.6.5.2; 48.6.5.1 – all from Marcian, 14 *inst.* It is possible that the compilers simply put the whole extract in the wrong place, but not very likely, since it is interrupted by other texts. Balzarini (1969b), 217-22, does not really clarify the situation by arguing that the same circumstances or deeds fell under *vis publica* if they affected public order in the strict sense, and under *vis privata* if it was such an injury to a private person that it was in the public interest to repress it criminally rather than allow a delictual remedy.

81. D 48.7.1.1-2, Marcian 14 *inst.*; 48.7.2, Scaevola 4 *reg.*; 48.7.3.2, Macer 1 *pub.* [*iud.*]; 48.7.7, Call. 5 *de cognit.*; 48.7.8, Mod. 2 *de poenis*.

82. PS 5.26.3; D 48.6.5pr, Marcian 14 *inst.*

83. D 48.7.6, Mod. 8 *reg.*; 47.8.2.1, 6, 9, Ulpian 56 *ad ed.* (abbreviated in 48.2.15); Vacca (1972), 89; 138f. Though physical force had surely already been excluded as a necessary element by Marcus Aurelius.

84. D 48.19.32, Ulpian 6 *ad ed.*; but Ulpian spoke of a governor who did not distinguish 'utrum Iulia publicorum an Iulia privatorum'.

85. G 3.209; *Inst.* 4.2; CJ 9.33. Cf. CJ 3.39.4 (330); 8.4.7 & 10 (389 & 484).

86. Cicero II *Verr.* 3.65.152; cf. *pro Tullio* 3.7-5.11.

87. He was the peregine praetor – Asconius *in toga cand.* 84 (Stangl 65), but this did not prevent his edict being absorbed into that of the urban praetor – Guarino (1956), 140ff.; Serrao (1954), 74ff.; Kelly (1966), 163ff.

88. D 47.8.2.20, Ulpian 56 *ad ed.*

89. *Inst.* 4.2.2.

90. D 4.2.13 (= 48.7.7), Callistratus 5 *de cogn.*: Caesar dixit: tu vim putas esse solum si homines vulnerentur? vis est et tunc quotiens quis id quod deberi sibi putat non per iudicem reposcit. Contrast 43.16.1.27: vim vi repellere licere Cassius scribit, idque ius natura comparatur. D 43.16.1.2, Ulpian 69 *ad ed.*, on the interdict *de vi*, appears to say that *vis* was also repressed by the *leges Iulia publicorum et privatorum* and by imperial enactments; the latter must surely include this. See also CJ 9.12.5 (294); 9.12.6 (317); 9.12.7 (319); 9.33.3 (293).

91. CJ 8.4.7 (389).

92. *Inst.* 4.2.1; Gordian had limited the remedy to moveables – CJ 9.33.1 (242).

93. CJ 9.12.1 (205); 9.12.9 (415); see also CJ 9.33.2 (260); 9.33.4 (293); 9.33.5 (293); PS 1.7.9-10.

94. D 47.13.1, Ulpian 5 *opin.*; PS 5.26.4.

95. See Gnoli (1984). PS 5.3; CJ 9.32.

96. D 47.19.6, Paul 1 *ad Neratium*; PS 2.31.11. Cf. Thomas (1968); MacCormack (1978).

97. D 47.18.

98. D 47.19.2pr, Ulpian 9 *de off. proconsulis*.

99. D 47.19.1, Marcian 3 *inst.*: per accusationem expilatae hereditatis.

100. D 47.19.3, Marcian 2 *pub. iud.*

101. D 47.19.2.1, Ulpian 9 *de off. proconsulis*.

102. D 47.19.5, Hermogenianus 2 *iuris epit.*; CJ 6.2.17 (294). Even if this is an interpolation of the non-liability for theft of the wife, it illustrates the close connexion.

103. G 2.52-57, though, as Gaius explains, a resolution of the Senate under Hadrian had laid down that such usucapion could be annulled, and that the heir could bring a claim to the inheritance against the possessor.

104. D 47.11.3, Ulpian 3 *de adulteriis*.

105. D 48.13.6(5), Marcian 5 *reg.*

106. D 48.13.5.3(4.6), Marcian 14 *inst.*

107. D 48.13.1, Ulpian 44 *ad Sab.*; 48.19.16.4, Claud. Sat. *de poenis pag.*

108. Robinson (1973); Gnoli (1974), 414.

109. D 47.11.3, Ulpian 3 *de adulteriis*; CJ 9.34.3 (242). See Zilletti (1961); Brasiello (1971); Mentxaka (1988).

110. D 47.20.1, Papinian 1 *resp*.; paying off one's creditors could release one from criminal liability – CJ 9.34.1 (231).

111. D 47.20.2, Ulpian 8 *ad Sab*.; in 3.2.13.8 Ulpian, 6 *ad ed*., says that although not a public crime, *stellionatus* did bring infamy.

112. D 47.20.3pr, Ulpian 8 *de off. proconsulis*.

113. See chapter VII.

114. D 48.16.7.2, Ulpian 8 *disp*.

115. PS 1.8.2.

116. Mackenzie (1678), title xxviii, p. 286; Hume (1829³), 328, however, describes an injury to the person under this term; CC 2053.

117. CJ 9.34.1 (231); 9.34.2 (239); cf. 9.34.4 (244).

118. D 47.20.3.1, 3, Ulpian 8 *de off. proconsulis*; the Watson translation of s.3 as 'concealing wares' is wrong. Cf. also D 21.1.4.2, Ulpian 1 *ad ed. aed. cur*., where 'impostor' seems the right translation and 50.13.1.3, Ulpian 8 *de omn. trib*., where closer to 'charlatan'.

119. D 47.20.4, Modestinus 3 *de poenis*.

120. D 47.20.3.2, Ulpian 8 *de off. proconsulis*.

121. *Inst*. 4.18.10; implied in D 48.1.4, Paul 37 *ad ed*., and suggested too by its financial penalty; cf. CJ 9.20.3 (224); 9.20.13 (294). See the lengthy footnote to Lambertini (1980), 9.

122. PS 5.30B.1 = *Coll*. 14.2.2.

123. *Coll*. 14.3.2, Ulpian.

124. *Coll*. 14.3.1-3, Ulpian. Caracalla's ruling does not seem to have been long in force – CJ 9.20.4 (239); cf. Millar (1965), 365.

125. D 43.29.3.11, Ulpian 71 *ad ed*.; CJ 9.20.5 (259); unlike the interdict for production of a free man, the criminal charge is not likely to have been available to a *pupillus*. Lauria (1932) holds that only someone with an interest could make the accusation, but he seems too swayed by Mommsen's theory of 'usurpation of *potestas*'.

126. Before 63 BC, since Cicero, *pro Rab. Post*. 3.8, referred to 'servis alienis contra legem Fabiam retentis'; after the Social War, judging from the phrase in *Coll*. 14.3.4, Ulpian: ... qui civem romanum eumve qui in Italia liberatus sit celaverit ... It was presumably triggered by much the same conditions as led to the edict on *rapina*; compare too the unsettled conditions and the abuse of *ergastula* following on the civil wars after Caesar's death – Suet. *Aug*. 32; *Tib*. 8; Seneca *controv*. 10.4.18; *ILS* 8506 = *CIL* III 2544; Pliny *Ep*. 6.25.2-3; D 1.18.13pr, Ulpian 7 *de off. proconsulis*; 48.13.4.2, Marcian 14 *inst*.; cf. Cicero *pro Cluentio* 7.21. *Fugitivi* – PS 1.6A. Robinson (1968); Wacke (1978); van Hoof (1988) on equivalence of *plagiarii* and *latrones*, and their use in romances.

127. Apuleius *Met*. 8.24; the *lex Cornelia de iniuriis* presumably. The rubric of the *lex Fabia* may well have been *de suppressis* according to Lambertini (1980), 90ff., citing PS *Frag. Leid*. 12-14.

128. PS 5.30B.1 = *Coll*. 14.2.1; CJ 9.20.12 (294); 9.20.14 (294), stresses the necessary element of *dolus*; cf. 9.20.15 (294). What about peregrines?

129. *Coll*. 14.3.4, Ulpian.

130. *Coll*. 14.3.5, Ulpian. Cf. D 47.2.36pr, Ulpian 41 *ad Sab*.; CJ 9.20.2 (213), where an action for the corruption of a slave might lie.

131. E.g. D 48.6.6, Ulpian 7 *de off. proconsulis*; this could be *vis or plagium*. Coroï (1915), 210, held that under Pius the penalty for *plagium* was still a fine, and that some greater penalty was needed to fit this case, while Longo (1970) thinks the compilers brought much under *vis*.

132. D 48.15.6.2, Callistratus 6 *de cogn*.

133. And Gaius points out that a free person too can be stolen – G 3.199; the same remains true in *Inst.* 4.1.9. A kidnapped slave must have been classed as *res furtiva* in the context of usucapion, as in CJ 6.2.10 (293).

134. D 47.2.36pr, Ulpian 41 *ad Sab.*; other texts, such as 11.4.1pr, Ulpian 1 *ad ed.*, 47.2.48.1, Ulpian 42 *ad Sab.*, 47.2.63(62), Marcian 4 *reg.*, which talk of theft where there would seem to have been sufficient grounds for *plagium*, are probably angled towards giving the owner his delictual remedy where he would not want to be bothered with a criminal charge. There was also the delict of corrupting a slave – D 11.3 – introduced in the last century of the Republic by the praetor; see below. The 'theft' of the *veteres* was wide; the concept was narrowed in the Late Republic, but commentaries *ad Sabinum* would be influenced by the earlier interpretation.

135. D 47.2.83(82).2, Paul 2 *sent.* (= PS 2.31.31); cf. 47.2.39, Ulpian 41 *ad Sab.*; PS 2.31.12; CJ 9.20.1 (213); 9.20.9 (293). See Lambertini (1980), 105ff.

136. D 48.15.6pr-1, Callistratus 6 *de cogn.*

137. Lambertini (1980), 88ff.

138. D 48.15.1, Ulpian 1 *reg.*; CJ 9.20.7 (287); 9.20.10 (293).

139. The selling of a free person naturally did not affect his status – CJ 9.20.11 (293), unless he had shared in the profits or, at some periods, been abandoned as a baby; see Reggi (1958); Boswell (1988), 62-75.

140. D 48.15.4, Gaius 22 *ad ed. provinciale.*

141. PS 1.6A.2; D 48.15.2.3, Ulpian 9 *de off. proconsulis*; CJ 9.20.6 (287); cf. D 11.4 *de fugitivis.*

142. D 48.15.2pr-2, Ulpian, 9 *de off. proconsulis*; cf. 18.1.35.3, Gaius 10 *ad ed. prov.* and see Daube (1952). And juristic interpretation of the Senate's resolution held that fugitives could be taken account of without risk of the Fabian penalty in the division of common property, etc. – D 10.3.19.3, Paul 6 *ad Sab.*

143. D 48.15.5, Modestinus 17 *resp.*; cf. CJ 9.20.8 (290). One sees a link with *vis* as stated by Marcus Aurelius.

144. D 48.15.3pr, Marcian 1 *iud. pub.*; cf. 47.2.48.2, Ulpian 42 *ad Sab.*

145. CJ 6.1.4 (317).

146. *Inst.* 4.18.10. A rescript of Constantine to the Vicar of Africa is the only text in the CTh title and the last in the CJ title – CJ 9.20.16 (315); it refers to the miseries of parents bereft of their children.

147. This penalty is laid down in the *lex Iulia municipalis* for misdoings with the corn supply – *FIRA* i 13: *tab. Hera.* v. 19.

148. *Coll.* 14.3.5, 4. Paul simply said that the penalty was formerly a fine – Coll. 14.2.2 = PS 5.30B.1; so did another late jurist – D 48.15.7, Hermogenianus 5 *iuris epit.* Paul elsewhere talked of a fine under the *lex Fabia* following a successful interdict for the production of a free man who had been chained, abducted, or shut up – PS 5.6.14; this text is somewhat suspect, and may have come from elsewhere when PS was being compiled. Cf. PS 1.6A.2

149. D 48.15.1, Ulpian 1 *reg.* Cf. CJ 4.55.4 (224): death? or status loss?

150. PS 5.30B.1-2 = *Coll.* 14.2.2-3. This is interesting as an example of a slave not necessarily being punished more heavily than a free man.

151. *Coll.* 14.3.6, Ulpian. This is not necessarily incompatible with the remark (D 48.15.7, Hermogenianus 5 *iuris epit.*) that the financial penalty had fallen into desuetude.

152. D 48.15.7, Hermogenianus 5 *iuris epit.*

153. D 40.1.12, Paul 50 *ad ed.*; this text is treated by Berger (1938), 289ff. The second part of this text, dating the postponement from the owner's death rather than the making of the will, seems to me be in a different context; although D 48.15.3.1, Marcian 1 *iud. pub.*, points out that the death of someone who ordered a kidnapping did not relieve the actual wrongdoer of liability (as with the *lex Aquilia*, he says). Cf. D 49.15.12.16, Tryphoninus 4 *disp.*

154. PS 1.6A.1. Was this in the SC? or was it interpretation of the SC? Its purpose must have been to prevent collusion between *fugitivus* and hunter. Lambertini (1980), 138ff., thinks there may have been another resolution of the Senate on this.

155. CJ 9.20.6 (287); so also PS 1.6A.2; *Coll.* 14.3.5, Ulpian.

156. Moreover, there would still have been at this period great flexibility in the choice of penalty by the judge having *cognitio*; see e.g. de Robertis (1954), Sez. I, cap. iii.

157. PS 1.6A.3 & 6.

158. CJ 6.1.3 (317-23).

159. CJ 9.20.7 (287). This may have been an instance where crucifixion was the penalty. See Lambertini (1980), 174ff.

160. CTh 9.18.1 = CJ 9.20.16 (315).

161. D.11.3; cf. 47.1.2.5, Ulpian 43 *ad Sab.*; CJ 6.2; *Inst.* 4.1.8. See Albanese (1959).

162. D 47.11.5, Ulpian 5 *de off. proconsulis*: severe animadvertitur.

163. PS 1.13A.5-6; such deeds might give rise to an Aquilian action.

164. PS 5.3; CJ 6.2.18 (294). Treated by Longo (1970), 469-75, who examines the texts closely and somewhat doubtfully, excluding frr. 9-12 from the context of *incendio ruina naufragio*.

165. Why a raft? does this refer to goods floated down the Tiber to Rome?

166. D 47.9.1.2-5, 3pr, Ulpian 56 *ad ed.*

167. D 47.9.1pr-1, Ulpian 56 *ad ed.*; cf. PS 5.3.2. The comment about the utility of the edict is almost certainly the compilers' editing of the text.

168. PS 5.20.1-2.

169. D 48.8.10, Ulpian 18 *ad ed.*

170. PS 5.20.3-5; although in *Coll.* 12.6 Ulpian cites a rescript of Severus to the effect that a harsher penalty might be appropriate.

171. Kocher (1965) thinks there was one law, while Crook (1987a) rather prefers the theory that there were two.

172. Cicero *de nat. deorum* 3.30.74; II *Verr.* 1.42.108.

173. D 48.10.7, Marcian 2 *inst.*, citing Marcus Aurelius and Commodus; cf. CJ 9.22.19 (294).

174. D'Ors (1971).

175. CJ 9.23.1 (212); See also Albanese (1976); Robinson (1992b).

176. D 48.10.22pr, Paul *ad SC Libonianum*; 48.10.1pr, Marcian 14 *inst.*; CJ 9.22.20 (294).

177. D 48.10.22.7, Paul *ad SC Libonianum*.

178. D 48.10.1.8, Marcian 14 *inst.*; 48.10.15.3, Callistratus 1 *quaest.*

179. D 48.10.6.pr, Africanus 3 *quaest.*; 48.10.15.1, Callistratus 1 *quaest.*; CJ 9.23.2 (213); 9.23.6 (290).

180. D 48.10.1.7, Marcian 14 *inst.*; most formal requirements were relaxed for soldiers' wills.

181. D 48.10.1.4, Marcian 14 *inst.*; 48.10.16.2, Paul 3 *resp.*

182. D 48.10.15pr, Callistratus 1 *quaest.*; cf. CJ 9.23.3 (223) which links the edict to the resolution of the Senate; both texts stress that they apply even if the scribe is writing at the dictation of the testator. Dodges might clearly be tried – D 48.10.15.6, ibid.

183. *Coll.* 8.7.2, Ulpian 8 *de off. proconsulis.*

184. *Coll.* 8.7.3, Ulpian 8 *de off. proconsulis.*

185. D 48.10.1pr-2, Marcian 14 *inst.*; 48.10.9.3-4, Ulpian 8 *de off. proconsulis*; 48.10.20, Hermogenianus 6 *iuris epit.*; 47.13.2, Macer 1 *pub. iud.*; *Coll.* 8.2.1, Paul; cf. 48.11.6pr, Venuleius Saturninus 3 *pub. iud.*, who writes under the rubric of the *lex Iulia repetundarum*; Lenel accepted this, but there is perhaps a contrast between s.2 and the earlier sentences. See also Archi (1941), 1524ff.

186. D 48.10.27pr-1, Modestinus 8 *reg.*; PS 5.15.5 = *Coll.* 8.3.1; cf. CJ 9.22.4(3) (227); CTh 11.39.2 (333).

187. Cf. D 48.2.4, Ulpian 2 *de adulteriis.*

188. D 48.10.1.2, Marcian 14 *inst.*; cf. 3.6.1.3, Ulpian 10 *ad ed.*; PS 5.25.2, 13; Caracalla wrote that nobody concerned with a case should be given money – CJ 7.49.1 (212). The mention of corrupting a judge in D 48.10.21, Paul *ad SC Turpillianum*, must surely be a scribal error since this, unlike the fraud of selling the same thing twice, can hardly have been regarded as a relatively minor offence.

189. PS 5.25.6; cf. Suet. *Nero* 17; D'Ors (1971) thinks that this was part of the *SC Libonianum*, but there is no good reason for not accepting further senatorial legislation. There had been earlier requirements for sealing wills – Cicero II *Verr.* 1.45.117.

190. D 48.10.21, Paul *ad SC Turpillianum.*

191. D 48.10.1.9-12, Marcian 14 *inst.*

192. D 48.10.19.1, Paul 5 *sent.*; 48.10.30.1, Modestinus 12 *pand.*

193. D 48.10.32.1, Modestinus 1 *de poenis*; 47.11.6, Ulpian 8 *de off. proconsulis.*

194. D 48.10.2, Paul 3 *ad Sab.*; PS 4.7.1; PS 5.25.1.

195. PS 4.7.3-5.

196. PS 4.7.2.

197. Livy 39.8 & 18.

198. D 48.10.30pr, Modestinus 12 *pand.*

199. D 48.10.9.3, Ulpian 8 *de off. proconsulis*; cf. *Coll.* 8.7.1 where this is ascribed to a resolution of the Senate in AD 45.

200. D 48.10.16.1, Paul 3 *resp.*

201. D 48.10.1.4, Marcian 14 *inst.*; 48.10.16.2, Paul 3 *resp.*

202. D 48.10.27.1, Modestinus 8 *reg.*

203. CJ 4.21.2 (223); D 48.10.3, Ulpian 4 *disp.*; 48.10.24, Scaevola 22 *dig.*; 48.10.29, Modestinus *de enuc. casibus*; 48.10.31, Callistratus 3 *de cogn*, citing Pius and Marcus Aurelius; PS 1.12.2; PS 5.25.3 = *Coll.*8.6.1; PS 5.25.9.

204. D 48.10.13.1, Papinian 15 *resp*; he was banned from the class of decurions for ten years.

205. D 48.10.25, Ulpian 7 *ad ed.*; or tampering with an edict – 48.10.32pr, Modestinus 1 *de poenis.*

206. D 48.10.33, Modestinus 3 *de poenis*; CJ 9.22.3(4) (227).

207. D 48.10.1.3, Marcian 14 *inst.*; cf. PS 5.25.4. Could there be a development here of the quasi-delictual liability of the *iudex qui litem suam facit*?

208. D 48.10.13pr, Papinian 15 *resp.*; PS 5.25.11; Suet. *Claudius* 25; Dio 60.17.4-7.

209. D 48.10.27.2, Modestinus 8 *reg.*; PS 5.25.12.

210. D 48.10.16pr, Paul 3 *resp.*

211. PS 5.25.5: Qui rationes, acta, libellos, album propositum, testationes, cautiones, chirographa, epistulas sciens dolo malo in fraudem alicuius deleverit mutaverit subjecerit subscripserit ... falsi poena coercetur; cf. CJ 9.22.23.1 (376).

212. D 48.10.1.6, Marcian 14 *inst.*; cf. 48.19.38.8-9, Paul 5 *sent.*; cf. PS 5.25.8, which includes the *cognitor*.

213. D 48.10.1.5, Marcian 14 *inst.*; 48.19.38.7, Paul 5 *sent.*

214. Cf. D 48.10.23, Paul *de poenis pag.*, mentioning misstatement in reckoning and accounting, in contrast to imitating another's handwriting.

215. D 47.20.3.1, Ulpian 8 *de off. proconsulis.*

216. *Const. Tanta* 19 & 21-2; *const. Deo Auctore* 13; *const. Cordi* 5; see D'Ors (1971), 558.

217. CTh 9.19.1 = CJ 9.22.21 (316).

218. D 48.10.1.13, Marcian 14 *inst.*; 48.10.33, Modestinus 3 *de poenis*; *Coll.* 8.5.1, Paul; 8.3.1, Paul, speaks of exile or removal from the decurionate.

219. D 47.11.8, Ulpian 9 *de off. proconsulis*; cf. Schiller (1936).

220. D 48.10.23, Paul *de poenis pag.*

221. See above; 'dolo' or 'inimicitiarum gratia' is several times stressed – PS 5.20.2 & 5; *Coll.* 12.6.1, Paul; 12.7.2, Ulpian.

222. XII T. 8.11; PS 5.20.6.

223. D 47.12.3pr-1, 6-7, 11-12, Ulpian 25 *ad ed.*; PS 1.21.4-9, 12; PS 5.19A.1; CJ 9.19.2 (340); 9.19.4 (357).

224. The Emperor Gordian could say such violators 'laesae tamen religionis in crimen inciderunt' – CJ 9.19.1 (240); the language of Christian Constantius and pagan Julian did not differ much – 9.19.4 & 5 (357 & 363).

225. Although the latter could often fall under *vis* – PS 5.26.3; cf. CJ 9.19.6 (526).

226. D 47.21.3.2, Callistratus 5 *de cogn.*; PS 5.22.2.

227. D 47.21.2, Callistratus 3 *de cogn.*; *Coll.* 13.3.1-2, Ulpian; see also *Coll.* 13.2.1, Paul = PS 1.16.1.

228. D 47.21.1, Modestinus 8 *reg.*; 47.21.3pr-1, Callistratus 5 *de cogn.*; CJ 9.2.1 (222).

IV. Violence Against the Person

1. However, see the very full treatment of the Republican state of affairs in Lintott (1968).

2. Held to be one statute, but establishing two *quaestiones perpetuae* by Ferrary (1991); Cloud (1968 & 1969). The more normal word was 'veneficiis'.

3. D 47.11.4, Marcian 1 *reg.*, citing a rescript of Severus and Antoninus; 48.8.8, Ulpian 33 *ad ed.*

4. Though see e.g. Juvenal 3.281-308 on the possible perils of the streets. The upper classes were not necessarily – even if usually – immune (Tac. *Annals* 13.25), and modern experience suggests that the poor suffer worse from crime than the middle classes; the conclusion seems to be that Rome's streets were relatively safe – Robinson (1992a), 212.

5. In English see especially Lawson (1950), or any textbook of Roman law.

6. Cantarella (1976).

7. Tac. *Annals* 4.22. Silvanus claimed to have been asleep, but Tiberius went to the house, examined the scene and saw clear evidence of a struggle. Silvanus committed suicide, and an attempt to charge his previous wife with affecting his reason by drugs and spells failed.

8. Russi (1986); Harris (1982); Boswell (1988).

9. Kunkel (1962), 40-5 & 98-105.

10. *ILS* 45 = *CIL* VI 1283; cf. Cicero *pro Rosc. Am.* 4.11.

11. After the Bacchanalian affair, there were several special courts concerned with poisoning: Livy 39.38.3, of 184 BC; 40.37 & 43, of 180 BC; 40.44, of 179 BC; *per.* 48, of between 154 and 150 BC, on which also see Val. Max. 6.3.8. See Monaco (1984).

12. Paul (PS 5.23.2) defines a *homicida* as one who kills a man with any sort of weapon, or brings about a death.

13. Cicero *fin.* 2.16.54: 'qui cum praetor quaestionem inter sicarios exercuisset, ita aperte cepit pecunias ob rem judicandam' that the following year a tribune of the people got the plebs to demand that the matter be investigated, and by decree of the Senate a *quaestio* was set up under one of the consuls. Kunkel (1962), 45 held it permanent, Jones (1972), 54, and also Gruen (1968a), 29, special; see also Bauman (1983), 234ff.

14. Asconius *in Milon.* 45 (Stangl 39); cf. *Auct. ad Her.* 4.41.53; Cicero *de inv.* 2.60. See Strachan-Davidson (1912), I 227f.

15. *Coll.* 1.3.1-2, Ulpian 7 *de off. proconsulis.* See also Cicero *pro Cluentio* 55.151 & 56.154.

16. D 48.8.3pr, Marcian 14 *inst.*

17. D 48.8.1pr-1, Marcian 14 *inst.*; firesetting is also mentioned, presumably when it caused a death.

18. PS 5.23.1-2; Nörr (1986b), 98-100.

19. Nörr (1986a).

20. Cicero *pro Cluentio* 53.147.

21. *Coll.* 1.3.1, Ulpian 7 *de off. proconsulis.* Strachan-Davidson (1912), II 149, suggested, reasonably, that there might have been another chapter in the statute for crimes committed outside the City.

22. Cicero *ad Att.* 3.15.5; cf. *pro Sestio* 25.53. It was only the second *lex Clodia*, the one specifically imposing interdiction on Cicero, which had to be repealed to enable Cicero to return from exile.

23. D 48.8.1.3, Marcian 14 *inst.*; cf. *Coll.* 1.6.2-4, Ulpian 7 *de off. proconsulis*; D 48.8.17, Paul 5 *sent.*; cf. PS 5.23.3 = *Coll.* 1.7.2. See Balzarini (1982).

24. D 48.8.1pr & 2, Marcian 14 *inst.*; PS 5.23.1-2; *Coll.* 1.3.2, Ulpian 7 *de off. proconsulis*; CJ 9.16.6 (294).

25. Suet. *Claudius* 25; G 3.213; *Inst.* 4.3.11.

26. D 48.8.11.1-2, Modestinus 6 *reg.*

27. G 1.53; PS 5.23.6; in D 1.6.2 (= *Coll.* 3.3.1-6) Ulpian (8 *de off. proconsulis*) cites several rescripts of Hadrian and Pius on this point; *Coll.* 3.4.1 is a rescript of Diocletian.

28. CTh 9.12.1 = CJ 9.14.1 (319) – the language is particularly ghoulish – & 2 (326/9).

29. D 48.8.1.1, Marcian 14 *inst.*; viewed as particularly reprehensible – CJ 9.18.1 (Caracalla); cf. 9.4.3 (216).

30. D 48.8.3.1-2, Marcian 14 *inst.*; Tacitus *Annals* 3.7 speaks of Martina as a notorious dealer in poison; in *Annals* 12.66 Agrippina sought out Locusta, 'a person of well-known skill in the trade of poisoning' for aid in poisoning Claudius; later (13.15) she was used for poisoning Claudius' son Britannicus. See Höbenreich (1988).

31. D 48.8.3pr-3, Marcian 14 *inst.*; 48.19.38.5, Paul 5 *sent.*; PS 5.23.14 & 19; cf. D 9.2.7.6 & 9pr, Ulpian 18 *ad ed.*; 9.2.8pr, Gaius 7 *ad ed. prov.* On the subjectivity of the norms concerning poison see Rodriguez-Alvarez (1991).

32. D 25.4.1.1, Ulpian 24(?34) *ad ed.*; 47.11.4, Marcian 1 *reg.*; 48.8.8, Ulpian

33 *ad ed.*; 48.19.39, Tryphoninus 10 *disp.*; cf. Cicero *pro Cluentio* 11.32; Juvenal 6.594-7; Gellius *NA* 12.1.8-9. See Nardi (1980a).

33. D 48.8.1pr-1, Marcian 14 *inst.*; 48.8.3.4, Marcian 14 *inst.*; 48.8.4pr, Ulpian 7 *de off. proconsulis*; PS 5.23.1 & 11(10).

34. D 48.8.1pr, Marcian 14 *inst.*; CJ 9.1.11 (244); cf. D 47.9.9, Gaius 4 *ad XII Tab.*; 48.8.10, Ulpian 18 *ad ed.*; PS 5.20.2 – 'inimicitiarum gratia'.

35. D 48.8.1pr & 3.4, Marcian 14 *inst.*; cf. 47.9.3.8, Ulpian 56 *ad ed.*

36. D 48.8.13, Modestinus 12 *pand.*, records that a SC brought under the penalty of the statute one who performed or organized *mala sacrificia*; PS 5.23.15-16; CTh 9.14.1 = CJ 9.16.7 (374) specifies a slain child – *necandi infantis piaculum.*

37. E.g. Tac. *Annals* 6.26. See Wacke (1983), with a bibliography; Pascale (1985) on the soldier.

38. PS 5.23.10.

39. D 48.8.12, Modestinus 8 *reg.* It is not clear in CJ 9.16.5 (294) whether it is the innocence or the youth which clears the accused.

40. D 48.5.39.8, Papinian 36 *quaest.*; CJ 9.9.4.1 (Severus Alexander). See Höbenreich (1990).

41. PS 5.23.3 = *Coll.* 1.7.1.

42. D 48.8.14, Callistratus 6 *de cogn.*; *Coll.* 1.6.2-4, Ulpian 7 *de off. proconsulis.* Cf. *Coll.* 1.12.1, Modestinus 6 *diff.*; CJ 9.16.1 (215); 9.16.4 (290).

43. D 48.8.15, Ulpian 8 *ad l.Iuliam et Papiam*; PS 5.23.5; CJ 9.16.5 (294); see also Nörr (1986b), 86-115.

44. D 48.8.7, Paul *de pub. iud.*; PS 5.23.12; CJ 9.16.4 (290). *Coll.* 1.11.1-4, Ulpian 7 *de off. proconsulis*, mentions a case in Baetica under Hadrian when relegation for five years was the sentence for the death of a young man, dying after being tossed in a blanket or cloak at a dinner party.

45. Tac. *Annals* 14.42-5; Wolf (1988a) has shown convincingly that what this records is probably not the real speech of Cassius Longinus but a rhetorical exercise expressing Tacitus' own views.

46. PS 3.5.2-3 & 6-8 & 11-12; D 29.5.1.31, Ulpian 50 *ad ed.*; 29.5.6pr, Paul 46 *ad ed.*; 29.5.17, Modestinus 8 *reg.* The suspicious circumstances were violence – 29.5.1.17, ibid. citing Labeo; where the death was by poison the slaves could not be expected to have prevented it, and so only those guilty, at least as accomplices, would be executed – 29.5.1.18 & 21, ibid.

47. PS 3.5.1 & 6 & 9 & 12a; D 29.5.3.18-32, Ulpian 50 *ad ed.*; 29.5.6.1, Paul 46 *ad ed.*; CJ 6.35.3 (222). There was a five-year prescriptive period for the crime of opening a will contrary to the *SC Silanianum* – D 29.5.13, Venuleius Saturninus 2 *pub. iud.*

48. PS 3.5.5.

49. Tac. *Annals* 13.32; D 29.5.3.16-17, Ulpian 50 *ad ed.*; 29.5.10.1, Paul *ad SC Silanianum*; 29.5.1.5, Ulpian 50 *ad ed.*; cf. 29.5.25.1, Gaius 17 *ad ed. prov.*

50. D 29.5.1.13 & 26, Ulpian 50 *ad ed.*, quoting Scaevola in the earlier sentence; 29.5.3.17, ibid.

51. D 29.5.1.1 & 28, Ulpian 50 *ad ed.*; in the latter sentence Hadrian is cited as saying that the maid's admission that the murderer had threatened her with death if she cried out showed that she could have at least done this, so she was deservedly put to death as an awful warning to other slaves. Cf. 29.5.14, Maecian 11 *pub. iud.*; 29.5.19, Modestinus 8 *pand.*

52. D 48.8.3.6, Marcian 14 *inst.*

53. D 48.8.1.4, Marcian 14 *inst.*; 48.8.9, Ulpian 37 *ad ed.*; cf. 9.2.5pr, Ulpian 18 *ad ed.*; PS 5.23.7-9; CJ 9.16.2 (243); 9.16.3(4) (265). See Luzzatto (1956).

54. See chapter V on when killing was permitted in cases of adultery.

55. CTh 9.14.2 = CJ 3.27.1 (391); the actual ground given was that it was 'better for a man to fight back at the proper time than for him to be avenged after his death'.

56. D 48.8.1.5, Marcian 14 *inst.*; see chapter V.

57. D 48.8.2, Ulpian 1 *de adulteris*; cf. 48.9.5, Marcian 14 *inst.*

58. CTh 9.13.1 = CJ 9.15.1 (365).

59. Tac. *Annals* 13.44; when his term as tribune had expired, Octavius was exiled under the *lex Cornelia*.

60. CTh 9.7.4.1 = CJ 9.16.8 (385). On the interrogation of slaves against their owners see Robinson (1981), 223ff.

61. D 48.2.1, Pomponius 1 *ad Sab.*; 48.2.2pr, Papinian 1 *de adulteriis*; or her cousin – CJ 9.1.4 (222); 9.1.9 (239).

62. D 48.2.2.1, Papinian 1 *de adulteriis*.

63. D 48.2.4, Ulpian 2 *de adulteriis*.

64. D 48.2.8-11pr, Macer 2 *pub. iud.* & Paul 5 *sent.* & Hermogenian 6 *iuris epit.* & Macer 2 *pub. iud.*

65. D 48.8.3.5, Marcian 14 *inst.*; 48.8.16, Modestinus 3 *de poenis* – the emperor was to be consulted before death could be inflicted on decurions. PS 5.23.1 says that the statutory penalty had been replaced with simple death for *honestiores*, crucifixion or the beasts for *humiliores*.

66. Festus p. 247: *leges regiae: Numa* 12; XII T. 9.4. E.g. Cloud (1971); Y. Thomas (1981); MacCormack (1982). Paul Jeffreys-Powell tells me that the etymology of the word suggests that it means simply the killing of a relation.

67. Livy *per.* 68; Orosius 5.16.23; Livy's epitomator describes this as the first use of the sack as penalty. Zucotti (1991).

68. Cf. Livy 40.8-16 or some of the mass poisoning cases.

69. Cicero *pro Rosc. Am.* 23.64.

70. In spite of D 1.2.2.32, Pomponius *enchiridion*, cf. CTh 9.19.4 (376), it is not credible that Sulla created a standing jury court for parricide, although he may have passed a law on the matter.

71. Suet. *Aug.* 33.1. See Kupiszewski (1971); Fanizza (1979).

72. PS 5.24.1.

73. D 48.9.9pr, Modestinus 12 *pand.*

74. D 48.9.5, Marcian 14 *inst.*, does not use it for the killing of a son.

75. By Zumpt (1865-9) II 2.361-3; see Gruen (1974), 257.

76. D 1.18.14, Macer 2 *iud. pub.*, citing a rescript of Marcus and Commodus; 48.9.9.1, Modestinus 12 *pand.*; cf. 1.18.13.1, Ulpian 7 *de off. proconsulis*.

77. D 48.9.1 & 3, Marcian 14 *inst.*; 48.9.9.1, Marcian 14 *inst.*

78. Cicero *pro Rosc. Am.* 25.70-26.72; *Auct. ad Her.* 1.13.23. Cloud (1971) points out that the period of the Punic Wars was morally shattering; we find human sacrifice after Cannae – Livy 22.57.

79. D 48.9.9pr, Modestinus 12 *pand.*, citing Hadrian; PS 5.24.1.

80. CTh 9.15.1 = CJ 9.17.1 (318-19); 11.36.4 (339); *Inst.* 4.18.6; the first text restricts to snakes the animals enclosed with the guilty man.

81. Lear (1965), 81.

82. D 48.9.6, Ulpian 8 *de off. proconsulis*, citing Maecian; 48.9.7, Ulpian 29 *ad ed.*; cf. 48.9.2, Scaevola 4 *reg.*

83. D 48.9.8, Ulpian 8 *disp.*

84. D 48.9.10, Paul *de poenis omnium legum*.

85. The principal treatment of *vis* will be found in chapter VI, under sedition.

86. Injury to life or limb arising from a mob or sedition, which was to be punished *extra ordinem*, seems comparable – PS 5.3.1.

87. D 48.6.3.4, Marcian 14 *inst.*; 48.5.40(39)pr, Papinian 15 *resp.*; PS 5.22.5 gives the penalty for the rape of a pre-pubertal girl as condemnation to the mines for *humiliores*, and for *honestiores* relegation to an island or exile.

88. D 48.6.5.2, Marcian 14 *inst.*

89. D 48.6.6, Ulpian 7 *de off. proconsulis*; CJ 9.20.5 (259); 9.12.3 (Diocletian).

90. CTh 9.24.1-3 (320/6, 349, 374); 9.25.1-3 (354, 364, 420).

91. CJ 9.13.1 (533); cf. Evans-Grubb (1989).

92. See chapter III.

93. D 48.6.3.2, Marcian 14 *inst.*; 48.6.11pr, Paul 5 *sent.*, gives a capital penalty, but cf. PS 5.26.3. This would appear to be the motive for the slaves' violence in CTh 9.10.4 = CJ 9.12.8 (390).

94. D 48.6.3.6, Marcian 14 *inst.* Such expulsion, using an unarmed mob, fell in the classical period under *vis privata* – 48.7.5, Ulpian 69 *ad ed.*; PS 5.26.3.

95. D 48.6.5pr, Marcian 14 *inst.*; this would also fall under *iniuria* – 47.10.1.6, Ulpian 56 *ad ed.*

96. D 48.6.10pr, Ulpian 68 *ad ed.*

97. D 48.7.2, Scaevola 4 *reg.*; 48.6.10pr-1, Ulpian 68 *ad ed.*, where the jurist adds (s.2) that the penalty is interdiction from fire and water. In CJ 9.12.4.1 (293) it seems to be classed under *vis privata* because the beating was by a gang.

98. CTh 9.10.1 = CJ 9.12.6 (317) & 2 (317/8).

99. D 48.7.7, Callistratus 5 *cognit.*; 48.7.8, Modestinus 2 *de poenis*; CJ 9.12.5 (294); CTh 9.10.3 = CJ 9.12.7 (319).

100. D 48.7.4.1, Paul 55 *ad ed.*, citing Labeo.

101. PS 5.26.1. See also chapter VI.

102. *Coll.* 9.2.1-2, Ulpian 9? *de off. proconsulis.*

103. CJ 9.5.1 (486); 9.5.2 (529); cf. 9.12.3 (Diocletian). See also Wacke (1978), Robinson (1968). Compare too the prohibition on keeping armed gangs, presumably for terrorizing people – CJ 9.12.10 (468).

104. See Manfredini (1979), Balzarini (1983), Polay (1986).

105. Cicero *pro Caec.* 12.35; D 47.10.5pr, Ulpian 56 *ad ed.*, is suggestive. If there was a *quaestio*, it was not rated as one of the *iudicia publica* – 3.3.42.1, Paul 8 *ad ed.*

106. Cloud (1994), 525.

107. G 3.220-5; *Inst.* 4.4. The praetor had powers of punishment where reparation was not possible because of low estate and poverty – D 47.10.35, Ulpian 3 *de omn. trib.*

108. D 47.10.1.1, Ulpian 56 *ad ed.*, citing Labeo; CJ 9.35.3 (239).

109. CJ 9.35.1 (222); 9.35.8 (294).

110. D 47.10.1.5, Ulpian 56 *ad ed.*

111. D 47.10.3.1-2, Ulpian 56 *ad ed.*; PS 5.4.2.

112. D 47.10.37.1, Marcian 14 *inst.*; CJ 9.35.7 (293).

113. D 47.10.5.6-7, Ulpian 56 *ad ed.*; cf. 44.7.9, Paul 9 *ad Sab.*

114. G 3.220.

115. PS 5.4.1.

116. That is, his place of residence, quite widely defined, but not *meritoria vel stabula* – D 47.10.5.2-5, Ulpian 56 *ad ed.*; PS 5.4.8; *Inst.* 4.4.8. It was more than mere invasion of privacy; compare the Scottish crime of hamesucken.

117. D 47.10.5pr-1, Ulpian 56 *ad ed.*; 47.10.7.1, Ulpian 57 *ad ed.*

118. Tac. *Annals* 13.25.

119. This could include the flogging or torture of a slave 'for it is clear that a slave suffers', and also sometimes gross verbal abuse – D 47.10.15.35 & 44, Ulpian 77 *ad ed.*

120. D 47.10.7.1, Ulpian 57 *ad ed.*

121. E.g. alleging slavery – CJ 9.35.9 (294); 9.35.10 (294).

122. D 47.10.18pr, Paul 55 *ad ed.*; CJ 9.35.5 (290).

123. D 47.10.5.9-11, Ulpian 56 *ad ed.*: in what seem to be the words of the statute: Si quis librum ad infamiam alicuius pertinentem scripserit composuerit ediderit dolove malo fecerit.

124. D 47.10.6, Paul 55 *ad ed.*

125. D 47.10.15.13, Ulpian 77 *ad ed.*

126. CTh 9.34.7 = CJ 9.36.2 (365/73); 9.34.9 (386); 9.34.10 (406); so also CJ 9.36.1, undated and lacking any rubric.

127. CTh 9.34.1-8 (313-68), but see also PS 5.4.11, with which compare 5.4.15-21.

128. D 47.10.1.2, Ulpian 56 *ad ed.*; 47.10.15.15-22, Ulpian 77 *ad ed.*; PS 5.4.4-5, on which see Desanti (1990a).

129. PS 5.4.21; Jos. *AJ* 20.108.

130. D 47.10.9.4, Ulpian 57 *ad ed.*; 47.10.25, Ulpian 18 *ad ed.*

131. D 47.11.1pr & 2, Paul 5 *sent.* = PS 5.4.5 & 14.

132. D 47.10.11.9, Ulpian 57 *ad ed.*; 47.10.12, Gaius 22 *ad ed. prov.*; CJ 9.35.9 (294).

133. D 47.11.1.1, Paul 5 *sent.* = PS 5.4.13, where it is added that such doings are severely punished.

134. D 47.10.26, Paul 19 *ad ed.*; there might be an alternative in the *actio servi corrupti*. For the impropriety of the better sort frequenting cookshops, see Robinson (1992a), 135-8; Ammianus reports that the Urban Prefect forbade any *honestus* to eat in public – 28.4.4.

135. D 47.11.9, Ulpian 9 *de off. proconsulis*; this, which appears to have been a crime peculiar to the province, was to be punished capitally, as amounting to death threats. It does not seem to be treated as magic, merely as intimidation.

136. D 47.11.11, Paul 1 *sent.*

137. D 47.10.15.30, Ulpian 77 *ad ed.*, citing Papinian.

138. D 47.10.38, Scaevola 4 *reg.*

139. D 47.10.45, Hermogenianus 5 *epit.*

140. D 48.2.12.4, Venuleius Saturninus, 2 *de iud. pub.*; PS 5.4.22.

141. D 47.10.45, Hermogenianus 5 *epit.*; PS 5.4.17; for an aggravated *iniuria* slaves might be condemned to the mines – PS 5.4.22.

142. PS 5.4.22. What happened if an owner did not put his slaves in chains is unknown, although it presumably happened.

143. PS 5.4.15-17.

144. D 9.2.27.28, Ulpian 18 *ad ed.*, citing Vivian. It has been argued that the fourfold penalty arose from a separate *actio popularis* or praetorian delict; see Dalla (1978), 76f.

145. Val. Max. 6.1.13; cf. Martial 2.60.

146. Suet. *Dom.* 7; cf. Philostratus *A of T* 6.42; Dio 67.2.3, but 68.2.4 ascribes this to Nerva; since we have Dio only in epitome, the ascription to Domitian seems preferable, especially in view of Martial 6.2; 9.6.

147. D 48.8.6, Venuleius Saturninus 1 *de off. procons.*; what is a little odd is such a restriction on an owner's powers so early.

148. D 48.8.3.4, Marcian 14 *inst.*

149. D 48.8.4.2, Ulpian 7 *de off. procons.*

150. D 48.8.5, Paul 2 *de off. procons.*; e.g. the normal method of castrating lambs is to tie off their testicles so that they atrophy – it appears to be painless.

151. Justin I *Apol.* 29, cited by Dalla (1978), 95.

152. PS 5.23.13.

153. SHA *Hadrian* 14. Circumcision seemed strange and disgusting to many Romans – e.g. Juvenal 14.96-106 – and it is possible that the *lex Cornelia* had generally forbidden mutilation. See Marotta (1983/84).

154. Dio 69.12. See Grant (1973), 244-7; Smallwood (1959), 334.

155. D 48.8.11pr, Modestinus 6 *reg.*

156. PS 5.22.3-4.

157. CTh 16.9.1 (336) & 2 = CJ 1.10.1 (339); 16.8.26 =CJ 1.9.16 (423).

158. CJ 4.42.1 (Constantine).

159. CJ 4.42.2 (457/65).

160. Compare the new value of virginity, in man as well as woman, in the Christian Empire.

161. NovJ 142 (558); cf. Procopius *Anec.* 11.34.

V. Sexual Offences

1. See for the late Republic Asconius *in toga cand.* 91 (Stangl 70); cf. *in Milon.* 46 (Stangl 40); Marshall (1985), 309-11.. This lack of chastity was classed as incest, see Cornell (1981); interestingly, he points out that the only other (mythical) example of a wilful religious offence by a priest was the case, in regal times, of M. Atilius, who was thrown into the sea in a sack, as if a parricide – DH 4.62.4; Val. Max. 1.1.13.

2. E.g. Plut. *Marc.* 2; Val. Max. 6.1.7-8 & 11; Livy 25.2.9; cf. Gellius *NA* 4.14.3; Bauman (1974b).

3. See (still) Lotmar (1912); Guarino (1943); Manfredini (1987); Treggiari (1991), 37-9.

4. 'Serviles quoque cognationes in hoc iure observandae sunt', and also illegitimate ones – D 23.2.14.2, Paul 35 *ad ed.*; *Inst.* 1.10.10; see also D 23.2.8, Pomponius 5 *ad Sab.*: a freedman cannot marry his freed mother or sister, because this rule was introduced by custom not statute – 'moribus, non legibus'.

5. D 23.2.39.1, Paul 6 *ad Plaut.*

6. *Coll.* 6.4.1-8, an enactment of Diocletian and Maximian, is couched in moralizing terms, although it granted an amnesty to couples who parted within a given date. *Coll.* 6.7.1-9 appears to be Mosaic.

7. Guareschi (1993) is the latest to express this general view.

8. D 48.5.8(7.1), in 2º *de adulteriis Papiniani* Marcian notes: Incesti commune crimen adversus duos simul intentari potest; so too 48.5.40(39).7, Papinian 15 *resp.*; in adultery, as we shall see, one party must first be convicted and only then the other accused – D 48.5.16(15).9, Ulpian 2 *de adult.*; 48.5.18(17).6, ibid.

9. Mommsen (1899), 688, says simply 'Zeugnisse mangeln gänzlich' – 'there's a total lack of evidence'.

10. D 48.5.40(39).5, Papinian 15 *resp.*

11. Cicero *pro Milone* 22.59; cf. Val. Max. 6.8.1.

12. D 48.5.40(39).8, Papinian 15 *resp.*; 48.18.4, Ulpian 3 *disp.*; cf. 48.18.17.1, Papinian 16 *resp.*, where a charge of adultery, not just *stuprum*, was required.

13. D 48.5.45(44), Papinian 4 *resp.*

14. CTh 9.7.8 = CJ 9.9.33(34) (393).

15. Ulpian *Reg.* 5.6; *Coll.* 6.2.2, Ulpian; *Inst.* 1.10.4. To establish the degree of relationship, the Romans counted from one party up to the common ancestor and then down to the other party.

16. G 1.62, though still recorded by Ulpian in *Coll.* 6.2.2.

17. Suet. *Claud.* 26; Tac. *Annals* 12.5-7; cf. Suet. *Dom.* 22.

18. *Coll.* 6.6.1, Papinian *de adulteris*; cf. D 48.5.39(38).1, Papinian 36 *quaest.*; Diocletian in *Coll.* 6.4.5.

19. D 3.2.10, Paul 8 *ad ed.*, states that the emperor was customarily requested for permission to marry within the mourning period; Dio 68.2 reports that Nerva forbade a man to marry his niece; cf. CTh 3.10.1 = CJ 5.8.1 (409) although it is unclear what kind of forbidden marriages are being sought.

20. CTh 3.12.1 (342).

21. CJ 5.8.2 (no date); 5.5.9 (476-84).

22. D 23.2.40, Pomponius 4 *ex Plautio*; *Inst.* 1.10.6 & 7.

23. Augustus extended this to cover the mother of one merely betrothed – D 23.2.14pr-1, 4, Paul 35 *ad ed.*

24. G 1.58, 63; D 23.2.68, Paul *ad SC Turpillianum*; *Coll.* 6.3.1-3 (= PS 2.19.3-5). This also covered aunts and uncles, great-aunts and great-uncles, and so on – G 1.62; *Inst.* 1.10.1, 3 & 5.

25. D 23.2.12.3, Ulpian 26 *ad Sab.*; *Inst.* 1.10.9.

26. G 1.61; *Coll.* 6.3.2, Paul; *Inst.* 1.10.2, 3. It was also allowed for the husband's child by a previous marriage to marry the wife's child by a previous marriage – *Inst.* 1.10.8.

27. CTh 3.12.2 (355), 4 (415); CJ 5.5.8 (475).

28. CTh 3.10.1, *interp.* (409); cf. Ambrose *Ep.* 60 (Mauer) = 58 in *CSEL*.

29. D 23.2.56, Ulpian 3 *disp.*; 25.7.1.3, Ulpian 2 *ad legem Iuliam et Papiam*, where Ulpian describes such behaviour as almost criminal and forbidden, but a soldier having the daughter of his sister as his concubine seems held liable for adultery, not incest – D 48.5.12(11).1, Papinian *de adulteris*. Children were also forbidden to marry their fathers' concubines, as irreligious, but the offence was classed as *stuprum*: CJ 5.4.4 (228).

30. D 48.18.5, Marcian 2 *inst.*; cf. Cicero *pro Cluentio* 5.

31. D 48.5.39(38)pr, Papinian 36 *quaest.*

32. Tac. *Annals* 6.49; cf. D 48.5.45, Papinian 4 *resp.*, where an incestuous relationship seems to have existed between mother-in-law and son-in-law.

33. D 48.5.39(38).2, Papinian 36 *quaest.*; PS 2.26.15; *Coll.* 6.3.3, Paul; CJ 5.5.4 (Val., Theo., Arc.) – though not always: CTh 3.12.3 = CJ 5.5.6.5 (396). There were also distinctions here as to whether she could recover something given as dowry: D 12.7.5, Papinian 11 *quaest.*

34. D 48.5.39(38).4, 7, Papinian 36 *quaest.*

35. D 48.5.39(38).1, Papinian 36 *quaest.*

36. D 48.5.39(38).3, 7, Papinian 36 *quaest.*

37. D 48.5.39(38).4-6, Papinian 36 *quaest.*

38. *Coll.* 6.5.1, Diocletian.

39. Tac. *Annals* 6.19; Dio 58.22; CTh 3.12.1 (342); CJ 9.9.33 (393).

40. D 48.18.5, Marcian 2 *inst.*; PS 2.26.15.

41. PS 2.26.15 (= *Coll.* 6.3.3), where there was no question of adultery, but an error of law that was pardonable in her; NovJ 12 (535), although generally stricter, only punished the woman equally with the man if she knowingly failed to observe the law.

42. G 1.64; *Coll.* 6.2.4, Ulpian; *Inst.* 1.10.12.

43. D 48.5.14(13).4, Ulpian 2 *de adult.*; logically of course the accusation should have been of *stuprum* rather than adultery.

44. D 23.2.66, Paul 2 *sent.*, where the tutor was punished in accordance with the status of his pupil; 48.5.7, Marcian 10 *inst.*, stating that a tutor who married his pupil could be accused of adultery under a resolution of the Senate (probably of 175/80) if her father had not indicated his wish for such a marriage; 25.2.17pr, Ulpian 30(34?) *ad ed.*; CJ 5.6 passim. See Desanti (1986A).

45. D 23.2.63, Papinian 1 *definitionum*; 23.2.38, Paul 2 *sent.*

46. D 23.2.42.1, Modestinus *de ritu nupt.*; 23.2.44, Paul 1 *ad l. Iuliam et Papiam*; Ulpian *Reg.* 13.1-2.

47. PS 2.19.9;. CTh 9.9.1 = CJ 9.11.1 (326/9) dealt severely with women having – secret – sexual relations with their own slaves. The *SC Claudianum* of the Principate was concerned with property rights in children rather than sexual morals. Compare the calm acceptance of cohabitation between a free-born woman and a slave in D 16.3.27, Paul 7 *resp.*

48. CTh 9.7.5 = 3.7.2 = CJ 1.9.6 (388); a purported marriage of this sort was to be held the equivalent of adultery.

49. CTh 3.14.1 (368/73).

50. D 48.5.30.1, Ulpian 4 *de adulteriis.*

51. D 23.2.48.1, Ter. Clemens 8 *ad l. Iuliam et Papiam*, regards a forbidden marriage as existing but deprived of privilege; Ulpian *Reg.* 16.2 points out that such a marriage does not count for relief from the anti-celibacy provisions of Augustus' legislation.

52. See still Volterra (1934).

53. There is Cicero's story of the man from Spain with the the two sets of children – *de or.* 1.40.183. Hadrian relegated for three years a man who *domum suam duxisset* a married woman, and from there sent a notice of divorce – D 24.2.8, Papinian 2 *de adulteriis* – but this seems closer to adultery or *stuprum* than bigamy; cf. 48.5.12.12, Papinian *de adulteris.*

54. D 3.2.1, Julian 1 *ad ed.*

55. CJ 9.9.18 (258).

56. CJ 5.5.2 (285).

57. CJ 5.17.7 (337); 9.9.34 (421).

58. See, for example: Esmein (1886), still the simplest exposition; Volterra (1930b); Bandini (1934); Biondi (1938); de Dominicis (1950); Andréev (1957); Thomas (1961) & (1970); Astolfi (1986[2]); Rizzelli (1990); Vitali (1972); Venturini (1988).

59. E.g. Livy 10.31; 25.2; Cicero *pro Rab. Post.* 3.8.

60. *Coll.* 4.2.2, Paul.

61. DH 2.25 for a husband with *manus* power over her acting as her judge; cf. Gellius *NA* 10.23 on Cato's views.

62. DH 4.66ff; Livy 1.58. It would presumably have been the cognatic family, to cope with cases of *manus*.

63. E.g. Livy *per.* 48; Val. Max. 6.3.7 & 8; cf. Livy 13.18; Val. Max. 5.8.2-3; 5.9.1; Suet. *Tib.* 35; Tac. *Annals* 2.50; 13.32.

64. Plautus *Curc.* 28-31; Horace *Sat.* 1.2.41-6; Val. Max. 6.1.13, which mentions cudgelling, punching, castrating (twice), and handing the lover over to the husband's slaves to be sexually abused; Quintilian's rhetorical exercises may reflect this earlier state of affairs, which was also the case in Greek law, see Carey (1993); cf. D 48.5.24pr, Ulpian 1 *de adulteriis*, which cites Solon and Dracon as demanding 'in the very act'.

65. D 22.5.14, Papinian *de adulteriis* and 22.5.18, Paul 2 *de adulteriis*, may go back to the Republican situation, joked about by Plautus.

66. For example, it was *iniuria* to abduct the chaperones of a respectable woman or a boy – *Coll.* 2.5.4, Paul.

67. Acron. *in Horat. Sat.* 2.1.46, ed. Orelli: 'prius adulterii poena pecuniaria erat' – crudely, a ransom when he was caught in the act; cf. D 12.5.4pr, Ulpian 26 *ad ed.*; 4.2.7.1, Ulpian 11 *ad ed.* However, this became *lenocinium* under the *lex Iulia*.

68. D 23.4.5pr, Paul 7 *ad Sab.*; Ulpian *Reg.* 6.12-13; cf. D 24.3.39, Papinian 11 *quaest.*; CTh 3.13.1 (349); Watson (1967), 29.

69. Giunti (1990); Nörr (1981); Raditsa (1980), esp. 334-9; cf. Horace *Odes* 4.5.21ff. See also Andréev (1963) who sees class-hatred as the explanation of the husband's *ius occidendi*, however limited.

70. D 48.5.1, Ulpian 1 *de adulteriis*.

71. CJ 9.9; D 48.5.6.1, Papinian 1 *de adulteris*; 50.16.101, Modestinus 9 *diff.*

72. D 48.5.28.16, Ulpian 3 *de adulteriis*.

73. E.g. D 48.5.11.2, Papinian 2 *de adulteris*; 48.5.15.1, Scaevola 4 *reg.*; 48.5.30.8, Ulpian 4 *de adulteriis*.

74. E.g. D 48.5.6.2, Papinian 1 *de adulteris*; 48.5.30.5, Ulpian 4 *de adulteriis*.

75. E.g. overtly D 48.5.2.5, Ulpian 8 *disp.*; 48.5.12(11).13, Papinian *de adulteris*; 48.5.14(13).1, Ulpian 2 *de adulteris*, citing Africanus.

76. Suet. *Aug.* 5; Tac. *Annals* 2.85; 3.22-3; 4.42; 6.48; but 2.50 & 3.38 seem to refer to senatorials tried by a *quaestio*.

77. Based on Dio 76.16; see Brasiello (1962); Garnsey (1967); Bauman (1968); Pugliese (1982), 745.

78. D 48.5.18.6, Ulpian 2 *ad l. Iuliam de adulteriis*.

79. D 48.2.3, Paul 3 *de adulteriis*.

80. CJ 9.9.1 (197).

81. PS 2.26.11; CJ 9.9.22 (290); 9.9.24(25) (291); CTh 9.7.1 = CJ 9.9.28 (326). The term *materfamilias* covered widows as well as married women – D 48.5.11pr, Papinian 2 *de adulteriis*. Presumably the kind of girl who would on marriage become a *materfamilias* was also implied, but spinsters were not a Roman concept, partly as a consequence of Augustus' *lex Iulia de maritandis ordinibus* penalizing the (rich) unmarried and childless.

82. D 48.5.6pr, Papinian 1 *de adulteris*; CJ 9.9.24(25) (291).

83. PS 2.26.16; CJ 9.9.23pr (290); 9.9.(24) (Arcadius).

84. CJ 9.9.25(26) (293).

85. D 48.5.14.3, Ulpian 2 *de adulteris* – here a rescript of Severus and Caracalla amplified the scope of the law; *Coll.* 4.6.1, Paul; cf. CTh 3.5.4 (332); Rizzelli (1987). See also, re D 48.5.12.7, Papinian *de adulteris*, Ankum (1987) and Daube (1955) at end. Daube holds that the father probably became infamous, and that the text reveals that there had been recent legislation allowing a *sponsa* to be accused *iure mariti*.

86. PS 2.26.12. The Romans did not legislate about lesbian relationships.

87. D 48.5.13, Ulpian 1 *de adulteriis*: 'sciens dolo malo'; cf. 48.5.44pr, Gaius 3 *ad leg. XII T*, citing Julian; CJ 9.9.20 (290).

88. D 48.5.14.5, Ulpian 2 *de adulteris*.

89. D 48.5.12.12, Papinian *de adulteris*.

90. CJ 9.9.34(35) (421).

91. PS 5.4.1, 4-5, 14. *Iniuria* could even include, it seems, a man exposing himself – *inferiore parte corporis nudatus* – PS 5.4.21; cf. Josephus *AJ* 20.108. The corruption of a pre-pubertal girl was also criminal – PS 5.22.5.

92. D 50.16.101pr, Modestinus 9 *diff.*: Modestinus can still say 'quidam putant' of the distinction.
93. CJ 9.9.29(30) = CTh 9.7.2 (326); Constantine seems to have thought that there was no time limit for husbands.
94. D 48.5.21, Papinian 1 *de adulteriis*; 48.5.23pr, 2, idem; PS 2.26.1; *Coll.* 4.2.3, 5, Paul; 4.8.1, Papinian; 4.12.1, Paul.
95. D 48.5.23.3, Papinian 1 *de adulteriis*.
96. D 48.5.22, Ulpian 1 *de adulteriis*; 48.5.24.1, ibid.; PS 2.26.2; *Coll.* 4.2.4, Paul; 4.7.1, Papinian, allows the father of an emancipated daughter the prior right of accusation but not the right to kill.
97. D 48.5.24pr, Ulpian 1 *de adulteriis*.
98. D 48.5.24.2-3, Ulpian 1 *de adulteriis*.
99. *Coll.* 4.2.6-7, Paul; 4.9.1, Papinian.
100. D 48.5.24.4, Ulpian 1 *de adulteriis*.
101. D 48.5.33pr, Macer 1 *de pub. iud.*
102. CJ 9.9.4 (Severus Alexander); PS 2.26.4, 7; *Coll.* 4.3.1-4, Paul; 4.12.3, 6, Paul.
103. D 48.5.25.1, Macer 1 *pub. iud.*
104. PS 2.26.6; *Coll.* 4.3.5, Paul, and 4.10.1, Papinian, which state that otherwise he would be liable for the killing; 4.12.5.
105. D 48.5.26pr, 2, 5, Ulpian 2 *ad l. Iuliam de adulteris*; 23.2.43.13, Ulpian 1 *ad l. Iuliam et Papiam*; the *paterfamilias* also could choose this course – 48.5.26.1, Ulpian 2 *ad l. Iuliam de adulteris*; PS 2.26.3. See Rizzelli (1990) 459-64. It is not clear quite what evidence was admissible.
106. D 48.5.26.3-4, Ulpian 2 *ad l. Iuliam de adulteris*.
107. *Coll.* 4.10.1, Papinian. The explanation given by Papinian (D 48.5.23.4, 1 *de adulteris*) was that the passion of a husband might need to be restrained from jumping to conclusions over-readily.
108. PS 2.26.8; *Coll.* 4.12.7, Paul.
109. D 48.5.39.8, Papinian 36 *quaest.*, citing Marcus Aurelius with Commodus, and Antoninus Pius; PS 2.26.5; *Coll.* 4.3.6, Ulpian, citing a rescript of Marcus Aurelius and Commodus, and a pardon granted by Caracalla; *Coll.* 4.10.1, Papinian; 4.12.4, Paul.
110. D 29.5.3.3, Ulpian 50 *ad ed.*
111. D 48.5.39.9, Papinian 36 *quaest.*
112. CJ 9.9.2 (199), else he was liable for *lenocinium*, but this did not apply if he had merely a suspicion, only if the adultery was so notorious that he could not feign ignorance – CJ 9.9.2 (199); 9.9.17.1 (257).
113. D 48.5.12.13, Papinian *de adulteris*; CJ 9.9.17.1 (257).
114. D 48.5.12.6, Papinian *de adulteris*; 48.5.15.2, Scaevola 4 *reg.*; CJ 9.9.6 (223). The period when a husband was holding a magistracy was not viewed as 'available', and so the better view was that the right of the *paterfamilias* should also be suspended along with that of the husband – D 48.5.16pr, Ulpian 2 *de adulteriis*.
115. D 48.5.4pr, Ulpian 8 *disp.*
116. D 48.5.12.5, Papinian *de adulteris*; CJ 9.9.21 (290).
117. D 48.5.4.1, Ulpian 8 *disp.*
118. D 48.5.4.2, Ulpian 8 *disp.*
119. D 48.5.12.6, Papinian *de adulteris*; CJ 9.9.6 (223).
120. Thomas (1970).
121. Implied in D 48.5.12.4, Papinian *de adulteris*, and stated in CJ 9.9.5

(223). CJ 9.9.27(28) (295), provided this period for accusing the woman too, clearly being aimed in part against hasty marriage to evade the law.

122. D 48.5.2.8, Ulpian 8 *disp.*; 48.5.3, Ulpian 2 *de adulteriis*.

123. D 48.5.6.2, Papinian 1 *de adulteris*; 48.5.38, Papinian 5 *quaest.*

124. D 48.5.6.3, Papinian 1 *de adulteris*.

125. D 48.5.4pr, Ulpian 8 *disp.*

126. D 48.5.16.5, Ulpian 2 *de adulteriis*.

127. D 48.5.2.9, Ulpian 8 *disp.*

128. D 48.5.16.6, Ulpian 2 *de adulteriis*. The statute itself almost certainly did not limit a minor's rights, but by the time of Ulpian minors no longer had full capacity and a limitation to accusation *iure mariti* is quite likely, just as a freedman or an *infamis* could accuse his own wife by a husband's right despite the former's disability *more maiorum* and the latter's statutory restriction – 48.2.4, Ulpian 2 *de adulteriis*; 48.2.8 & 11pr, Macer 2 *pub. iud.*

129. D 48.5.16.7, Ulpian 2 *de adulteriis*.

130. CJ 9.9.11 (226). It is not clear whether 9.9.29(30).2 (326) changes this.

131. Implied in CTh 9.7.7 = CJ 9.9.32 (392).

132. Not certainly in her husband's adultery – CJ 9.9.1 (197).

133. CJ 9.9.7.1 (223): the adult victim of a rape is expected to pursue her wrongs with the assistance of her curators.

134. D 48.5.14.9-10 & 6, Ulpian 2 *de adulteris*: 'for it is too late for him to impugn the morals which he has sanctioned by marriage.'

135. D 48.5.2pr, Ulpian 8 *disp.*; 48.5.5, Julian 86 *dig.*; 48.5.16.8, Ulpian 2 *de adulteriis*; CJ 9.9.12(14) (239), with the exception of when the charge was laid before her new marriage.

136. CJ 9.9.8 (224).

137. D 48.5.18.6, Ulpian 2 *ad l. Iuliam de adulteriis*; 48.5.20.3, ibid.; CJ 9.9.13(12) (240).

138. D 48.5.20.2-3, Ulpian 2 *ad l. Iuliam de adulteriis*. CJ 9.9.26(27) (294): Commissum ante adulterium cum eo cui se postea nuptiis sociavit velamento matrimonii non extinguitur.

139. D 48.5.8(7.1), Papinian 2 *de adulteriis*; 48.5.16.9, Ulpian 2 *de adulteriis*. PS 2.26.10 allows two male adulterers, but not more, to be accused at the one time; perhaps this arose from a particular case? or else was a misunderstanding of a husband's right to accuse an *adulter* when already accusing two other persons of other crimes.

140. D 48.5.12.4, Papinian *de adulteris*; 48.5.18.7-20pr, Ulpian 2 *ad l. Iuliam de adulteriis*.

141. D 48.5.12.11, Papinian *de adulteris*; cf. 48.5.27pr, Ulpian 3 *disp.*

142. D 48.5.17, Ulpian 1 *de adulteriis*.

143. D 48.5.18.1-2, Ulpian 2 *ad l. Iuliam de adulteriis*; cf. CJ 9.9.12(14) (239).

144. D 48.5.14.4, Ulpian 2 *de adulteris*.

145. D 48.5.14.1, Ulpian 2 *de adulteris*, citing Sextus Caecilius Africanus (himself citing Homer) by whose time an *uxor iniusta* seems therefore to have become liable, but still only *iure extranei* in Papinian's time – *Coll.* 4.5.1, Papinian.

146. CTh 9.7.2 (326), but the *constitutio Antoniniana* (of *c.* 212) must have made such distinctions less material.

147. *Coll.* 4.6.1, Paul; Ankum (1987).

148. D 48.5.14pr, Ulpian 2 *de adulteris*; clearly there is no husband's right of accusation, but her concubinage must be 'respectable'. Daube (1955) thought that her liability was introduced soon after the passing of the *lex Iulia*.

149. CJ 9.9.7 (223); see Ankum (1987).

150. D 48.5.14.7, Ulpian 2 *de adulteris*. Ankum (1985).

151. D 48.5.14.2, Ulpian 2 *de adulteris*. It is clear from Ulpian *Reg.* 13 that it was only senatorials who were forbidden to marry (ex-)prostitutes, although other free born persons were also forbidden to marry a *lena*, a woman manumitted by a pimp or madam, a woman caught in the act of or condemned for adultery, and an actress; cf. D 23.2.43, Ulpian 1 *ad l. Iuliam et Papiam*.

152. PS 2.26.11; CJ 9.9.22 (290); CTh 9.7.1 (326); as Rizzelli (1988) points out, anyone with the capacity to be guilty of *stuprum* could also be guilty of adultery; cf. Ankum (1987).

153. D 48.5.14.8, Ulpian 2 *de adulteris*. Daube (1955) thinks it was because she was not a proper *sponsa* either, and that the implication is that the fiancé would normally have the *ius mariti*; this seems to be true in AD 223 – CJ 9.9.7.

154. CJ 9.9.3 (213).

155. *Coll.* 4.11.1, Papinian; CJ 9.9.6.1 (223).

156. In CJ 9.9.35(36) (532), Justinian laid down the same period, even when the suspect wife had died, in order for the fate of the dowry to be settled.

157. D 48.5.34(33)pr, Marcian 1 de *pub. iud.*

158. D 3.6.9, Papinian 2 *de adulteriis*; this does not suggest that the slave would be fit for much after being put to the question.

159. PS 2.26.9; *Coll.* 4.12.8, Paul; CJ 9.9.31(32) = CTh 9.7.4pr (385). The Code puts it this way round, rather oddly when it was her slaves which classically would be interrogated when she was suspect – though PS allows for the questioning of the husband's also.

160. CTh 9.7.4.1-2 (385); the *interpretatio* sees such plotting by a wife to arise from her adultery. Treason had always been an exception to the rule prohibiting interrogation – CTh 9.6.2, 3 (376 & 397).

161. For more about calumny, *tergiversatio, praevaricatio* and annulments, see chapter VII.

162. D 4.4.37.1, Tryph. 3 *disp.*; *Coll.* 4.4.1, Paul.

163. CJ 9.9.6.1 (223). But Scaevola seems to say – D 48.5.15.3, 4 *reg.* – that he is at risk, even *iure mariti*.

164. CJ 9.9.17pr (257).

165. D 48.5.16.6, Ulpian 2 *de adulteriis*.

166. D 48.5.31pr, Paul 1 *de adulteriis*.

167. D 48.5.2.1, Ulpian 8 *disp.*; CJ 9.9.16 (256).

168. D 48.5.41.1, Paul 19 *resp.*

169. D 48.5.12.3, Papinian *de adulteris*.

170. CJ 9.9.29(30) (326).

171. CJ 9.9.10 (225); a soldier who made a pact with his wife's lover should be dismissed the service and deported – D 48.5.12pr, Papinian *de adulteris*.

172. D 48.5.32, Paul 2 *de adulteriis*.

173. D 48.5.12.2, Papinian *de adulteris*.

174. CJ 9.9.14(13) (242), but the original accusation could not be made in her absence – CJ 9.9.15pr (242).

175. D 48.5.18.4-5, Ulpian 2 *ad l. Iuliam de adulteriis*. For an absent military husband, see CJ 9.9.19 (287).

176. CJ 9.9.12(14) (239).

177. D 48.5.16.1-2, 4, Ulpian *de adulteriis*.

178. D 48.5.16.3, Ulpian *de adulteriis*.

179. D 48.5.16.4, Ulpian *de adulteriis*.

180. CTh 9.7.9 (393).

181. D 48.5.12.8-9, Papinian *de adulteris*.

182. CJ 9.9.25(26) (293).

183. CTh 9.7.7 = CJ 9.9.32(33) (392).

184. CJ 9.9.27(28) (295).

185. PS 2.26.14; PS probably reflects the state of affairs at the end of the third century. Cf. Pliny *Ep.* 6.31.5.

186. Kaser (1949).

187. D 48.5.30.1, Ulpian 4 *de adulteriis*; CJ 9.9.9 (224); 9.9.17.1 (257).

188. D 34.9.13, Papinian 32 *quaest.*

189. Ulp. *Reg.* 13.2; 16.2; D 23.2.43.12-13, Ulpian 1 *ad l. Iuliam et Papiam*.

190. D 22.5.14, Papinian *de adulteriis*; 22.5.18, Paul 2 *de adulteriis*; 28.1.20.6, Ulpian 1 *ad Sab.*

191. D 22.5.14, Papinian *de adulteriis*.

192. D 48.5.43, Tryphoninus 2 *disp.*

193. D 47.11.1.2, Paul 5 *sent.*; the capital sentence mentioned in CJ 9.9.9 (224), must refer to exile.

194. CJ 9.9.29(30), 4 (326). However, Ammianus 28.1.16 remarks on its infliction as an instance of the cruelty of Valentinian I, so it may have been seldom enforced; CTh 11.36.4 (339) imposes the penalty of the sack on adulterers.

195. CJ 9.10.1 (326).

196. CTh 11.36.4 (339); it was not taken into CJ.

197. See Solazzi (1943); Rizzelli (1990); Formigoni Candini (1990).

198. D 48.5.2.2, Ulpian 8 *disp.*; 48.5.13, Ulpian 1 *de adulteriis*. The word *leno* (and its derivatives), meaning a pimp or procurer, and linked with *meretrix*, are much older, being common in Plautus.

199. CTh 15.8.2 (428).

200. Including women – D 48.5.11(10).1, Papinian 2 *de adulteriis*.

201. Although he was infamous by reason of his trade as *leno*, even if he held himself out to be *caupo*, *stabularius* or *balneator*; this infamy seems to be the penalty rather than that of the *lex Iulia* – D 3.2.4.2, Ulpian 6 *ad ed.*; s.3 extended this on manumission to the former slave who had prostituted the slaves in his *peculium*. The infamous but non-criminal status of the *leno* is confirmed from the disabilities expressed in D 3.1.1.8, Ulpian 6 *ad ed.*, as applying to the infamous.

202. D 23.2.43pr-9, Ulpian 1 *ad l. Iuliam et Papiam*; 38.1.38pr, Callistratus 3 *ed. mon.*; more spectacularly, 23.2.47, Paul 2 *ad l. Iuliam et Papiam*; cf. Suet. *Tib.* 35; restricted in SHA *Hadrian* 18. The neatest expression I know is in D 12.5.4, Ulpian 26 *ad ed.*, where money given to a prostitute cannot be recovered by the *condictio ob turpem causam*: 'illam enim turpiter facere, quod sit meretrix, non turpiter accipere, cum sit meretrix'; on which see Formigoni Candini (1991).

203. A woman who became a madam to avoid the penalty of adultery which her 'respectable' status would otherwise have incurred, fell under the resolution of the Senate extending the *lex*: D 48.5.11.2, Papinian 2 *de adulteriis*; cf. Tac. *Annals* 2.85.

204. D 48.5.2.2, Ulpian 8 *disp.*; 48.5.30(29)pr, Ulpian 4 *de adulteriis*; D 48.2.3.3, Paul 3 *de adulteriis*; CJ 9.9.2 (199); 9.9.11 (226); PS 2.26.8 = *Coll.* 4.12.1.7. The complaisant husband might be proceeded against *de plano* by the judge hearing the adultery charge, as happened under Severus: D 48.5.2.6, Ulpian 8 *disp.*

205. D 24.2.9, Paul 2 *de adulteriis.*

206. D 48.5.12.10, Papinian *de adulteris.*

207. D 48.5.30(29).1, Ulpian 4 *de adulteriis*; CJ 9.9.9 (224).

208. D 23.2.26, Modestinus 5 *resp.*, but this may apply only where she has no defence (other than rape?) because she was caught in the act; cf. 23.2.43.12-13, Ulpian 1 *ad l. Iuliam et Papiam*; 29.1.41.1, Tryph. 18 *disp.*

209. D 48.5.12.13, Papinian *de adulteris.*

210. D 48.5.2.5, Ulpian 8 *disp.*; cf. the need for the husband to set an example of virtue – 48.5.14.5, Ulpian 2 *de adulteris*. This last is a very odd text, because it suggests mutual condonation as a good thing, not as *lenocinium*; presumably it is Justinianic.

211. D 48.5.30.3-4, Ulpian 4 *de adulteriis.*

212. CJ 9.9.10 (225).

213. CJ 9.9.17pr (257) – and recall his wife.

214. D 4.2.7.1, Ulpian 11 *ad ed.*; the references to the risk of death make it clear that the jurist was thinking of a husband, or father, catching the couple *in flagrante.*

215. D 4.2.8.2 & pr, Paul 11 *ad ed.*; 48.2.3.3, Paul 3 *de adulteriis*; 48.5.11(10).1, Papinian 2 *de adulteriis* (on women); 48.5.15(14)pr, Scaevola 4 *reg.*; 48.5.30.2, Ulpian 4 *de adulteriis*; CJ 9.9.10 (225); 9.9.23 (290). Rizzelli (1990), 473ff., argues that the explanation given by Ulpian suggests strongly that this was extended from the husband to others; Daube (1972) has pointed out that *ope consilio* covers the principal as well as accomplices.

216. D 48.5.2.2, Ulpian 8 *disp.*; 48.5.9pr, Papinian 2 *de adulteriis*; 48.5.30.3-4, Ulpian 4 *de adulteriis*, but not the husband who merely let the lover go – as in the preceding sentence.

217. D 48.5.34.2, Marcian 1 *pub. iud.*; the extension of liability to women was probably later than the *lex*, as also in 48.5.11.1, Papinian 2 *de adulteriis* – Daube (1972).

218. D 48.2.3.3, Paul 3 *de adulteriis*; 48.5.9, Papinian 2 *de adulteris*; 48.5.10, Ulpian 4 *de adulteriis* – the term *'balneum'* signifies small-scale or private baths; 48.5.11.1, Papinian 2 *de adulteriis*; 48.5.33.1, Macer 1 *pub. iud.*

219. D 48.5.12.3, Papinian *lib. sing. de adulteris*; we have already looked at this case in the context of withdrawing the accusation.

220. CJ 9.9.10 (225) talks of the penalties for compromising with, not just ignoring, the adulter, or prevaricating, and also of someone (a husband presumably) drawing back from an investigation into the truth.

221. D 48.5.15(14).1, Scaevola 4 *reg.*; the Senate, we are told, was responsible for the extension of the *lex Iulia* to this case, and it seems likely that it did arise from a particular case in front of the Senate.

222. D 48.5.9(8), Marcian 2 *de adulteris*. The shape of the text suggests extensions to the statute from adultery in the strict sense – a married woman is more likely to have difficulty in finding an opportunity than a widow, or a man. Also, a woman friend might well be the one to help, which would explain the stress on women too being liable under this chapter of the statute – 48.5.11(10).1, Papinian 2 *de adulteriis.*

223. D 48.5.10(9).1-2, Ulpian 4 *de adulteriis*; 48.2.3.3, Paul 3 *de adulteriis*, but is this, more sinisterly, the man who lends a house into which his friend may lure an unwitting lady? the seduction in 24.2.8, Papinian 2 *de adulteriis*, led to letters of divorce being sent to the lady's husband and, subsequently, relegation for three years for the man.

224. D 48.5.10(9)pr, Ulpian 4 *de adulteriis*, specifying 'amici'.

225. D 48.5.34(33).1, Marcian 1 *pub. iud.*; cf. perhaps 48.5.12(11)pr, Papinian *de adulteris*.

226. CJ 9.9.2 (199), of a husband who only suspected but could not prove the adultery.

227. D 48.5.2.3, Ulpian 8 *disp*.

228. D 48.5.30(29).4, Ulpian 4 *de adulteriis*; CJ 9.9.17.1 (257): ut ignorationem simulare non possit.

229. D 48.5.12.10, Papinian *de adulteris*; CJ 9.9.11 (226). Cf. Guarino (1993).

230. *Lex Iulia municipalis* (*FIRA* i 13), vv. 122-3; D 3.2.1, Julian 1 *ad ed.*; 3.2.4.2-3, Ulpian 6 *ad ed.*; 23.2.43pr-9, Ulpian 1 *ad l. Iuliam et Papiam*. Formigoni Candini (1990), 104, cites, as the sole recorded threat of criminal proceedings in the Republic, Plautus' *Asinaria* 130-3, where a character threatens to lay a charge before the *tresviri*; but this could be for theft or swindling rather than brothel-keeping. Cf. D 5.3.27.1, Ulpian 15 *ad ed.*, on the propriety of rents from brothels; 37.12.3pr, Paul 8 ad *Plaut*.

231. D 48.5.25(24)pr, Macer 1 *pub. iud.* I think, nevertheless, that the term *leno* is here more likely to have meant someone technically 'respectable' but convicted of *lenocinium* than an actual brothel keeper; actors, on the other hand, must often have been objects of adulation, e.g. Juvenal 6.69ff. They all fell outside the provisions of the *lex Iulia de vi* – PS 5.26.2.

232. D 48.5.11(10).2, Papinian 2 *de adulteriis*; 48.5.2.6, Ulpian 8 *disp.*; Suet. *Tib.* 35; *Dom.* 8.

233. Suet. *Cal.* 40; SHA *Sev. Alex.* 24. see McGinn (1989).

234. D 1.6.2, Ulpian 8 *de off. procon.*: impudicitiam turpemque violationem; 1.12.1.8, Ulpian *de off. p. u.*; cf. SHA *Hadrian* 18: lenoni et lanistae servum vel ancillam vendi vetuit, causa non praestita.

235. E.g. D 13.7.24.3, Ulpian 30 *ad ed.*; CJ 4.56.1-3 (223, 223, 225). Cf. McGinn (1990).

236. SHA *Sev. Alex.* 24; *Tacitus* 10; cf. Aurelius Victor 28.6. St Jerome, however, ascribes the abolition of male prostitution to Constantine – *Comm. in Isaiam* 1.2.7.

237. CJ 8.50(51).7 (291). Unless it can be taken as denying a claim with a *turpis causa*.

238. CTh 15.8.1 (343). Presumably the bishop would see that this was observed.

239. CTh 15.8.2 =CJ 11.41.6 (428).

240. NovTh 18 (439).

241. CJ 11.41.7 (457-67). This would seem open to abuse.

242. NovJ 14 (535).

243. *Bas*. 21.2.4.4, the comment of Stephen on D 3.2.4.2.

244. See Boswell (1980); Manfredini (1985); Dalla (1987); cf. Daube (1986). See also Lilja (1983); Williams (1962); Griffin (1976); Cantarella (1988).

245. E.g. Martial 1.90; 7.70.

246. Cantarella (1987) 86-9 (on Greeks), 157, 178; yet another example of the 'private' nature of women's life in the ancient world.

247. D 48.5.35(34).1, Modestinus 1 *reg.*, although it is possible that 'vel puero' is interpolated here to bring homosexuality within the *lex Iulia de adulteriis*; cf. 50.16.101pr, Modestinus 9 *diff*.

248. An attempt – presumably unsuccessful – might amount to *iniuria* – D 47.10.9.4, Ulpian 57 *ad ed.*; PS 5.4.5.

249. E.g. Petronius *Sat.* 9-11; Juvenal 6.33-7; cf. Seneca *controv.* 4.10: 'impudicitia in ingenuo crimen est, in servo necessitas, in liberto officium'. The references to infamy and consequent legal disabilities which have already been cited in relation to prostitution clearly applied, if anything with more force since they had more capacity to lose, to male whores. One of Valerius Maximus' more distasteful tales (6.1.6) has a former male prostitute righteously putting to death his daughter for *stuprum*.

250. The date of the law is uncertain; it must have been passed before 50 BC, because it is referred to in Cicero *ad fam.* 8.12 & 14. It seems to be placed in 227 BC by Valerius Maximus (6.1.7), but he is unreliable, and it remains unlikely that a law would be named after a culprit, despite the *SC Macedonianum*. Ryan (1994) suggests that it provided for a civil suit not a criminal prosecution, at least in Cicero's time.

251. *Stuprum* is seen as *iniuria* in PS 5.4.1 & 4 & 14; Desanti (1990a).

252. Val. Max. 6.1.7; 6.1.10; 6.1.12 – cf. Plut. *Marcellus* 2, where the penalty is given as a fine, which is right for an aedilician prosecution before the tribes, and is confirmed by Quintilian *inst.* 4.2.69, 71, as a fine of 10,000 sesterces (though Quintilian is of very dubious worth as evidence for legal practice in the Empire).

253. Cicero *ad fam.* 8.12 & 14.

254. D 48.5.9(8)pr, Papinian 2 *de adulteris*.

255. Suet. *Dom.* 8; the *lex* is also reliably mentioned as complementary to the *lex Iulia* in Juvenal 2.43-7; Ausonius *epig.* 92.

256. *Coll.* 5.2.1-2 (=PS 2.26.12, 13); cf. *Auct. ad Her.* 4.8.12, which alleged the aggravated death penalty as the traditional penalty for such male rape. D 48.6.3.4, Marcian 14 *inst.*, places it as falling under the *lex Iulia* on *vis*, like any other rape; so too 48.5.30(29).9, Ulpian 4 *de adulteriis*.

257. PS 5.4.14 = D 47.11.1.2); the term he uses is *puer praetextatus*.

258. *Coll.* 5.1, where Moses laid down burning alive for both parties; cf. Leviticus 20.13. See also Paul I *Cor.* 6.9; Aug. *Conf.* 3.8.15; Orosius 1.5.

259. See chapter IV.

260. CTh 9.7.3 = CJ 9.9.30(31) (342), in Pharr's translation.

261. *Coll.* 5.3.1, an enactment of Theodosius, abbreviated in CTh 9.7.6 (390). The Romans seem to have thought that sexual role-playing was always stereotyped. Cf. D 3.1.1.6, Ulpian 6 *ad ed.*, where a catamite is distinguished from a man raped by brigands or the enemy.

262. *Inst.* 4.18.4; NovJ 77 (undated) forbade homosexuality and blasphemy, authorising the Urban Prefect to impose *ultimis suppliciis*; NovJ 141 (559), addressed to the people of Constantinople, was concerned only with homosexual practices, and is a call to repentance, failing which *acerbiores poenas* are prescribed; Procopius *Anec.* 11.34-6, gives castration as the penalty, and NovJ 142 of AD 558 indeed laid that down as the fitting punishment for making eunuchs.

263. D 48.5.30(29).9, Ulpian 4 *de adulteriis*; 48.6.3.4, Marcian 14 *inst.*; CJ 9.12.3 (293). CJ 9.20.1 (213) shows that slave women were also comprised.

264. D 48.6.5.2, Marcian 14 *inst.*, generalizing about the rape of single or married women; 48.6.6, Ulpian 7 *de off. procons.*, concerning a particular abduction of a freeborn boy.

265. CJ 9.9.20 (290).

266. See, however, D 48.5.14(13).7, Ulpian 2 *de adulteriis*, concerning a wife subject to violence while in enemy hands. It seems probable that, as happens even nowadays, many women kept quiet about rape because they felt ashamed – cf. 48.5.40pr, Papinian 15 *resp.*

267. This is why the rather old-fashioned term 'ravisher' seemed appropriate for what may be either abduction with intent to force a marriage or just rape. See Nörr (1986a), 42ff.; Desanti (1986b); Evans-Grubb (1989); cf. most recently (though silent about earlier literature) Haase (1994); see also Goria (1987).

268. CTh 9.24.1.2 (320/6).

269. CTh 9.24.1 (320/6); it is interesting to note that informal manumission must still have been common enough for there to be significant numbers of Junian Latins.

270. CTh 9.24.2 (349).

271. CTh 9.25.1-3 (354, 364, 420).

272. CTh 9.24.3 (374).

273. CJ 9.13.1 (533).

274. NovJ 143 (563).

VI. Offences Against the State

1. See e.g. Rogers (1933), (1952), (1959a & b); Cramer (1951-2); Chilton (1955); Lear (1965); MacMullen (1966); Bauman (1967) & (1974a).

2. Lear (1965), 69.

3. Most recently Cloud (1994), 502.

4. E.g. (as cited by Cloud (1994), 514) taking an army out of one's province, or making unauthorized war; also the original limitation to senators.

5. As with Milo's successive condemnations in 52 for *vis* and *ambitus*.

6. PS 5.29.1.

7. Cloud (1994) 518. Under the *lex Mamilia* those citizens who had colluded with Jugurtha were condemned, but this was a special court.

8. Cloud (1994), 519.

9. Val. Max. 8.5.2 describes it as a *publica quaestio*; cf. Cicero *de or.* 2.107 & 199.

10. Cicero *Brutus* 89.304; Asconius *in Scaurian.* 22 (Stangl 24-5).

11. Allison & Cloud (1962); Cloud (1963).

12. Dio 44.10.

13. D 48.4.1.1, Ulpian 7 *de off. proconsulis*; 48.4.2, Ulpian 8 *disp.*; PS 5.21A.2; 5.29.1. Carsidius Sacerdos was acquitted in AD 23 of supplying grain to the *hostis* Tacfarinas – Tac. *Annals* 4.13.

14. D 39.4.11pr, Paul 5 *sent.*; CTh 9.40.24 = CJ 9.47.25 (419).

15. D 48.4.3, Marcian 14 *inst.*

16. D 48.4.4pr, Scaevola 4 *reg.*; 48.4.10, Hermogenianus 6 *iuris epit.*

17. Cicero *in Pis.* 21.50; cf. *pro Cluentio* 35.97 & 36.99; II *Verr.* 1.5.12; 4.41.88; 5.20.50; *ad fam.* 3.11.2.

18. D 48.4.1.1, Ulpian 7 *de off. proconsulis*.

19. D 48.4.2, Ulpian 8 *disp.*; 48.4.3, Marcian 14 *inst.*

20. D 48.4.3, Marcian 14 *inst.*; PS 5.29.1; cf. Dio 54.3 on M. Primus making unauthorized war in Macedonia.

21. D 48.4.4, Scaevola 4 *reg.*

22. D 48.4.3, Marcian 14 *inst.* 'Temere' seems the better reading, and surely must govern both forms of surrender. To abandon one's *imperium* presumably here implies cowardice, as generals must sometimes have needed sick-leave.

23. D 49.16.6.4, Arrius Menander 3 *de re militari*; 49.16.3.4, Modestinus 4 *de poenis*.

24. D 48.4.2, Ulpian 8 *disp.*; 49.16.3.10-11, Modestinus 4 *de poenis*; 49.16.5.1, Arrius Menander 2 *de re militari*.

25. D 49.16.6.1, Arrius Menander 3 *de re militari*; 49.16.13.4, Macer 2 *de re militari*.

26. D 48.4.7.4, Modestinus 12 *pand.*

27. D 48.4.1.1, Ulpian 7 *de off. proconsulis*; CJ 9.8.5pr (397).

28. D 48.4.4pr, Scaevola 4 *reg.*

29. Cicero II *Verr.* 2.41.100; cf. PS 5.26.3.

30. D 48.4.2, Ulpian 8 *disp.*

31. CJ 9.8.1 (223).

32. D 48.4.3, Marcian 14 *inst.*

33. D 50.10.3.2, Macer 2 *de off. praesidis*; 50.10.4, Modestinus 11 *pand.*; CTh 15.1.31 (394); cf. Dio 53.23, telling of Cornelius Gallus' exile for putting his name on a pyramid.

34. CJ 9.8.5.2 (397).

35. D 3.2.11.3, Ulpian 6 *ad ed.*, citing Neratius; 11.7.35, Marcellus 5 *dig.*

36. Vespasian on his death-bed joked that he was turning into a god – 'Vae, inquit, puto deus fio' – but actually struggled to rise, saying that an emperor should die on his feet – Suet. *Vesp.* 23 & 24. Caligula may have been mad enough, but his reign is unimportant in the legal sources.

37. D 48.4.4.1, Scaevola 4 *reg.*; presumably the case of AD 22 recorded in Tac. *Annals* 3.70.

38. D 48.4.5pr-1, Marcian 5 *reg.*

39. D 48.4.5.2, Marcian 5 *reg.*; 48.4.6, Venuleius Saturninus 2 *iud. pub.*; cf. 47.10.38, Scaevola 4 *reg.*

40. CJ 11.9.4 (424); 1.23.6 (470).

41. *Coll.* 15.2.1-6, Ulpian 7 *de off. proconsulis*; Cramer (1954). Yet emperors themselves were interested in astrology, e.g. Tiberius – Tac. *Annals* 6.20-1 – or Hadrian – SHA *Hadrian* 14.8; 16.7.

42. D 12.2.13.6, Ulpian 22 *ad ed.*, citing a rescript of Severus and Caracalla; no mention is made of the wrongdoer's status.

43. CJ 9.7.1 (393).

44. D 48.4.7pr-2, Modestinus 12 *pand.*; 48.4.8, Papinian 13 *resp.*

45. D 48.4.7.3, Modestinus 12 *pand.*

46. PS 5.29.2.

47. CJ 9.8.3 (314); PS 5.29.2.

48. D 48.4.9, Hermogenianus 5 *iuris epit.*

49. D 48.2.20, Modestinus 2 *de poenis*; 48.4.11, Ulpian 8 *disp.*; 49.14.22pr, Marcian *de delatoribus*, citing rescripts of Severus and Caracalla; CJ 9.8.6pr, Paul *pub. iud.*; cf. Tac. *Annals* 4.19-20; 6.29 for the early Principate.

50. CTh 9.14.3 = CJ 9.8.5.1 (397); firmly rejected in CTh 9.40.18 = CJ 9.47.22 (399), but the compilers of each code preserved both texts.

51. CJ 9.8.6.2, Marcian 1 *iud. pub.*

52. Sall. *Cat.* 31.4; *invect.* 2.3. Other trials under this statute were those of Caelius in 56 and of a friend of Milo in 52 BC.

53. Lintott (1968), ch. viii, especially pp. 110ff. Gruen (1974), 225-7 does not think that 'contra rem publicam' was necessarily in the *lex Plautia*; it could simply have extended the remit of the *quaestio* to deal with private violence. Cf. for other trials, *Schol. Bob. pro Sulla* Stangl 84; Cicero *pro Sulla* 19.54-21.60; *pro Milone* 13.35; *ad fam.* 8.8.1; *pro Caelio* 29.70; *de har. resp.* 7.15; *ad Att.* 2.24;

pro Sestio 39.84; Asconius *in Milon.* 55 (Stangl 46) re Saufeius; Quintilian *inst.* 9.3.56.

54. Cicero *ad Q. fr.* 2.3.5; cf. D 47.22.2, Ulpian 6 *de off. proconsulis.*

55. Cf. Cicero *pro Caec.* 12.35; D 3.3.42.1, Paul 8 *ad ed.*; 47.10.5-6, Ulpian 56 *ad ed.* & Paul 55 *ad ed.*

56. Longo (1970a), 531, sees a change of interpretation under Constantine, when there was an attempt to include in *vis* any form of violent behaviour; Justinian tried to go back to classical precision.

57. D 43.16.1.2, Ulpian 69 *ad ed.*, is one of the few texts that uses the plural – *de legibus.*

58. Consider D 47.1.3, Ulpian 2 *de off. proconsulis*; cf. 47.8 passim.

59. Cloud (1988a, 1989); Longo (1970a), 475ff., is in agreement about the tralatician nature of the legislation.

60. Pliny *NH* 20.46.117; Tac. *Annals* 4.13, records of AD 23 that the provincial governor of Further Spain was convicted of *vis publica* and deported to an island, but this is only evidence of usage by Tacitus himself.

61. *Inst.* 4.18.8; CTh 9.10, rubric.

62. Livy 10.9.4; this is further argument that there was an Augustan *lex Iulia.*

63. PS 5.26.1, 3; this is the view of classical law held by Vacca (1972), 87.

64. D 48.6.12, Paul *ad SC Turpillianum.*

65. D 48.6.3pr, Marcian 14 *inst.*; arson in such circumstances is specifically mentioned in 48.6.5pr, idem; PS 5.26.3.

66. D 48.6.3.1, Marcian 14 *inst.*

67. PS 5.26.3.

68. D 48.6.7, Ulpian 8 *de off. proconsulis*; PS 5.26.1.

69. Cicero *in Pis.* 4.8; Marshall (1985), pp. 94 & 262-3; Asconius *in Pison.* 7 (Stangl 15); *in Corn.* 75 (Stangl 59). And see below.

70. Gruen (1974), 229.

71. Cicero *pro Plancio* 3.8 & 33.79; *pro Sulla* 31.89-32.90; *pro Sestio* 69.146; Dio 39.37.1.

72. D 47.22 passim; 3.4.1, Gaius 3 *ad ed. prov.*; 47.11.2, Ulpian 4 *opin.*; 50.6.6.12, Callistratus 1 *de cognit.*

73. D 47.22.1pr, Marcian 3 *inst.*; Pliny *Ep.* 10.93; Bruns #175; cf. Duff (1938), 110ff.

74. D 47.22.2, Ulpian 6 *de off. proconsulis.*

75. D 1.12.1.14, Ulpian *de off. p. u.*

76. CJ 9.30.1 (384); 9.30.2 (466).

77. PS 5.22.1; the penalty under the *lex Iulia de vi* became capital for *humiliores* and deportation for *honestiores* – PS 5.26.2.

78. Lintott (1968); Cloud (1988a) & (1989).

79. PS 5.26.2, citing actors, judgment debtors, those who had been led off to jail, or been guilty of contempt of court, or done something against public discipline; similarly, military commanders were not restricted by the *lex Iulia* in their exercise of discipline. Manfredini (1991).

80. D 48.6.7, Ulpian 8 *de off. proconsulis*; PS 5.26.1.

81. D 48.6.8, Maecian 5 [*iud.*] *pub.*

82. Pontenay de Fontette (1954); Lintott (1981).

83. See Richardson (1987).

84. The *tabula Bembina*: *FIRA* i 7; *ARS* #45; Cloud (1994), 508, who cites Stockton (1979) and Lintott (1981), holds it as Gracchan but doubts the role of M'. Acilius Glabrio. Mattingly (1975a) suggested that the Gracchan *lex repetun-*

darum might be the *lex Iunia* which, as the *tabula Bembina* tells us, had come after the *lex Calpurnia*.

85. *FIRA* i 7, vv. 1 & 78.

86. Cicero's comments (*Inv. Rhet.* 1.92; *De or.* 2.199) on the hatred of the equestrian order for the statute suggest that it restored the court entirely to the Senate, and this is what Tacitus thought (*Annals* 12.60).

87. Cicero II *Verr.* 1.9.26; cf. Asconius *in Scaurian.* 21 (Stangl 24).

88. Cicero *pro Rab. Post.* 4.8-9.

89. Cicero *de off.* 2.75. Cicero refers to the Servilian and Cornelian laws in *pro Rab. Post.* although that trial was under Caesar's Julian law.

90. Cicero *ad fam.* 8.8.3 for at least 101 clauses; 2.17.2, like *ad Att.* 6.7.2, refers to the departing governor's depositing his accounts in two leading cities of his province; 5.20.2 refers explicitly to the deposit of another copy of these accounts in the *aerarium*.

91. E.g. accepting money to make military appointments or to give a stated opinion – whether in a formal assembly or in an official advisory body: CJ 4.7.3 (290). cf. D 1.9.2, Marcellus 3 *disp.*, citing Cassius Longinus on the inability of someone removed from the senatorial order for turpitude, as though for *res repetundae*, to act as judge or give evidence; the *lex Iulia de repetundis* did not, however, prohibit someone convicted of calumny from giving evidence – 22.5.13, Papinian 1 *de adulteriis*.

92. Cicero *ad fam.* 8.8; *pro Flacco* 33.82; Val. Max. 8.1.10.

93. D 48.11.1pr, Marcian 14 *inst.*

94. D 48.11.8, Paul 54 *ad ed.*

95. D 48.11.5, Macer 1 [*iud.*]. *pub*; Pliny *Ep.* 3.9; cf. Cicero *pro Rab. Post.* 5.12.

96. D 1.16.4.2, Ulpian 1 *de off. proconsulis*, ascribes this to AD 20; Tacitus refers it to AD 24, after a previous debate in 21 – *Annals* 4.20; 3.33-4.

97. D 48.11.1.1, Marcian 14 *inst.*; 48.11.7.1, Macer 1 *iud. pub.*

98. D 1.16.6.3, Ulpian 1 *de off. proconsulis*; 18.1.46, Marcian *de delatoribus*; 49.14.46.2, Hermogenianus 6 *iuris epit.*; 50.5.3, Macer 2 *de officio praesidis*; cf. 48.11.8.1, Paul 54 *ad ed.*; Cicero II *Verr.* 4.5.9-10 on replacing slaves, to allow more would 'ereptionem esse non emptionem' – not purchase but pillage; in *ad Att.* 5.10.2 & 5.16.3 & 5.21.5, he refers to various allowances lawfully made to governors; cf. D 1.16.4pr, Ulpian 1 *de off. proconsulis*.

99. CJ 2.19.11 (326); 9.27.1 (382); 4.2.16 (408).

100. D 48.11.3, Macer 1 [*iud.*]. *pub.*; 48.11.7pr & 3, idem; PS 5.28.1 applies the ruling to judges delegate.

101. D 48.11.4, Venuleius Saturninus 3 *pub. iud.*; 48.11.9, Papinian 5 *resp.*; cf. 1.16.10.1, Ulpian 10 *de off. proconsulis*.

102. D 48.11.6pr-2, Venuleius Saturninus 3 *pub. iud.*

103. D 48.11.7pr, 2-3, Macer 1 *iud. pub.*

104. There seems to have been a wider scope for *res repetundae* under Caesar's law, before the Augustan legislation, judging by the range of misdeeds of which Piso was accused in 55 BC, such as leaving the province, or dismissal of legates before authorized departure from the province – Cicero *in Pis.* 21.50; 34.83-4; 37.90-1.

105. CJ 9.27.4 (386); 9.27.5 (390).

106. Cicero *Phil.* 1.9.23.

107. Cicero *pro Cluentio* 41.115-16.

108. D 48.11.7.3, Macer 1 *iud. pub.*; PS 3.4.14 & 9 remarks that a man statutorily convicted of *repetundae* had no testamentary powers, whereas someone relegated or sentenced to a spell of forced labour did.

109. D 48.11.2, Scaevola 4 *reg.*; CJ 9.27.1 (382), with a fourfold penalty like 9.27.6 (439); see also 9.27.2 (382); 9.27.3 (383).

110. PS 5.28.1, on the *iudex pedaneus*.

111. Cicero *pro Cluentio* 53.147; *pro Mur.* 20.42; and particularly *de nat. deorum* 3.30.74; cf. I *Verr.* 13.39; II *Verr.* 1.4.11; 3.36.83.

112. Plut. *Pomp.* 2.2 & 4. Was the case of L. Lucullus in 102 BC the *casus* for the creation of a standing court?

113. PS 5.27.1 seems almost to view peculation as a delict with fourfold damages.

114. D 48.13.11(9).2, 4, Paul *iud. pub.*; cf. CJ 9.28.1 (415).

115. D 48.13.1, Ulpian 44 *ad Sab.*

116. D 48.13.8pr(6.1), Ulpian 7 *de off. proconsulis.*

117. D 48.13.8.1(6.2), Ulpian 7 *de off. proconsulis.*

118. D 48.13.15(13), Modestinus 2 *de poenis.*

119. D 48.13.11(9).3, Paul *iud. pub.*, citing Labeo.

120. D 48.13.14(12), Marcellus 25 *dig.*

121. D 48.13.5.4(4.7), Marcian 14 *inst.*

122. D 48.13.10(8), Venuleius Saturninus 3 *iud. pub.*; cf. 48.13.12(10)pr, Marcian 1 *iud. pub.*, where a smaller sum than was actually received was written into the public records.

123. D 48.13.11(9).5, Paul *iud. pub.*

124. D 48.13.2, Paul 11 *ad Sab.*; 48.13.11(9).6, Paul *iud. pub.*, cites Labeo to the effect that a returning governor was, after rendering his accounts, only civilly liable as a private person to the aerarium; under the *lex Iulia*, however, after a year of grace he became criminally liable *de residuis.*

125. D 48.13.5pr-1(4.3-4), Marcian 14 *inst.*

126. D 48.13.11(9).2, Paul *iud. pub.*, citing Labeo.

127. D 48.13.4pr-1, Marcian 14 *inst.*; 48.13.11(9).1, Paul *iud. pub.* One example given was boring a hole through a wall to extract something – 48.13.13(11), Ulpian 68 *ad ed.* See also Robinson (1973).

128. CJ 9.29.1 (380).

129. CJ 9.29.2 (384); 9.29.3 (385).

130. Marcian also tells us for his time – D 48.1.6, 14 *inst.* – that the same court should have jurisdiction in any claim for reparation, even where the criminal charge failed through the death of the accused; cf. 48.2.20, Modestinus 2 *de poenis.*

131. D 48.13.3, Ulpian 1 *de adulteriis.*

132. D 48.13.5.2(4.5), Marcian 14 *inst.*

133. D 48.13.16(14), Papinian 36 *quaest.*

134. D 48.13.4, Marcian 14 *inst.* Cf. 48.13.6(5), Marcian 5 *reg.*; 48.13.7(6), Ulpian 7 *de off. proconsulis*; 48.13.11(9)pr-1, Paul *iud. pub.*; 48.13.13(11), Ulpian 68 *ad ed.*; see also Gnoli (1974a & b).

135. D 48.13.7(6), Ulpian 7 *de off. proconsulis*; PS 5.19.1. D 48.13.11(9)pr-1, Paul *iud. pub.*, also suggests a range of punishment, depending on circumstance; 48.13.12(10).1, Marcian 1 *iud. pub.*, cites deportation for a young man of senatorial family who master-minded an ingenious 'Trojan horse' theft from a temple.

136. D 48.13.9(7), Venuleius Saturninus 2 *iud. pub.*

137. The views of Fascione (1984), the most recent monograph, have not found support.

138. D 48.14.1pr, Modestinus 2 *de poenis*: 'The law is nowadays of no effect in Rome, since the creation of magistrates is a matter for the attention of the emperor and not for the favour of the people.'

139. See particularly Gruen (1968a) & (1974).

140. E.g. Suet. *Vesp*. 2.3; Pliny *Ep*. 3.20; 6.19.

141. PS 5.30A.1, equates this form of *ambitus* with *vis publica*, bringing deportation.

142. D 48.14.1.1, Modestinus 2 *de poenis*.

143. CJ 9.26.1 (400); 9.27.6 (439).

144. E.g. Plut. *Marius* 5.3-4; Dio 36.38.2.

145. Livy 4.25.9-14; 7.15.11-13; 40.19.11.

146. Livy *per*. 47. See Fascione (1984), 44-7.

147. A lost law placed by Gruen (1968a), 124-5 & (1974), 212 in *c*. 120 BC, i.e. between the Gracchan law and the trial of Marius; Cloud points out, (1994), 506, that Cicero, in *Brutus* 34.130, by speaking of the appearance of professional prosecution, attests several *quaestiones perpetuae* by this time. Fascione (1984), 53-9, argues that Mommsen has made us all take for granted that the first *quaestio perpetua* was that created by the *lex Calpurnia repetundarum* of 149 BC, but that there is nothing inherently unlikely – against the same background of special commissions – in a standing jury court being created ten years earlier. Of Cicero's two texts (*de off*. 2.21.75; *Brutus* 27.106), however, it is particularly difficult to interpret the *Brutus* in Fascione's way.

148. Plutarch *Marius* 5; Scaurus and Rutilius also charged each other with *ambitus* in that year – Cicero *Brutus* 30.113; there is nothing explicit about the court, but if Marius was tried by *iudices*, as he must have been to be acquitted on a tied vote – Cloud (1994), 515, e.g. Cicero *ad fam*. 8.8.3 – then so presumably were they.

149. *Schol. Bob. pro Sulla* Stangl 78.

150. Appian *BC* 1.100 describes it as dealing with the order of holding magistracies, and prohibiting anyone seeking to hold the same office for a second time within ten years.

151. Asconius *in Corn*. 69 & 74-5 (Stangl 55 & 58-9); Dio 36.38.

152. Cicero *pro Murena* 23.47; Gruen (1974), 214-15, citing McDonald (1929), argues convincingly (and against Mommsen) that this provides the best explanation of the recorded events.

153. Asconius *in Corn*. 69 (Stangl 55).

154. E.g. *Schol. Bob. pro Sulla* Stangl 79; it was perhaps based on a proposed SC of the previous year – Asconius *in toga cand*. 83 (Stangl 64).

155. Cicero *pro Plancio* esp. 18.45-19.48; *Schol. Bob. pro Plancio* Stangl 152.

156. Asconius *in Pison*. 17 (Stangl 21).

157. Cicero *pro Plancio* 15.36-7; *Schol. Bob. pro Plancio* Stangl 152 & 160.

158. Cf. Cicero *ad fam*. 8.2.1 & 8.4.1; Val. Max. 5.9.2. Gruen (1974), 236-7, argues from the absence of the specifics in the *lex de vi* and from the statements of Appian (*BC* 2.23) and Plutarch (*Cato minor* 48.3) that the law was retroactive, and from the fact that Messalla was prosecuted under both the *lex Licinia* and the *lex Pompeia* (where he thinks the former had previously dealt with all such crimes) that Pompey's law was now the basis of the *quaestio perpetua*. Pliny *pan*. 29.1 certainly praises Pompey's measure; cf. Vell. Pat. 2.47.3.

159. Asconius *in Milon*. 36 (Stangl 34).

160. Asconius *in Milon*. 39 & 53 (Stangl 36 & 46).

161. Tac. *dial. de or*. 38; Dio 40.52.3.

162. Cicero *pro Murena* 32.67; cf. the Eatanswill election in Charles Dickens' *The Pickwick Papers*, ch. 13.

163. Cicero *pro Sestio* 64.133-5; *in Vat.* 15.37; *Schol. Bob. pro Sestio* Stangl 140; cf. *de har. resp.* 26.56.

164. Cicero *in Vat.* 15.37; but he was charged under the more recent *lex Licinia de sodaliciis* – *Schol. Bob. pro Plancio* Stangl 160.

165. Asconius *in toga cand.* 88 (Stangl 68); Marshall (1985), 300-1.

166. Cicero contrasted the ambiguity of *maiestas* with the clarity of *ambitus* – *ad fam.* 3.11.2 – but I think this ambiguity lies at the heart of treason.

167. *Lex Fabia de numero sectatorum*, mentioned in Cicero, *pro Murena* 34.71, but without detail, but probably of the mid-60s; cf. Plut. *Cato minor* 8.2.

168. XII T. 8.27.

169. D 48.14.1.3, Modestinus 2 *de poenis*, mentions this as falling, by resolution of the Senate, under the penalty of the statute that was undoubtedly otherwise dealing with *ambitus*; in 48.6.12, Paul *ad SC Turpillianum*, we are told 'Qui nova vectigalia exercent, lege Iulia de vi publica tenentur'. But was this the same case? the same SC?

170. D 48.14.1.4, Modestinus 2 *de poenis*; cf. 48.10.1.2, Marcian 14 *inst.*

171. *Schol. Bob. pro Sulla* Stangl 78.

172. *Schol. Bob. pro Sulla* Stangl 78-9. The *lex Calpurnia* is also mentioned in Dio 36.21; cf. 37.25; Cicero *pro Murena* 23.46; 32.67. On his own *lex Tullia*, see e.g. *pro Murena* 2.3; 41.89; *in Vat.* 15.37.

173. Dio 37.29.

174. Cicero *pro Murena* 23.47; *pro Plancio* 34.83.

175. Cicero *pro Plancio* 3.8; Dio 39.37.

176. Cicero *pro Cluentio* 36.98; cf. Gruen (1974) 323; D 48.14.1.2, Modestinus 2 *de poenis*.

177. Dio 40.52.3-4.

178. D 48.14.1.1, Modestinus 2 *de poenis*.

179. Crawford (1985), 30ff.

180. Cicero II *Verr.* 1.42.108. See also Grierson (1956); Santalucia (1979).

181. Pliny *NH* 33.132; Cicero *de off.* 3.20.80; Lo Cascio (1979); see also Seager (1994), 180-1.

182. Kocher (1965); Crook (1987a).

183. D 48.10.9pr, 2, Ulpian 8 *de off. proconsulis*.

184. Ulpian's statement (D 48.10.9pr) that adding base metal to gold fell under the law must reflect regulation of the purity of gold, perhaps because payments might be made with gold by weight. Cf. SHA *Tacitus* 9 on the standards of gold and other metals.

185. Grierson (1956), at 251 & 255.

186. CTh 9.21.1 (318); 9.21.3 (326): ut in monetis tantum nostris cudendae pecuniae studium frequentetur; cf. 9.21.10 = CJ 9.24.3 (393). The relative mildness of the penalty laid down in AD 318 makes it clear that this concerned copper coinage.

187. CTh 9.21.6 (349); 9.23.1 (356); 11.21.1 (371).

188. See the citation by Grierson (1956) of Blackstone IV,6,2.

189. D 5.1.53, Hermogenianus 1 *iuris epit.*, allows torture of slaves against their owners when 'rei criminis falsae monetae', though against this is PS 1.12.3.

190. Suet. *Tib.* 58.

191. CTh 9.22.1 (317).

192. CJ 9.24.2, dated 326, which appears to be a conflation of CTh 9.21.3 (326), and 9.21.5 (343) and 9.21.9 (392).

193. CTh 9.21.5 (343).

194. CTh 9.21.9 (392).

195. PS 5.25.1: ... qui nummos aureos argenteos adulteraverit, lavaverit, conflaverit, raserit, corruperit, vitiaverit; D 48.10.8, Ulpian 7 *de off. proconsulis*, refers to those who 'partim raserint partim tinxerint vel finxerint' gold coins, seemingly shaving, rubbing or washing non-gold with gilt.

196. D 48.10.19pr, Paul 5 *sent.*; see Grierson (1956), 244.

197. D 48.10.9.1, Ulpian 8 *de off. proconsulis*.

198. D 48.13.8pr, Ulpian 7 *de off. proconsulis*; Grierson (1956), 246-7, remarks that this may prove the fraudulent origin of the plated *denarii* which have survived from the late Republic and early Empire.

199. D 48.13.8.1, Ulpian 7 *de off. proconsulis*.

200. CTh 9.21.2 (321); 9.21.4 (329); largely reproduced in CJ 9.24.1 dated AD 321.

201. CTh 9.21.6 (349) at Rome.

202. PS 5.25.1; D 48.10.8, Ulpian 7 *de off. proconsulis*.

203. CTh 9.22.1 (317); CTh 9.21.5 (343).

204. Not in CTh 9.38.1-4, between 322 and 368, but from 9.38.6 (381), which includes *const. Sirm.* 8, it was classed among the unpardonable crimes, and defined there as treason as well as in CTh 9.21.9 (389). It is uncertain whether the legislation applied to silver as well as gold coinage; it seems quite likely that it did, since by contrast, coining bronze was explicitly not capital.

205. CTh 9.21.1 (318); 9.21.2, cf. CJ 9.21.2 (326); 9.21.10 (393) is so moderate in its language that it can hardly mean the crime was capital, but presumably refers to Constantine's legislation.

206. CTh 9.21.2 & 4 (321 & 329).

207. CTh 9.23.1 (356); 11.21.1 (371).

208. Sirks (1991); Robinson (1992a), ch. 10.

209. Cf. D 48.19.37, Paul 1 *sent.*; 47.11.6pr, Ulpian 8 *de off. proconsulis*; Pollero (1991). See also chapter VII.

210. D 48.2.13, Marcian 1 *pub. iud.*; 48.12.1, Marcian 2 *inst.*; 48.12.3.1, Papirius Iustus 1 *de const.*

211. Although it had needed legal protection in the Republic too – Livy 38.35; cf. Dio 52.24.

212. D 48.12.2pr, Ulpian 9 *de off. proconsulis*; cf. 47.11.6pr, Ulpian 8 *de off. proconsulis*. For later frauds see e.g. CTh 14.17.6 (370).

213. Later, see e.g. CTh 13.5.38 (414) on corruption within the service.

214. D 48.12.2.1-2, Ulpian 9 *de off. proconsulis*, given as a fine of 20 *aurei*, therefore probably 20,000 sesterces.

215. D 48.19.37, Paul 1 *sent.*; PS 1.20A.1.

216. D 48.12.3pr-1, Papirius Justus 1 *de const.* – I follow Gothofredus' reading of 'invehitur'; PS 1.1A.27.

VII. Other Offences: Against Good Morals or Public Discipline

1. In this category falls the pursuit of those falsely claiming citizenship under the *lex Licinia Mucia* of 95 BC, and perhaps of those guilty of usury.

2. Greenidge (1894); Pommeray (1937).

3. Treggiari (1991), 60-80.

4. G 1.53; D 1.6.2, Ulpian 8 *de off. proconsulis*; *Coll.* 3.2.1, Paul; 3.3.5-6, Ulpian.

5. D 1.12.1.8, Ulpian *de off. p. u.*: saevitiam, duritiam, famem, obscenitatem.

6. Suet. *Tib.* 37; cf. Tac. *Annals* 3.60-3 – and also 3.36.

7. Gellius *NA* 2.24.1-14; Cicero *ad Att.* 12.36.1; *ad fam.* 7.26.2; Plut. *Sulla* 35; Dio 43.25. See also Slob (1986).

8. Gellius *NA* 2.24.15, citing the jurist Ateius Capito; Tac. *Annals* 2.33; 3.52ff.; Dio 57.15.

9. Suet. *Tib.* 34; *Claudius* 38; *Nero* 16; Dio 65.10.

10. *ILS* 642 = *CIL* III 2, 824ff., esp. ii 19-21; *ARS* #299 §7; cf. Lactantius *de mort. pers.* 7.6.7.

11. Livy 35.41, of 192 BC; Cato *de r. r.* pr. 1; Festus p. 259 on *quadruplatores*.

12. G 4.23; Tac. *Annals* 6.16ff.; CJ 2.11.20 (290); CTh 2.33.1.2 (325); cf. D 47.11.6pr, Ulpian 8 *de off. proconsulis*, which probably also included usurers.

13. CTh 2.33.2 (386) imposes a penalty for the future of fourfold restitution, for the past of twofold; CJ 4.32.28 (529).

14. SHA *Sev. Alex.* 24; Suet. *Vesp.* 23 – cf. Robinson (1992a), 121; D 30.39.5, Ulpian 21 *ad Sab.*; Dio 55.25 & 31.

15. NovVal 15 (444-5); NovVal 24 (447).

16. de Laet (1949); Palmer (1980).

17. CJ 4.63.4 & 6 (408 or 409); cf. CTh 9.23.1 (356).

18. E.g. D 49.14.1, Callistratus 1 *de iure fisci*; 34.9.1, Marcian 6 *inst.*; PS 5.13.1; CJ 9.41.1pr (196); cf. 9.35.3 (239).

19. D 39.4.11.2, Paul 5 *sent.*

20. E.g. D 39.4.6, Modestinus 2 *de poenis*; 39.4.12, Ulpian 38 *ad ed.*; CTh 11.7.1 (313); 1.16.11 (369); 11.8.1 = CJ 10.20.1 (397); 8.10.3 = CJ 12.61.3 (400), 4 (412). And see later in this chapter.

21. See Robinson (1992a), 162-8; 202-5.

22. D 11.5.1, Ulpian 23 *ad ed.*; 11.5.2pr, Paul 19 *ad ed.*

23. *Lex Cornelia de aleatoribus*: Cicero *Phil.* 2.23.56; D 11.5.3, Marcian 5 *reg.*

24. D.11.5.2.1, Paul 19 *ad ed.*; the *leges Titia* and *Publicia* quoted in 11.5.3, Marcian 5 *reg.*, are otherwise unknown.

25. Horace *Odes* 3.24; 3.58; Martial 5.84; 14.1.3.

26. Suet. *Aug.* 71; Juvenal 1.88-90; Fronto *ad Marcum de or.* 10.10 (Nab. 155).

27. CJ 3.43.1 & 2 (Justinian); NovJ 123.10.

28. *Lex repetundarum* of the *tabula Bembina* v. 16; *tabula Heracleensis* vv. 104 & 112-13; D 3.2.1, Julian 1 *ad ed.*; 3.2.2.5, Ulpian 6 *ad ed.*; 3.2.4.2-3, idem; cf. CJ 11.41.4 (394).

29. PS 5.26.2; Augustus restricted this power to the times of the games or at the theatre, but he himself could be severe with performers who overstepped the mark – Suet. *Aug.* 45; cf. Tac. *Annals* 1.77.

30. Tac. *Annals* 4.14; 13.25.

31. D 48.5.25pr, Macer 1 *pub.* [*iud.*]

32. D 48.5.11.2, Papinian 2 *de adulteriis*; cf. CTh 9.7.1 =CJ 9.9.28 (326); Suet. *Tib.* 35.

33. There appears to be a link in Suet. *Tib.* 36.

34. Suet. *de rhet.* i; Gellius *NA* 15.11.1; Val. Max. 1.3.3.

35. Suet. *de rhet.* i: praeter consuetudinem ac morem maiorum fiunt; Gellius *NA* 15.11.2.

36. Pliny *Ep.* 3.11; Gellius *NA* 15.11.3-5 refers to a SC authorising their expulsion under Domitian.

37. Dio 67.13.2-3.

38. Lucian in his biography of Peregrinus Proteus, who was converted first to Christianity and then to Cynicism; Philostratus in his life of the sophist, Apollonius of Tyana – see Dzielska (1986). So too did Tertullian, *apol.* 46.4.

Similarly, Simon Magus and the gnostics, significant if heretical in the Early Church, were close to being classifiable as astrologers.

39. Eusebius *HE* 6.3.9.

40. Despite D 48.19.5pr, Ulpian 7 *de off. proconsulis*, citing Trajan; but cf. 48.10.15.1-2, Callistratus 1 *quaest*. See also Sordi (1983), 29f.

41. Cf. Suet. *Tib*. 36, where all astrologers were banished, except those who asked for pardon and undertook to make no further predictions; Dio 57.15.8.

42. Gellius *NA* 1.9.6.

43. Tac. *Hist*. 1.22; Gellius *NA* 14.1; Ammianus 16.8.2; 19.12.14.

44. CJ 9.18.1 (Caracalla).

45. Dio 49.43.5; 56.25; cf. on the early second century BC, Livy 39.8.3; 39.16.8. Pliny *NH* 18.8.42, tells us of aediles prosecuting for magicking away crops.

46. Suet. *Tib*.36 & 63; Tac. *Annals* 2.32 and Dio 57.15.8 put the SC in AD 16.

47. *Coll*. 15.2.1-2, Ulpian.

48. Tac. *Annals* 12.52; Philostratus *A of T* 4.35 (cf. 5.19); Suet. *Vit*. 14; Tac. *Hist*. 2.62; Dio 65.9; 65.13; Suet. *Dom*. 10; Philostratus *A of T* 7.4; Pliny *Ep*. 3.11.

49. *Coll*. 15.2.3-6, Ulpian; D 48.19.30, Modestinus 1 *de poenis*.

50. CJ 9.18.2 (294); *Coll*. 15.3, from the *Codex Gregorianus*, citing a rescript of Diocletian and Maximian to a proconsul of Africa. It is possible that this refers to Christians, since the *Collatio* was probably compiled under Jewish rather than Christian influence.

51. PS 5.21.1-3.

52. PS 5.21.4.

53. PS 5.23.17-18.

54. CTh 9.16.9 (371); 16.10.1.

55. *Coll*.15.2, Ulpian; PS 5.21; CTh 9.16.3 = CJ 9.18.4 (321/4); 9.16.9 (371).

56. CTh 9.16.1-2 = CJ 9.18.3 (319); 16.10.1 (320/1).

57. CTh 9.16.4-5 = CJ 9.18.5-6 (357); 9.16.6 = CJ 9.18.7 (358).

58. CTh 9.16.12 = CJ 1.4.10 (409); Desanti (1991).

59. CTh 9.16.7 (364) & 8 = CJ 9.18.8 (370/3) & 11 = CJ 9.18.9 (389).

60. G 1.27; CJ 6.1.3 (317/23).

61. *FV* 6; CJ 4.55.4 & 5 (224 & 225).

62. D 28.3.6.5, Ulpian 10 *ad Sab*.; 40.13.3, Pomponius 11 *ep. et var. lect.*; 1.5.21, Modestinus 7 *reg*.; 40.12.23, Paul 50 *ad ed*.; CJ 7.18.1 (239); *Inst*. 1.3.4; 1.16.1. Cf. D 48.19.14, Macer 2 *de re mil*.

63. G 1.91; 1.160. PS 2.21a; Ulpian *Reg*. 11.11; cf. CTh 4.12.5, 6 (362 & 366); 10.20.10 = CJ 11.8.7 (380); Tac. *Annals* 12.53; Suet. *Vesp*. 11.

64. D 37.14.5, Marcian 13 *inst*.; 25.3.6.1, Modestinus *de manumiss.*, citing Commodus; 4.1.6, Ulpian 13 *ad ed*.; 40.9.30pr, Ulpian 4 *ad leg. Ael. Sent.*; 4.2.21pr, Paul 11 *ad ed*.; 50.16.70pr, Paul 73 *ad ed*.; 40.2.15, Paul 1 *ad leg. Ael. Sent.*; CJ 6.7.1 (214); CTh 4.10.1 = CJ 6.7.2 (332), 2 = CJ 6.7.3 (423), 3 = CJ 6.7.4 (426); NovVal 24; *Inst*. 1.16.1; Suet. *Claudius* 25; Tac. *Annals* 13.26f.; Dio 60.13.

65. D 11.4.2, Callistratus 6 *cogn.*; PS 5.22.6. Tac. *Annals* 13.26-7

66. G 4.44; CJ 7.20.2 (294); 9.21.1 (300); cf. CTh 9.20.1 = CJ 9.31.1 (378); *Inst*. 4.6.13; cf. Quintilian 3.6.19; Suet. *Claudius* 25 refers to usurpation of equestrian status punished with confiscation; Pliny *NH* 33.2.33; Dio 78.13.

67. Cicero *Balb*. 21.48; *Brutus* 16.63; cf. Livy 41.8.9.

68. Cicero *Balb*. 23.52; *ad Att*. 4.18.4; *de off*. 3.11.47; Val. Max. 3.4.5; Dio 37.9.5.

69. Suet. *Claudius* 25 where we are told that those who usurped citizen privileges were executed (on the Esquiline); cf. *Claudius* 15.

70. CJ 9.25.1 (293); cf. PS 5.25.11, where such change was fraudulent. D

48.10.13pr, Papinian 15 *resp*. Suet. *Claudius* 25 forbidding peregrines to use the *tria nomina*.

71. PS 5.25.12; 48.10.27.2, Modestinus 8 *reg*.; cf. 48.10.13.1, Papinian 15 *resp*.

72. D 48.3.13, Callistratus 6 *de cognit*.

73. D 48.3.4, Ulpian 9 *de off. proconsulis*.

74. Cicero *de leg*. 2.8.19-9.22. C. Rabirius was prosecuted before *iudices* in 73 for violating sacred groves (Cicero *pro Rab. perd*. 7); this was presumably a *quaestio extraordinaria*, like the *Bona Dea* affair. See also Robinson (1975).

75. This explains why our sources are more literary than legal.

76. Cicero *de leg*. 2.8.19; 2.9.22; 2.10.25; Tac. *Annals* 1.73; cf. Dio 57.8-9; Severus Alexander – CJ 4.1.2 (223).

77. Livy 39.8-19; *FIRA* i 30 (pp. 240f.); dealt with at great length by Pailler (1988); see also Bauman (1990).

78. Cf. PS 5.23.15-16 which almost certainly reflects the pagan law; the penalties were crucifixion or the beasts – an expression of Roman revulsion.

79. Pliny *NH* 30.4.13; Suet. *Claudius* 25.5; Pliny *NH* 29.12.54; and see Last (1949).

80. Val. Max. 1.3.4.

81. Tac. *Annals* 2.85; Dio 53.2.4; 54.6.6. (The *pomerium* was the ritual City boundary.)

82. Josephus *AJ* 18.65-80.

83. D.48.19.30, Modestinus *de poenis*; PS 5.21.2. (Cf. Livy 4.30.9 for persons turning others' superstitious fears to their own advantage when drought led to plague in 428 BC.)

84. D.48.19.18, Ulpian 3 *ad ed*., though cf. 50.16.225, Tryphoninus 1 *disp*.

85. D.48.19.16.10, Claud. Sat. *de poenis pag*.

86. See Robinson (1990-2) for detail. The problem has been to distinguish conceptually between what the victims – understandably – see as persecution, and the Roman government's attitude of normal indifference and occasional restoring of order.

87. Suet. *Nero* 16.2; like Tacitus, he wrote less than fifty years after the event.

88. Tac. *Annals* 15.44.

89. Tertullian *apol*. 5; Lactantius *de mort. pers*. 2.5-3.1; Eusebius *HE* 4.26.9.

90. Dio 67.14.

91. Pliny *Ep*. 10.96-7; cf. Tertullian *apol*. 2.10.

92. SHA *Sept. Sev*. 17.1.

93. E.g. St Perpetua and Companions – *ACM*; cf. Eusebius *HE* 6.3.3.

94. Lactantius *de mort. pers*. 3.4-4.1.

95. CTh 16.1.2 = CJ 1.1.1 (380).

96. Tac. *Annals* 2.85; Suetonius *Tib*. 36; Josephus *AJ* 18.81-84.

97. Suet. *Claudius* 25; Dio 60.6.6.

98. 'antiquitate defenduntur' said Tacitus, *Hist*. 5.5; cf. Josephus *AJ* 16.6.2.

99. Dio 68.1.2: Nerva 'released all those on trial for treason and recalled the exiles ... and thereafter nobody was permitted to accuse anyone of *maiestas* or of adopting the Jewish mode of life'; see also Eusebius *HE* 3.20.8.

100. D.48.8.11pr, Modestinus 6 *reg*.; cf. 48.8.3.4-5, Marcian 14 *inst*.; 48.8.4.2, Ulpian 7 *de off. proconsulis*; PS 5.23.13. See Smallwood (1959 & 1961).

101. CTh 16.8.1 = CJ 1.9.3 (315); 16.8.5 (335); 16.8.28 (426).

102. CTh 16.8.18 (408).

103. CTh 16.9.1 & 2 = CJ 1.10.1 (339); 16.9.5 (423); milder were 16.9.3 & 4 (415 & 417).

104. CTh 16.8.7 = CJ 1.7.1 (357); cf. 16.8.19 (409).

105. CTh 9.7.5 = CJ 1.9.6 (388).

106. CTh 16.8.9 (393); 16.8.12 (397); 16.8.21 = CJ 1.9.14 (412/18); 16.8.25-7 (423).

107. CTh 16.8.2 (330) & 4 (331); 7.8.2 = CJ 1.9.4 (368/73); 16.8.8 (392) & 9 (393); 16.8.20 (412); 16.10.24 = CJ 1.11.6 (423); although immunity might also mean prohibition on holding office – CTh 16.8.16 (404); 16.8.24 (418); CJ 1.9.18 (439).

108. Mommsen (1887), II 2, 1108, says that Gratian in AD 375 was the first not to use the title.

109. CTh 16.8.19 = CJ 1.9.12 & 1.12.2 (409); CTh 15.4.1 = CJ 1.24.2 (372); CTh 9.44.1 = CJ 1.25.1 (386); *const. Sirm.* 13 (419); CJ 1.12.3 (431).

110. E.g. CJ 1.1.3 (448); NovJ 77.

111. CTh 16.10.3 (342/6); 16.10.15 = CJ 1.11.3 (399); cf. 16.10.14 (396); 16.10.24 = CJ 1.11.6 (423); but 16.10.16 & 19 (399 & 408); 16.10.25 (435).

112. CTh 16.10.4 = CJ 1.11.1 (346/54); 16.10.11 (391).

113. CTh 16.10.19 & 20 (408 & 415).

114. CTh 16.10.8 (382); 16.10.13 (395).

115. CTh 16.10.17 & 18 (399); CJ 1.11.7 (451).

116. CTh 16.2.5 (323); 16.7.1 (381); 16.7.4-5 (391); cf. CJ 1.7.2; CTh 16.7.7 = CJ 1.7.4 (426).

117. E.g. CTh 16.2.31 = CJ 1.3.10 (398); *const. Sirm.* 14 (409).

118. CJ 1.5.12.5 (527).

119. CJ 1.5.18.4 (Justinian).

120. CTh 16.4.1 (386).

121. D 3.6, the title on calumny, is mainly concerned with when money can properly change hands without any 'squalid extortion' – 3.6.1.3, Ulpian 10 *ad ed.*; cf. 48.1.10, Papinian 2 *def.*; CJ 9.46.

122. D 48.2.7.1, Ulpian 7 *de off. proconsulis*; 48.2.18, Modestinus 17 *resp.*

123. D 48.3.6.1, Marcian 2 *iud. pub.* Sometimes these offences counted as *falsum* – 48.10.1.2-3, Marcian 14 *inst.*; 48.10.25, Ulpian 7 *ad ed.*; 48.10.33, Modestinus 3 *de poenis.*

124. D 23.2.43.11, Ulpian 1 *ad l. Iuliam et Papiam*; 47.15.1.1, Ulpian 6 *ad ed.*; however, some jurists held it was possible for there to be *praevaricatio* in an offence against *bonos mores* – 47.15.3pr & 3, Macer 1 *pub. iud.* Those charges where, we are told, an accusation could be dropped without incurring liability under the *SC Turpillianum* were, indeed, offences outside the *iudicia publica* – except for *iniuria* – but the judge could impose punishment at his discretion – D 48.16.7.1, Ulpian 8 *disp.*

125. D 48.16.1pr-1, Marcian *ad SC Turpillianum.*

126. Regularly in Tacitus, e.g. *Annals* 3.37; 4.31; 4.36; 4.66; 11.5-7; 13.5; 13.23; 15.33.

127. D 48.16.10pr, Papinian 2 *de adulteriis*; 48.16.15.5, Macer 2 *pub.* [*iud.*].

128. D 48.16.14, Ulpian 7 *de off. proconsulis*, citing a rescript of Hadrian; cf. CJ 9.1.2 (205).

129. D 48.16.15.3-4, Macer 2 *pub.* [*iud.*]; CJ 9.6.3 (216); the death, naturally, must precede the dropping of the accusation.

130. CJ 9.43.1 (215).

131. D 48.16.8-9, Papinian 2 *de adulteriis* & Macer 2 *pub.* [*iud.*]. Naturally an accuser was under no obligation to renew the charge after the senate had declared such an amnesty – 48.16.12, Ulpian 2 *de adulteriis*.

132. Cicero refers to it in *pro Rosc. Am.* 19.55.

133. D 48.2.3.2, Paul 3 *de adulteriis*; 48.2.7pr, Ulpian 7 *de off.proconsulis*; CTh 9.1.5 (326); 9.1.9 = CJ 9.46.7 (366); 9.1.11 (373); 9.1.14 (383); 9.1.19 = CJ 9.2.17 (423).

134. D 48.16.1.3-5, Marcian *ad SC Turpillianum*; G 4.178; CJ 9.46.3 (Severus Alexander); a 'not proven' verdict could never therefore ground calumny. CTh 9.37.3 = CJ 9.46.9 (382) lays less stress on actual bad faith; cf. CJ 9.46.10 (423).

135. D 48.16.1.13, Marcian *ad SC Turpillianum*; 48.16.15pr, Macer 2 *pub.* [*iud*]; CTh 9.5.1pr = CJ 9.8.3.1 (314); 9.39.2 =CJ 9.46.8 (385).

136. D 48.16.6.4, Paul 1 *sent.*; PS 1.5.1; 1.6B.1e.

137. D 48.16.15.2, Macer 2 *pub.* [*iud.*].

138. CJ 9.9.6.1 (223); 9.46.2 (224); CTh 9.7.2 = CJ 9.9.29.2 (326).

139. D 48.1.14, Papinian 16 *resp.*; 48.2.4, Ulpian 2 *de adulteriis*; CJ 9.46.2 (224); 9.46.4 (283).

140. CJ 9.1.13 (294); cf. 9.1.14 (294); 9.1.18 (304).

141. PS 5.13.3; CTh 9.6.3 = CJ 9.1.20 (397); 9.1.21 (423); Tac. *Annals* 13.10.

142. Tac. *Annals* 4.28-30.

143. CTh 9.39.2 = CJ 9.46.8 (385).

144. Tac. *Hist.* 2.10 describes the trial of an *eques* simply for being a *delator* early in Galba's reign, but professional prosecutors were being defended in the Senate under Vespasian – Tac. *Hist.* 4.44.

145. PS 5.13.1-2.

146. D 48.16.1.6, Marcian *ad SC Turpillianum*; CJ 9.9.10 (225); 9.42.2.1 (319); Tac. *Annals* 14.41; cf. Pliny *Ep.* 3.9.29-33.

147. D 47.15.1, Ulpian 6 *ad ed.*

148. D 47.15.3.1, Macer 1 *pub. iud.*; CJ 9.2.11 (292).

149. Tac. *Annals* 14.41 – for procuring or conducting a collusive action; D 47.15.7, Ulpian 4 *de censibus*; CJ 9.9.10 (225); 9.9.23.1-2 (290).

150. CJ 9.1.3 (222); 9.45.2 (239); CTh 9.36.1 = CJ 9.44.1 (385); CTh 9.36.2 = CJ 9.44.2 (409). The penalty originally seems to have been unspecified punishment *extra ordinem*, and infamy; in the Later Roman Empire, the penalty was confiscation of a quarter of his estate, as well as infamy; those who would not be harmed by infamy – the meaner sort – were to be exiled.

151. CJ 9.42.2pr & 2 (319): 'through error or rashness or anger'; cf. Pliny *Ep.* 5.13, where fear was successfully pleaded, though the advocate had to return his fee.

152. D 48.16.1.7-9, Marcian *ad SC Turpillianum*; permission from the emperor was sufficient – 48.16.13.1, Paul 3 *de adulteriis*; CJ 9.45.1 (Caracalla); cf. 9.45.2 (239); 9.42.2 (319).

153. CJ 9.42.1 (287).

154. D 48.16.15.2, Macer 2 *pub.* [*iud.*]; CJ 9.42.2.1-2 (319); 9.42.3pr (369).

155. D 49.14.15pr, Iunius Mauricianus 3 *ad legem Iuliam et Papiam*; CJ 9.46.1 (Severus Alexander); 9.42.2pr (319).

156. D 48.2.3.4, Paul 3 *de adulteriis*; 48.16.18, Papirius Justus 1 *de const.*

157. CJ 9.42.3.1-3 (369).

158. CJ 9.46.6 (290/3).

159. D 48.16.2, Paul *de poenis omnium legum*; 48.16.4.1, Papinian 15 *resp.*; 48.16.13pr, Paul 3 *de adulteriis*; 48.16.15.4, Macer 2 *pub.* [*iud.*]; PS 1.6B.1-3 (or even his son); CJ 9.1.6 (224); 9.45.3 (258); 9.45.4 (260); 9.42.1 (287); 9.45.6 (Diocletian).

160. CJ 9.9.16.1-2 (256), citing the *lex Petronia* as well as the *SC Turpillianum*; his immunity from calumny did not extend to tergiversation; cf. 9.9.17pr (257).

161. D 48.16.1.14, Marcian *ad SC Turpillianum*.

162. D 48.16.17, Modestinus 17 *resp.*

163. D 48.16.16, Paul *de adulteriis*, citing a rescript of Domitian.

164. See chapter V.

165. D 48.16.1.10, Marcian *ad SC Turpillianum*. Papinian held that a time-barred accuser of adultery could not be held liable for calumny – 48.16.11, *de adulteriis*; after all he had not been able to make his accusation.

166. D 48.2.1 & 2, Pomponius 1 *ad Sab.* & Papinian 1 *de adulteriis*; cf. 3.1.1.5, Ulpian 6 *ad ed.*; CJ 9.1.8 (238); 9.1.10 (239); 9.1.12 (293); 9.1.15 (294).

167. D 48.16.4pr, Papinian 15 *resp.*; cf. CJ 9.45.5 (294).

168. PS 1.1.3-4 & 7.

169. D 48.16.6pr-3, Paul 1 *sent.*; PS 1.6B.1a-1d; CJ 9.1.7 (230).

170. D 48.16.1.11-12, Marcian *ad SC Turpillianum*.

171. D 48.16.7.1, Ulpian 8 *disp.*

172. D 48.16.5, Paul 2 *resp.*

173. D 48.16.7pr, Ulpian 8 *disp.*; PS 5.17.1 allows it only within thirty days.

174. D 48.16.10.1-2, Papinian 2 *de adulteriis*; cf. 48.16.15.6, Macer 2 *pub.* [*iud.*].

175. CJ 9.2.10 (290).

176. PS 5.25.13.

177. PS 5.28.1.

178. D 47.15.2, Ulpian 9 *de off. proconsulis*; 48.16.3, Paul 1 *sent.*; 48.16.15.1, Macer 2 *pub.* [*iud.*]; PS 1.5.2.

179. D 47.15.3.3, Macer 1 *pub. iud.*

180. D 47.15.5, Venuleius Saturninus 2 *pub. iud.*; cf. 47.15.4, Macer 2 *pub. iud.*

181. D 47.15.6, Paul *iud. pub.*; CJ 9.2.17pr (423); cf. G 4.174-81.

182. PS 5.4.11-12.

183. D 48.3.8, Paul *de poenis militum.*

184. D 48.3.10, Venuleius Saturninus 2 *de off. proconsulis.*

185. CTh 9.3.1 (320); 9.3.7 = CJ 1.4.9 (409).

186. D 48.3.12pr, Callistratus 5 *de cognit.*; 48.3.14.1.2, Modestinus 4 *de poenis.*

187. PS 5.31.1.

188. D 48.3.14.3-5, Modestinus 4 *de poenis.*

189. CTh 9.3.1 = CJ 9.4.1 (320); 9.3.5 = CJ 9.4.4 (371).

190. CJ 9.5.1 (486); Robinson (1968).

191. CJ 9.5.2 (529).

192. Noethlichs (1981).

193. MacMullen (1988).

194. CTh 9.1.4 (325); cf. 9.27.6 = CJ 9.27.4 (386), which worryingly begins 'We order, We urge ...'.

195. CTh 9.14.2 = CJ 3.27.1 (391).

196. CTh 9.1.7 (338); 9.17.2 (349); 9.3.6 = CJ 9.4.5 (380); 9.40.14 = CJ 9.47.21 (385); 9.1.18 (396).

197. CTh 9.40.8 (365); 9.27.1 = CJ 12.1.12 (380); 9.1.15 (385); 9.28.1 =CJ 9.28.1 (392).

198. CTh 9.42.7 (369); 9.3.6 = CJ 9.4.5 (380); CJ 9.2.16 (395).
199. CTh 13.5.38 (414).
200. CTh 9.26.1 & 2 (397 & 400); 9.26.3 (416).
201. Tac. *Annals* 3.31: fraude mancipum et incuria magistratuum.
202. XII T. 10.1; 10.10; D 47.12.3.5, Ulpian 25 *ad ed.* citing Hadrian; also Robinson (1975).
203. See Robinson (1992a), 34-8.
204. *FIRA* i 45; *ARS* #172; D 18.1.52, Paul 54 *ad ed.*; cf. 39.2.46, Paul 1 *sent.*; cf. CJ 8.10.3 (224). See also Rainer (1987); Lewis (1989); Robinson (1992a), 42-6.

Glossary of Technical Terms

This Glossary is designed to explain quickly those words which may be unfamiliar; however, the Index should be used for crimes, etc. The use of a classical dictionary is recommended for other institutions of Antiquity. The explanations relate to the period covered by this book, that is, from the last century BC onwards, and to its theme, the criminal law.

aediles: senatorial magistrates, junior to the praetors, who had in the Republic the general care of the City.

agnatic family: the patriarchal citizen family. Our surname system has the same base – a woman is born with, but does not transmit, her surname. Adoption could make someone a full member of an agnatic family, without any blood tie.

album: list of potential *iudices*, for civil causes as well as the standing jury-courts, drawn up annually by the Praetor; roughly comparable to a list of potential jurors in Britain when such service required a property qualification.

annona: the state-organized arrangements for the procurement and distribution of free or subsidized grain, and other foodstuffs, to the citizens of Rome, and Constantinople. The Prefect of the Grain Supply was in charge.

auxilium: the right and duty to bring aid to any unjustly afflicted citizen, which was one of the tribunician powers acquired by the emperors.

capital – as in offence/punishment: something putting at risk not always someone's physical life, as in modern usage, but also his (or her) civic life by status loss – *capitis deminutio*.

capitis deminutio: literally [a group's] reduction by a head; *c. d. maxima* meant loss of free status – of membership of the class of free men, *c. d. media* loss of citizenship, and *c. d. minima* change or loss of agnatic family. The last form was irrelevant to criminal law.

Code: literally a *codex*, a book bound at the spine, as are modern books, in contrast to a scroll. Perhaps because it is much easier for looking things up, the official collections of imperial enactments were in this format. The two Diocletianic Codes – Hermogenianus and Gregorianus – do not seem to have been concerned with criminal law, but the Theodosian Code of 438 had one of its sixteen books devoted to the topic, as Justinian's Code of 534 had one of its twelve.

coercitio: the power of a magistrate or official to enforce his orders in his sphere of office; it has a much wider range than our contempt of court, for it was applicable to offenders against public order.

cognatic: relationships by blood, whether through male or female.

cognitio: a magistrate's right to hear cases (in Scots law, his power to cognosce), but used primarily in contrast to the procedure and penalties of the *ordo*.

collegia: clubs, leagues, organized supporters, guilds; in the late Republic and early Empire the term was pejorative.

comitia: one of the assemblies – usually organized by centuries or by tribes – of the whole (male) Roman citizen body.

commentariensis: a rank below the centurionate, found on the office staff of most magistrates; his function was the keeping of records. At least by the Later Empire and probably before, he was particularly responsible for the custody of those accused, the keeping of records of criminal proceedings, and the supervision of putting into effect any sentence passed.

concilium plebis: the assembly by tribes of all (male) Roman citizens excluding the patricians.

concubinage: a stable relationship between an upper-class man and a lower-class woman, where marriage would have been improper or possibly illegal; not compatible with marriage.

condictio furtiva: an action to recover the value of something stolen, with no penal element.

consilium: a council to give counsel, whether within the family, or to someone holding office, or to the emperor.

constitutio Antoniniana: an edict of the Emperor Antoninus Severus, commonly known as Caracalla, in 212 which gave Roman citizenship to the free inhabitants of the Empire.

Corn Supply: see *annona*.

culleus: the penalty for parricide – being sewn up in a leather sack, perhaps with various animals, and flung into the sea or flowing water.

curia: as a criminal penalty, removal from the *curia* normally meant forfeiture of status as a decurion; probably its original use meant removal from the Senate.

cursus: public post service, i.e. the use of official stages for changing horses.

decurion: member of a town council – the *ordo decurionum*, and so a privileged citizen.

dediticius: a slave who had been condemned for a serious offence, and who was not allowed within 100 miles of Rome (or the emperor).

deportation: permanent exile with loss of citizenship, usually to a particular unpleasant site.

Digest: the edited collection of jurists' writings produced at the order of the Emperor Justinian in 533.

edicts/*edicta*: general enactments issued by the emperor with legislative force.

emancipate: to release by a juridical act from paternal power; cf. manumit.

equestrians/*equites*: the 'gentry' class of the late Republic and early Empire, overlapping at its upper end with senatorial families, and similarly defined by a property qualification.

exercitio iudicii publici: used for individual magistrates, including the emperor, who seem to have enjoyed the same powers as a standing jury court.

extra ordinem: offences dealt with other than by the *quaestiones perpetuae* and the legislation which created them.

familia: sometimes the family by blood, sometimes the extended household, sometimes even wider usage for an emperor.

fustigatio, verberatio, pulsatio: different levels of corporal punishment.

honestiores: the privileged classes of citizen, including veterans honourably discharged from the legions.

HS: the symbol for a sum given in sesterces; see money.

humiliores: the lower orders, the unprivileged within the citizen body.

imperium: the power of life and death inherent in military command, and symbolized by the lictors with fasces attending the two highest magistracies of the Republic, consuls and praetors.

intercessio: a veto on the act of any magistrate by a tribune of the people or the emperor using his tribunician power.

interdictio aquae et ignis: interdiction from water and fire, banishment from Roman territory; as the emperor came to control all territories within the Empire, it was replaced by more specific banishment.

Institutes: an elementary work of Roman law, in particular those of Gaius in the later second century and of Justinian.

iudex: a juror in a *quaestio perpetua*; in later usage, a provincial governor.

iudicia publica: the standing jury courts.

jurist: a man, normally of senatorial or other high rank, who specialized in the interpretation of law, particularly private law, roughly from the late first century BC until the mid-third century AD.

iustae nuptiae: marriage, with the full legal consequences of the father's paternal power over the children.

lex: a statute passed by one of the *comitia*.

manumit: to release from slavery by a juridical act.

matrimonium iniustum/non iustum: a marriage, but without the consequential paternal power.

metus: duress, threats; also a praetorian delict.

minor: a person less than 25 but over puberty, which was when Romans technically came of age.

money: the unit of account in the late Republic and the Principate was the *sestertius*, a silver coin; in the Later Empire sums such as fines were reckoned in gold, the *solidus* or *aureus*, with a rough conversion rate of 1 aureus to 100 sesterces, although there are also texts referring to pounds of gold.

nautae caupones stabularii: ship-masters, inn-keepers and keepers of stables with horses for hire, all of whom were strictly liable for the delicts of their servants because of the poor bargaining position of travellers.

Night Watch: see *vigiles*.

noxal liability/surrender: the vicarious liability of an owner or *paterfamilias* for the delicts of those in his power; he owed the victim reparation but could surrender the actual wrongdoer to work off the damages.

opus metalli: a slightly mitigated form of condemnation to the mines – *in metallum*.

opus publicum: forced labour on public works.

ordo: from perhaps the late second century on the term was used for membership of the decurionate, the governing class of the provincial municipalities – they would have mostly have been described as equestrians earlier.

ordo iudiciorum publicorum: the system of standing jury courts, as finalized under Augustus; variations from the practice of this system were sometimes described as *extra ordinem*, sometimes as falling under *cognitio*.

paterfamilias: the senior ascendant male in an agnatic family; his children, and his grandchildren through his sons, were in his paternal power as long as he lived. He had powers of life and death over them (although these became limited) as well as being noxally responsible for their delicts; he had also the only proprietary capacity in the group. His wife was not (normally) in his power, but in her own agnatic family.

patron: the technical term for the former owner of a former slave, whom he or she has now made a freedman/woman.

peregrine: a non-citizen, a foreigner by legal status, but the term included most (free) inhabitants of the Empire until the *constitutio Antoniniana*, q.v.

plebiscitum: a statute passed by the *concilium plebis*.

praefectus = Prefect.

praetor: a magistrate with *imperium*, and particularly the Urban Praetor who was responsible for all civil process in Rome; praetors were presidents of the *quaestiones*.

pulsatio: see *fustigatio*.

pupil: a child (not in paternal power) under puberty, and therefore to a greater or lesser extent incapable of juristic acts without the intervention of his or her tutor.

quaestio: originally a commission of inquiry; when ad hoc it could be described as *extraordinaria*; a *quaestio perpetua* was a permanent jury court, and this is the normal meaning of the term.

recuperatores: assessors of damages due with some judicial function.

relegation: exile, temporary or permanent, from Rome and the convict's native province, sometimes to a particular site.

rescripts: individual replies from emperors on points of law referred to them.

responsa: the legal opinions of jurists.

sack: see *culleus*.

SC and **SCC** – *senatusconsultum / -ulta*: a resolution or resolutions of the Senate – often equivalent to legislation, but also ad hoc.

sodalicia: see *collegia*.

sodalitates: see *collegia*.

stationarii: troops stationed along major land routes to keep the peace and check smuggling.

status loss: see *capitis deminutio*.

sui iuris: someone, male or female, no longer in paternal power but of independent capacity.

tresviri capitales: minor magistrates – young men who might become senators – with responsibility in the late Republic for fire control and public order.

tutor: the man who supplemented the legal incapacity of a pupil by his authorization and administration.

Urban Prefect: from the early Empire, the magistrate responsible for the administration of the City of Rome.

usucapion: the acquisition by lapse of time of good title to property originally taken in good faith and with good reason.

verberatio: see *fustigatio*.

vigiles: the Night Watch created by Augustus as a fire brigade; their Prefect functioned as the Urban Prefect's subordinate.

vindicatio: a claim to something as its owner.

Bibliography

Abbreviations

For periodicals I have followed the conventions of *L'Année Philologique*, with the following exceptions where either they are not listed or I have kept the normal Roman law usage (*AP* version in brackets):

ACM	*Acts of the Christian Martyrs*, ed. Musurillo
ANRW	*Aufstieg und Niedergang des Römischen Welt*, ed. Temporini, Berlin
AntCl	*L'Antiquité Classique* (AC)
ARS	*Ancient Roman Statutes*, ed. Johnson et al.
CIL	*Corpus Inscriptionum Latinarum*
EFR	*École Française à Rome*
F.	Festschrift for
FIRA	*Fontes Iuri Romani Anteiustiniani*
ILS	*Inscriptiones Latinae Selectae*, ed. Dessau
LQR	*Law Quarterly Review*
RE	*Real Encyclopaedie*, ed. Pauly-Wissowa
RHD	*Revue d'Histoire de Droit* (RD)
TR	*Tijdschrift voor Rechtsgeschiedenis* (RHD)
St.	Studies/Essays in honour of
SZ	*Savigny-Stiftung Zeitschrift*, Römanische Abteilung (ZRG)

Albanese, B. (1959) 27 *ASGP*, 5-152, 'Actio servi corrupti'.
—— (1967) 70 *BIDR*, 119-86, 'Sulla responsibilità del *dominus sciens* per i delitti del servo'.
—— (1976) 36 *ASGP*, 289-365, 'Sul senatoconsulto Liboniano'.
—— (1979) *St. Musotto* II, 5- 'Vitae necisque potestas paterna e lex Iulia de adulteriis coercendis'.
—— (1982) 48 *SDHI*, 455-70, 'Tacito, i cristiani e l'incendio neroniano (*Ann.* 15.44)'.
Albertario, E. (1936, Milan) *Studi di Diritto Romano* III, 141-95, '*Delictum* e *crimen*'.
Alexander, M.C. (1982) 1 *ClAnt*, 141-66, 'Repetition of prosecution and the scope of prosecutions in the standing criminal courts'.
—— (1985) 80 *CPh*, 20-32, '*Praemia* in the *quaestiones* of the Late Republic'.
Allison, J.E. & J.D. Cloud (1962) 21 *Latomus*, 711-31, 'The *lex Iulia maiestatis*'.
Amarelli, F. (1988) 54 *SDHI*, 110-46, 'Il processo di Sabrata'.
Amaya Garcia, V.M. (1993, Dykinson) *Coautoria y complicidad: Estudio historico y jurisprudencial*.
Amelotti, M. (1958, Milan) *La prescrizione delle azioni*.

Andréev, M. (1957) 35 *RHD*, 1-32, 'Divorce et adultère dans le droit romain classique'.
—— (1963) 5 *St. Clasice*, 165-80, 'La *lex Iulia de adulteriis coercendis*'.
Ankum, H. (1985) 32 *RIDA*, 153-205, 'La *captiva adultera*'.
—— (1987) *Estudios ... D'Ors*, 161-98, 'La *sponsa adultera*'.
Arcaria, F. (1992, Milan) *Senatus censuit. Attività giudiziaria ed attività normativa del Senato in età imperiale*.
Archi, G.G. (1941) *St. Pavia*, 'Problemi in tema di falso in diritto romano' (= *Scritti* III, 1981, Milan, 1487-587).
—— (1947) *Scr. Ferrini* I, '*Civiliter vel criminaliter agere* in tema di falso documentale' (= *Scritti* III, 1981, Milan, 1589-668).
—— (1950) 4 *RIDA* (= *Mél. de Visscher* III), 'Gli studi di diritto penale da Ferrini a noi' (= *Scritti* III, 1981, Milan, 1395-432).
—— (1956) *Studia Gaiana* IV, 'I nuovi frammenti e il diritto criminale romano' (= *Scritti* III, 1981, Milan, 1451-85).
—— (1957) 4^3 *RIDA*, 'Réscrits impériaux et littérature jurisprudentielle dans le développement du droit criminel' (= *Scritti* III, 1981, Milan, 1433-49).
—— (1961) 12 *IURA*, 1-23, 'La prova nel diritto del Basso-Impero'.
Arias Bonet, J.A. (1957-8) 27-8 *AHDE*, 197-219, 'Los *agentes in rebus*'.
Arnaud-Lindet, M.-P. (1980) 58 *RHD*, 411-22, '*Crimen Seiani*: sur quelques vers de Juvénal'.
Astolfi, R. (1986^2, Padua) *La Lex Iulia et Papia*.
Atkinson, K.M.T. (1960) 9 *Historia*, 440-73, 'Constitutional and legal aspects of the trials of M. Primus and Varro Murena'.
Austin R.G. ed. (1960^3, Oxford) *Cicero: pro Caelio*.
Avonzo, F. de Marini (1955) 6 *IURA*, 120-7, 'La repressione penale della violenza testamentaria (CJ 6.3.4.1)'.
—— (1956) 59-60 *BIDR*, 125-98, 'Coesistenza e connessione tra *iudicium publicum* e *iudicium privatum*'.
—— (1957, Milan) *La funzione giurisdizionale del senato romano*.
—— (1977, Turin) *Il senato romano nella repressione penale*.
Backhaus, W. (1989) 71 *Klio*, 321-9, '*Servi vincti*'.
Badian, E. (1954) 75 *AJPh*, 374-84, '*Lex Acilia repetundarum*'.
—— (1962) 11 Historia, 197-245, 'Forschungsbericht. From the Gracchi to Sulla'.
—— (1969) 18 *Historia*, 447-91, '*Quaestiones Variae*'.
—— (1974) *Polis and Imperium: St. Salmon*, 145-66, 'The attempt to try Caesar'.
Baldwin, B. (1963) 43 *Aegyptus*, 256-63, 'Crime and criminals in Graeco-Roman Egypt'.
—— (1964) 18 *Phoenix*, 39-48, 'Executions under Claudius: Seneca's *ludus de morte Claudii*'.
—— (1967) 22 *PP*, 425-39, 'Executions, trials and punishment under Nero'.
Balestri Fumagalli M. (1980, Milan) *Sem. rom. Gardesano Atti* II, 213-30, 'Il divieto di appello contro le sentenze del prefetto del pretorio (CTh 11.30.16)'.
Balsdon, J.P.V.D. (1938) 14 *PBSR*, 98-114, 'The history of the extortion court, 123-70 B.C.'.
Balzarini, M. (1969a) 11 *BIDR*, 203-311, 'In tema di repressione *extra ordinem* del furto nel diritto classico'.
—— (1969b, Padua) *Ricerche in tema di danno violento e rapina*.
—— (1982) 28 *Labeo*, 17-42, 'Appunti sulla *rixa*'.
—— (1983, Padua) *De iniuria extra ordinem statui*.

—— (1984) *Scr. Guarino – Sodalitas* VI, 2865-90, 'Pene detentive e *cognitio extra ordinem criminale*'.

—— (1988) *Idee* ed. Burdese, 159-69, 'Nuove prospettive sulla dicotomia *honestiores-humiliores*'.

Bandini, V. (1934) *St. Ratti*, 497-507, 'Appunti in tema di reato di adulterio'.

Barnes, T.D. (1968) 58 *JRS*, 32-50, 'Legislation against the Christians'.

—— (1984) 105 *AJPh*, 69-72, 'Constantine's prohibition of pagan sacrifice'.

Bassanelli Sommariva, G. (1983-4) 25-6 *BIDR*, 95-119, 'CTh 9.5 *ad legem Iuliam maiestatis*'.

—— (1985, Bologna) *Diritto criminale: Appunti per lezioni di diritto pubblico romano*.

Bauman, R.A. (1967, Johannesburg) *The crimen maiestatis in the Roman Republic and the Augustan Principate*.

—— (1968) 2 *Antichthon*, 68-93, 'Some remarks on the structure and the survival of the *quaestio de adulteriis*'.

—— (1969, Wiesbaden) *The duumviri in the Roman criminal law and the Horatius legend*.

—— (1972) 6 *Antichthon*, 63-73, '*Vim fieri veto*: à propos of a recent work'.

—— (1974a, Munich) *Impietas in principem*.

—— (1974b) 33 *Latomus*, 245-64, 'Criminal prosecutions by the aediles'.

—— (1974-5) 5 *Index*, 39-48, 'Discorso sulla giurisprudenza: I libri *de iudiciis publicis*'.

—— (1976) *St. Beinart* = *AJ*, 19-36, '*Maiestatem populi romani comiter conservanto*'.

—— (1980) *ANRW* II.13, 103-233, 'The *leges iudiciorum publicorum* and their interpretation in the Republic, Principate and Later Empire'.

—— (1982a) 110 *Hermes*, 102-10, 'Hangman! call a halt!'.

—— (1982b) 99 *SZ*, 81-127, 'The resumé of legislation in Suetonius'.

—— (1983, Munich) *Roman Lawyers in Roman Republican Politics*.

—— (1990) 39 *Historia*, 334-48, 'The suppression of the Bacchanals: five questions'.

Beard, M. (1980) 70 *JRS*, 12-27, 'The sexual status of Vestal Virgins'.

Beaucamp, J. (1976) 54 *RHD*, 485-508, 'Le vocabulaire de la faiblesse féminine'.

Beckingsale, B.W. (1963, London) *Elizabeth I*.

Beinart, B. (1975) *AJ*, 5-39, 'Crime and punishment in an historical setting'.

Bellen, H. (1962) 79 *SZ*, 143-68, 'Zur Appellation von Senat an den Kaiser'.

Berger, A. (1938) 45 *BIDR*, 267-93, 'Note esegetiche in tema di plagio'.

—— (1944) 2 *Seminar*, 23-40, 'Some remarks on cattle-stealing in Roman law'.

—— (1953, Philadelphia) *An Encyclopaedic Dictionary of Roman Law*.

Bianchini, M. (1964, Milan) *La formalità costitutive del rapporto processuale nel sistema accusatorio romano*.

Biondi, B. (1938) *Scr. Mancaleoni*, 63-96, 'La *poena adulterii* da Augusto a Giustineano'.

—— (1954, Milan) *Il diritto romano cristiano* III.

Birks, P.B.H. (1984) 52 *TR*, 373-87, 'A new argument for a narrow view of "litem suam facere" '.

Biscardi, A. (1960) 7 *RIDA*, 307-61, 'Sur la *litis contestatio* du procès criminal'.

—— (1986) 89 *BIDR*, 165-84, 'Il culto cristiano e la sua exclusione dal Pantheon di Roma imperiale'.

Bleicken, J. (1962, Göttingen) *Senatsgericht und Kaisergericht*.

Blockley, R.C. (1969) 30 *Cl. et Med.*, 403-19, 'Internal self-policing in the later Roman administration. Some evidence from Ammianus Marcellinus'.

164 Bibliography

Blum, W. (1969, Bonn) *Curiosi und Regendarii*.

Bonini, R. (1959) 10 *RISG*, 119-79, 'D 48.19.16: Claudius Saturninus, *de poenis paganorum*'.

—— (1964, Milan) *I libri de cognitionibus di Callistrato*.

—— (1990, Milan) *Ricerche di diritto Giustinianeo*.

Boswell, J. (1980, Chicago) *Christianity, Social Tolerance, and Homosexuality*.

—— (1988, New York) *The Kindness of Strangers*.

Bradley, K.R. (1973) 94 *AJPh*, 172-82, '*Tum primum revocata ea lex*'.

Braginton, M.V. (1943-4) 39 *CJ*, 391-407, 'Exile under the Roman emperors'.

Brand, C.E. (1968, University of Texas) *Roman Military Law*.

Brasiello, U. (1937, Naples) *La repressione penale in diritto romano*.

—— (1946) 12 *SDHI*, 148-74, 'Note introduttive allo studio dei crimini romani'.

—— (1962, Milan) *St. Betti* IV, 551-70, 'Sulla desuetudine dei *iudicia publica*'.

—— (1971) *St. Volterra* IV, 325-45, 'Sulla persecuzione degli eredi del colpevole nel campo criminale'.

—— (1976) 42 *SDHI*, 246-64, 'Sulla ricostruzione dei crimini in diritto romano: cenni sull'evoluzione dell'omicidio'.

Brecht, C.H. (1938, Munich) *Perduellio*.

—— (1944) 64 *SZ*, 354-9, '*Perduellio* und *crimen maiestatis*'.

Brunt, P. (1961) 10 *Historia*, 189-228, 'Charges of provincial maladministration under the early Principate'.

—— (1981) 97 *SZ*, 256-65, 'Evidence given under torture in the Principate'.

—— (1984a) 34 *CQ*, 423-44, 'The role of the Senate in the Augustan regime'.

—— (1984b) *Scr. Guarino – Sodalitas* I, 469-80, 'Did emperors ever suspend the law of *maiestas*?'.

Buckland, W.W. (1908, Cambridge) *The Roman Law of Slavery*.

—— (1937) 27 *JRS*, 37-47, 'Civil proceedings against ex-magistrates'.

—— (1963, Cambridge) 3rd ed. by P. Stein, *A Textbook of Roman Law*.

Burdese, A. ed. (1988, Padua) *Idee vecchie e nuove sul diritto criminale romano*.

Burillo, J. (1982) 7 *REHJ*, 13-20, 'La desprivatizacíon del *furtum* en el derecho postclasico'.

Busacca, C. (1968) 19 *IURA*, 83-93, 'Val. Max. 6.9.10 e la *quaestio* istituta dalla *lex Caecilia*'.

Busek, V. (1935) *Acta Cong. Iur. Int. Romae* I, 411-79, 'Die Gerichtsbarkeit in Strafsachen in römischen Reiche bis Justinian'.

Buti, I. (1982) *ANRW* II.14, 29-59, 'La *cognitio extra ordinem* da Augusto a Diocleziano'.

Callu, J.P. (1984) *EFR Du Châtiment*, 313-59, 'Le jardin des supplices au Bas-Empire'.

Calore, A. (1989) 35 *Labeo*, 194-214, 'L'aiuto ai proscritti sillani'.

Camiñas, J.G. (1983, Santiago) *Delator*.

—— (1984, Santiago) *La lex Remnia de calumniatoribus*.

—— (1990) 37 *RIDA*, 117-33, 'Le *crimen calumniae*'.

Camodeca, G. (1993) 21 *Index*, 353-64, 'Nuovi dati dagli archivi campani sulla datazione e applicazione del SC Neronianum'.

Campolunghi, M. (1972) 75 *BIDR*, 151-220, 'Gli effetti sospensivi dell'appello in materia penale'.

Cancelli, F. (1956) *St. de Francisci* III, 15-35, 'A proposito dei *tresviri capitales*'.

Cantarella, E. (1972) *St. Scherillo* I, 243-74, 'Adulterio, omicidio legittimo e causa d'onore in diritto romano'.

—— (1976, Milan) *Studi sull'omicidio in diritto greco e romano*.

—— (1987, Johns Hopkins University Press) *Pandora's Daughters*.
—— (1988, Rome) *Secondo natura*.
—— (1991, Milan) *I supplizi capitali*.
Capocci, V. (1956) 22 *SDHI*, 266-310, 'Sulla concessione e sul divieto di sepoltura nel mondo romano ai condennati a pena capitale'.
Cardascia, G. (1950) 28 *RHD*, 305-37; 461-85, 'L'apparition dans le droit des classes d'*honestiores* et d'*humiliores*'.
Carey, C. (1993) 18 *LCM*, 53-5, 'Return of the radish'.
Cavarzere, A. (1982) 27 *Atene e Roma*, 163-70, 'Asconio e il *crimen calumniae*'.
—— (1988a) *Sem. rom. Gardesano Atti* III, 233-50, 'La *lex Plautia de vi* nello specchio deformante della *pro Caelio*'.
—— (1988b) *Idee* ed. Burdese, 117-, 'De teste Fufio: Cicerone e il trattamento dei testimoni nella *pro Caelio*'.
Cerami, P. (1991) 41 *ASGP*, 31-51, '*Tormenta pro poena adhibita*'.
Cervenca, G. (1965) 31 *SDHI*, 312-18, 'Per la storia dell'editto *Quod metus causa*'.
Chastagnol, A. (1960, Paris) *La préfecture urbaine à Rome sous le Bas-Empire*.
Chevailler, L. (1953) 31 *RHD*, 200-43, 'Contribution à l'étude de la complicité en droit pénal romain'.
Chilton, C.W. (1955) 45 *JRS*, 73-81, 'The Roman law of treason under the early Principate'.
Christensen, T. (1984) 35 *Cl. et Med.*, 129-75, 'The so-called Milan Edict'.
Churruca, J. (1979) 26 *RIDA*, 227-38, 'Les procès contre les chrétiens dans la seconde moitié du deuxième siècle'.
Claasen, J.-M. (1992) 35 *Acta Classica* (S.A.), 19-47, 'Cicero's banishment: *tempora et mores*'.
Clark, A.C., ed. (1907, Oxford) *Q. Asconii Pediani orationum Ciceronis quinque enarratio*.
Classen, C.J. (1972) 89 *SZ*, 1-17, 'Die Anklage gegen A. Cluentius Habitus'.
Cloud, J.D. (1963) 80 *SZ*, 206-32, 'The text of D 48.4: *ad legem Iuliam maiestatis*'.
—— (1968) 18 *CR*, 140-3, 'How did Sulla style his law *de sicariis*?'.
—— (1969) 86 *SZ*, 258-86, 'The primary purpose of the *lex Cornelia de sicariis*'.
—— (1971) 88 *SZ*, 1-66, '*Parricidium*'.
—— (1984) *Scr. Guarino – Sodalitas* III, 1365-76, '*Provocatio*: two cases of possible fabrication in the annalistic sources'.
—— (1987) 12 *LCM*, 82-5, 'The Augustan authorship of the *lex Iulia de vi publica*'.
—— (1988a) 66 *Athenaeum*, 579-95, '*Lex Iulia de vi* – I'.
—— (1988b) 13 *LCM*, 69-72, 'Sulla and the praetorship'.
—— (1989) 67 *Athenaeum*, 427-65, '*Lex Iulia de vi* – II'.
—— (1993) 18 *LCM*, 39-43, 'Municipal capital jurisdiction over Roman citizens: a chimaera?'.
—— (1994) *CAH* IX², 491-530, 'The constitution and public criminal law'.
Cody, J.M. (1973) 68 *CPh*, 205-8, 'The use of *libero/damno* and *absolvo/condemno* in the judicial proceedings of the Late Republic'.
Cohen, B. (1949) 2 *RIDA* = *Mél de Visscher* I, 133-56, '*Contrectatio* in Roman and Jewish law'.
Coleman, K.M. (1990) 80 *JRS*, 44-73, 'Fatal charades: Roman executions staged as mythological enactments'.
Cornell, T. (1981) *EFR Le Délit réligieux*, 27-37, 'Some observations on the *crimen incesti*'.

Coroï, J. (1915, Paris) *La violence en droit criminel romain.*
Coster, C.H. (1935, Cambridge, Mass) *The iudicium quinquevirale.*
Cousin, J. (1943) 21 *RHD*, 88-94, *'Lex Lutatia de vi'.*
Craig, C.P. (1981) 111 *TAPhA*, 31-7, The *accusator* as *amicus'.*
Cramer, F.H. (1945) 6 *J. Hist. Ideas*, 157-, 'Bookburning and censorship in Ancient Rome'.
—— (1951) 12 *Cl. et Med.* 9-50, 'Expulsion of astrologers from ancient Rome'.
—— (1951-2) 9 & 10 *Seminar*, 1-35; 1-59, 'The Caesars and the stars'.
—— (1954, Philadelphia) *Astrology in Roman Law and Politics.*
Crawford, M. (1985, London) *Coinage and Money under the Roman Republic.*
Cremades, I. & Paricio, J. (1984) 54 *AHDE*, 179-208, 'La responsabilidad del juez'.
Crifò, G. (1961, Milan) *Ricerche sull'exilium nel periodo repubblicano.*
—— (1971) 2 *Index*, 389-94, 'Procedimento accusatorio criminale nel Basso Impero'.
—— (1985, Naples) *L'esclusione dalla città.*
Crook, J.A. (1955, Cambridge) *Consilium Principis.*
—— (1976) 66 *JRS*, 132-8, '*Sponsione provocare*: its place in Roman litigation'.
—— (1987a) 65 *Athenaeum*, 163-71, *'Lex Cornelia de falsis'.*
—— (1987b) 33 *PCPhS*, 38-52, 'Was there a doctrine of "manifest" guilt in the Roman criminal law?'.
Cuff, P.J. (1964) 14 *CR*, 136-7, 'Tacitus *Annals* 1.72'.
Dalla, D. (1978, Milan) *L'incapacità sessuale in diritto romano.*
—— (1980, Milan) *Senatusconsultum Silanianum.*
—— (1987, Milan) *Ubi Venus mutatur.*
Daly, L.J. (1983) 65 *Klio*, 245-61, 'The report of Varro Murena's death (Dio 54.3.5)'.
—— (1984) 66 *Klio*, 157-69, 'Augustus and the murder of Varro Murena'.
Daube D. (1952) *JR*, 12-28, 'Slave catching'.
—— (1955) 9 *Hellenika*, 8-21, 'The accuser under the *lex Iulia de adulteriis'.*
—— (1956) 72 *LQR*, 494-515, 'Defence of superior orders in Roman law'.
—— (1965) *St. Biondi* I, 199-212, 'Licinnia's dowry'.
—— (1972) 7 *IJ*, 373-80, 'The *lex Iulia* concerning adultery'.
—— (1986) 103 *SZ*, 447-8, 'The Old Testament prohibitions of homosexuality'.
David, J.M. (1984) *EFR Du Châtiment*, 131-76, 'Du *Comitium* à la Roche Tarpèienne'.
Davies, R.W. (1973) 4 *AncSoc*, 199-212, 'The investigation of some crimes in Roman Egypt'.
Dell'Oro, A. (1960, Milan) *I libri de officio nella giurisprudenza romana.*
Demougeot, E. (1986) 45 *Latomus*, 160-70, 'Le fonctionnariat du Bas-Empire éclairé par les fautes des fonctionnaires'.
Desanti, L. (1986a) 28 *BIDR*, 443-63, 'Costantino ed il matrimonio fra tutore e pupilla'.
—— (1986b) 52 *SDHI*, 195-217, 'Costantino – il ratto e il matrimonio riparatore'.
—— (1987) 1 *AUFG*, 187-201, 'Giustiniano e il ratto'.
—— (1988) *Idee* ed. Burdese, 225-40, 'La repressione della *scientia divinatoria* in età del Principato'.
—— (1990a) 4 *AUFG*, 129-42, '*Interpellare de stupro* e *iniuriae in corpus* – PS 5.4.4'.
—— (1990b, Milan) *Sileat omnibus perpetuo divinandi curiositas.*
—— (1991) 5 *AUFG*, 27-37, 'Astrologi: eretici o pagani? Un problema esegetico'.

De Zulueta, F. (1932) 22 *JRS*, 184-97, 'Violation of sepulture in Palestine at the beginning of the Christian era'.

Dignös, G. (1962, Munich diss.) *Die Stellung der Ädilen im römischen Strafrecht*.

D'Ippolito, F. (1964) *Synteleia Arangio-Ruiz*, 717-21, 'Una presunta disposizione del SC Silaniano'.

—— (1965) 11 *Labeo*, 42-6, 'Un caso di *ambitus* del 66 a.C.'.

Dixon, S. (1984) 52 *TR*, 343-71, '*Infirmitas sexus*: womanly weakness in Roman law'.

Dominicis, M. de (1950) 16 *SDHI*, 221-53, 'Sulle origini romano-cristiane del diritto del marito ad accusare *constante matrimonio* la moglie adultera'.

Dorey, T.A. (1958) 5 *G & R*, 175-80, 'Cicero, Clodia and the *pro Caelio*'.

D'Ors, A. (1971) *St. Volterra* II, 527-58, 'Contribuciones a la historia del *crimen falsi*'.

—— (1978) 24 *Labeo*, 42-51, 'Una nueva conjetura sobre CJ 7.12.1; D 48.19.33'.

—— (1982) 48 *SDHI*, 368-94, '*Litem suam facere*'.

Ducloux, A. (1991) 69 *RHD*, 141-76, 'L'Église, l'asile et l'aide aux condamnés d'après la constitution du 27 juillet 398'.

Ducos, M. (1979) 57 *REL*, 145-65, 'La crainte de l'infamie et l'obéissance à la loi'.

Duff, P. (1938, Cambridge) *Personality in Roman Private Law*.

Düll, R. (1953, Milan) *Atti Verona* III, 159-77, 'Studien zum römischen Sepulkralrecht'.

—— (1957) 74 *SZ*, 384-93, 'Fälle des *amburi* im Licht des Retorsions- und Kompensationens-gedankens im antiken Strafrecht'.

Dupont, C. (1953 & 1955, Lille) *Le droit criminel dans les constitutions de Constantin: Les Infractions; Les Peines*.

—— (1976) *RIDA*, 119-39, 'Peines et relations pécuniaires entre fiancés'.

Dzielska, M. (1986, Rome) *Apollonius of Tyana in Legend and History*.

École Française à Rome (1981, Rome) *Le Délit religieux*.

—— (1984, Rome) vol. 79, *Du Châtiment dans la cité*.

Eder, W. (1969, Munich) *Das Vorsullanische Repetundenverfahren*.

Ehrlich, J.D. (1986, Ann Arbor) *Suicide in the Roman Empire*.

Ehrman, R.K. (1987) 40 *Mnem*, 422-5, 'Martial *de spect.* 8: gladiator or criminal?'.

Eisenhut, W. (1972) *ANRW* I.2, 268-82, 'Die römische Gefangnisstrafe'.

Esmein, A. (1878) 2 *RHD* = *Mélanges* (1886), 1-35; 395-442, 'Le délit d'adultère à Rome'.

Evans-Grubb, J. (1989) 79 *JRS*, 59-83, 'Abduction marriage in Antiquity'.

Fallu, E. (1970) 48 *REL*, 180-204, 'La première lettre de Cicéron à Quintus et la *lex Iulia de repetundis*'.

Fanizza, L. (1977) 23 *Labeo*, 199-214, 'Il senato e la prevenzione del *crimen repetundarum* in età tiberiana'.

—— (1979) 25 *Labeo*, 266-89, 'Il parricidio nel sistema della *lex Pompeia*'.

—— (1982, Naples) *Giuristi, crimini, leggi mell'età degli Antonini*.

—— (1984) 96 *MEFRA*, 671-95, 'Il crimine e la morte del reo'.

—— (1988, Rome) *Delatori e accusatori*.

Fantham, E. (1975) 24 *Historia*, 423-43, 'The trials of Gabinius'.

Fascione L. (1984, Milan) *Crimen e quaestio ambitus nell'età repubblicana*.

—— (1988) 34 *Labeo*, 179-88, 'Le norme *de ambitu* nella *lex Ursonensis*'.

Ferrary, J.L. (1975) 87 *MEFRA*, 321-48, 'Cicéron et la loi judiciaire de Cotta (70 av. J.C.)'.

—— (1979) 91 *MEFRA*, 83-134, 'Recherches sur la législation de Saturninus et de Glaucia'.

—— (1983) *CRAI Paris*, 556-72, 'Les origines de la loi de majesté à Rome'.

—— (1991) 69 *Athenaeum*, 417-34, '*Lex Cornelia de sicariis et veneficis*'.

Ferrini, C. (1902, reprinted 1976, Rome) *Diritto penale romano – esposizione storica e dottrinale*.

—— (1930 reprinted) *Opere* V, 51-72; 73-105, 'Il tentativo nelle leggi e nella giurisprudenza romana; Ancora sul tentativo nel diritto romano'.

Fishwick, D. (1984) 9 *AmJAncH*, 123-7, 'Pliny and the Christians'.

Fontette, F. Pontenay de (1954, Paris) *Leges repetundarum*.

Forbes, C.A. (1936) 67 *TAPhA*, 114-25, 'Books for the burning'.

Formigoni Candini, W. (1990) 4 *AUFG*, 97-127, '*Ne lenones sint in ullo loco reipublicae romanae*'.

—— (1991) 5 *AUFG*, 17-25, ' "Quod meretrici datur repeti non potest." Ancora su D 12.5.4.3'.

Fraccaro, P. (1919) 52 *RIL* (= *Opuscula* II, 1956, Pavia, 225-86) 'Sulla *leges iudiciariae romanae*'.

Fraschetti, A. (1990, Bari) *Roma e il principe*.

Frend, W.H.C. (1965, Blackwell, Oxford) *Martyrdom and Persecution in the Early Church*.

Fridh, A. (1958) 75 *SZ*, 361-4, 'CTh 9.5.1'.

Frier, B.W. (1983) 113 *TAPhA*, 221-41, 'Urban praetors and rural violence'.

Garnsey, P (1966) 56 *JRS*, 167-89, 'The *lex Iulia* and appeal under the Empire'.

—— (1967) 57 *JRS*, 56-60, 'Adultery trials and the survival of the *quaestiones* in the Severan age'.

—— (1970, Oxford) *Social Status and Legal Privilege*.

Garofalo, L. (1989, Padua) *Il processo edilizio*.

—— (1990) 56 *SDHI*, 366-97, 'Il pretore giudice criminale in età repubblicana?'.

Gatti, T. (1935-6) 113 & 115 *AG*, 59-70; 44-59, 'I limiti delle *leges iudiciorum publicorum*'.

Gaudemet, J. (1957, Paris) *La formation du droit seculier et du droit de l'Église*.

—— (1962) *St. Betti* II, 481-508, 'Le problème de la responsibilité pénale dans l'Antiquité'.

—— (1964a) *Mnemeion: St. Solazzi*, 141-53, 'A propos du *furtum* à l'époque classique'.

—— (1964b) *Synteleia Arangio-Ruiz*, 699-709, '*Maiestas populi romani*'.

—— (1966) 1 *IJ*, 128-35, 'Les abus des *potentes* au Bas-Empire'.

—— (1981) 98 *SZ*, 47-76, 'Constitutions constantiniennes relatives à l'appel'.

—— (1984) *Scr. Guarino – Sodalitas* VI, 2569-74, 'De la responsabilité pénale dans la législation post-classique'.

Genin, G.C. (1968, Lyon) *La repression des actes de tentative*.

—— (1971) *Mél. Falletti* II, 233-93, 'Réflexions sur l'originalité juridique de la répression du suicide'.

Giardina, A. (1973-4) 13-14 *Helikon*, 184-90, 'Sulla problema della *fraus monetae*'.

Gioffredi, C. (1946a) 12 *SDHI*, 187-91, '*Ad statuas confugere*'.

—— (1946b) 12 *SDHI*, 191-3, 'Ancora sull'*aqua et igni interdictio*'.

—— (1970, Turin) *I principi del diritto penale romano*.

Giomaro, A.M. (1976-7) 29 *St. Urb.*, 1-52, 'Deperibilità dei mezzi di prova e diritto condizionato'.

Giovanni, L. de (1985, Naples) *Il libro XVI del Codice Teodosiano*.

—— (1988) 54 *SDHI*, 147-69, 'L'appello nel giuristo Marciano'.

Girard, P.F. (1913) 34 *SZ*, 295-372, 'Les *leges Iuliae iudiciorum publicorum et privatorum*'.

Giuffrè, V. (1981) 27 *Labeo*, 214-18, '*Latrones desertoresque*'.

—— (1989, Naples) *Il "diritto penale" nell' esperienza romana*.

—— (1991, Naples) *La "repressione criminale" nell' esperienza romana*.

—— (1994) 40 *Labeo*, 359-64, '*Nominis delatio* e *nominis receptio*'.

Giunti, P. (1990, Milan) *Adulterio e legge regie*.

Gladigow, B. (1972) *ANRW* I.2, 295-313, 'Die sakrale Funktion der Liktoren'.

Gnoli, F. (1972) 38 *SDHI*, 328-38, 'Sulla paternità e sulla datazione della *lex Iulia peculatus*'.

—— (1973) 107 *RIL*, 437-72, 'Sulla repressione penale della ritenzione di *pecunia residua* nella *lex Iulia peculatus*'.

—— (1974a) 40 *SDHI*, 151-207, '*Rem privatam de sacro surripere*'.

—— (1974b) 40 *SDHI*, 401-14, 'Seneca, *benef.* 7.7.1-4: prospettiva filosofica e prospettiva giuridica del *sacrilegium*'.

—— (1975) 109 *RIL*, 331-41, 'Cicero *nat. deor.* 3.74 e l'origine della *quaestio perpetua peculatus*'.

—— (1979, Milan) *Ricerche sul crimen peculatus*.

—— (1984, Milan) *Hereditatem expilare*.

Goria, F. (1973) 39 *SDHI*, 281-384, 'Ricerche sul impedimento da adulterio e obbligo di ripudio da Giustiniano a Leone VI'.

—— (1987) *ED* 38, 'Ratto (diritto romano)'.

Gotoff, H.C. (1986) 81 *CPh*, 122-32, 'Cicero's analysis of the prosecution speeches in the *pro Caelio*'.

Grant, M. (1973, London) *The Jews in the Roman World*.

Grasmück, E.L. (1978, Paderborn) *Exilium*.

Grelle, F. (1980) *ANRW* II.13, 340-65, 'La *correctio morum* nella legislazione flavia'.

Greenidge A.H.J. (1894, Oxford) *Infamia*.

—— (1895) 7 *JR*, 228-40, 'The conception of treason in Roman law'.

—— (1901, Oxford) *The Legal Procedure of Cicero's Time*.

Grierson, P. (1956, London) *Essays in Roman Coinage presented to H. Mattingly*, 240-61, 'The Roman law of counterfeiting'.

Griffin, J. (1976) 66 *JRS*, 87-105, 'Augustan poetry and the life of luxury'.

Griffin, M.T. (1973) 23 *CQ*, 108-26, 'The *leges iudiciariae* of the pre-Sullan era'.

Grisé, Y. (1982, Paris) *Le suicide dans la Rome antique*.

Grodzynski, D. (1984a) *EFR Du Châtiment*, 361-403, 'Tortures mortelles et catégories sociales'.

—— (1984b) 96 *MEFRA*, 697-726, 'Ravies et coupables'.

—— (1987) 53 *SDHI*, 140-218, 'Pauvres et indigents, vils et plebéiens'.

Gruen, E.S. (1964) 95 *TAPhA*, 99-110, 'Politics and the courts in 104 BC'.

—— (1965a) 55 *JRS*, 59-73, 'The *lex Varia de maiestate*'.

—— (1965b) 24 *Latomus*, 576-80, 'The exile of Metellus Numidicus'.

—— (1968a, Cambridge, Mass.) *Roman Politics and the Criminal Courts, 149-78 BC*.

—— (1968b) 111 *RhM*, 59-63, 'M. Antonius and the trial of the Vestal Virgins'.

—— (1974, U. of California Press) *The Last Generation of the Roman Republic*.

—— (1990, Brill) *Studies in Greek Culture and Roman Policy*.

Gualandi, G. (1963, Milan) *Legislazione imperiale e giurisprudenza*.

Guareschi, A. (1993) 21 *Index*, 453-88, 'Le note di Marciano ai *de adulteriis libri duo* di Papiniano'.

Guarino, A. (1943) 63 SZ, 175-267, 'Studi sull' *incestum*'.

—— (1956, Naples) *Ordinamento giuridico romano*.

—— (1975) 21 *Labeo*, 73-7, 'La *perduellio* e la plebe'.

—— (1989) 35 *Labeo*, 79-81, 'Variazioni sulla tema di Malleoli'.

—— (1990) 36 *Labeo*, 267-79, 'Cicerone come e quando'.

—— (1991) 37 *Labeo*, 5-13, '*Extremum atque ultimum*'.

—— (1993) 21 *Index*, 411-31, 'Lui, lei e l'altro nel matrimonio romano'.

Haase, R. (1994) 111 *SZ*, 458-70, 'Justinian I und der Frauenraub (*raptus*)'.

Habicht, C. & P. Kussmaul (1986) 43 *MusHelv*, 135-44, 'Ein neues Fragment des *Edictum de accusationibus*'.

Hands, A.R. (1962) 5 *PACA*, 27-31, 'The timing of suicide'.

Harries, J. & I. Wood (edd.) (1993a, London) *The Theodosian Code*.

Harries, J. (1993b) Harries & Wood (edd.) *The Theodosian Code*, 1-6, 'The background to the Code'.

Harris, W.V. (1982) 32 *CQ*, 114-16, 'The theoretical possibility of extensive infanticide in the Graeco-Roman world'.

Härtel, G. (1986) 22 *AC* (Hung), 69-86, 'Die Religionspolitik der römischen Kaiser von Diokletian bis Justinian'.

Henderson, M.I. (1951) 41 *JRS*, 71-88, 'The process de repetundis'.

Hengel, M. (1977, London) *Crucifixion*.

Hildebrandt, P. (ed.) (1971 repr. of 1907, Teubner) *Scholia in Ciceronis orationes Bobiensia*.

Hitzig, H.F. (1909, Zurich) *Der Herkunft des Schwurgerichts im römischen Strafrecht*.

Höbenreich, E. (1988) 208 *AG*, 75-97, 'Due SCC in tema di veneficio (Marcian 14 *inst.* D 48.8.3.2-3)'.

—— (1990) 107 *SZ*, 249-314, 'Überlegungen zur Verfolgung unbeabsichtigter Tötungen von Sulla bis Hadrian'.

—— (1992) *F. Wesener*, 187-99, 'Ulp. 8 *off. proc.* D 47.11.6'.

Hönig, R. (1960, Göttingen) *Humanitas und Rhetorik in spätrömischen Kaisergesetzen*.

Honoré, T. (1981, Oxford) *Emperors and Lawyers*.

Hoof, A.J.L. van (1988) 19 *AncSoc*, 105-24, 'Ancient robbers'.

Hough, J.N. (1930) 51 *AJPh*, 135-47, 'The *lex Lutatia* and the *lex Plautia de vi*'.

Houlou, A. (1974) 52 *RHD*, 5-29 'Le droit penal chez St Augustin'.

Howe, L.L. (1942, Chicago) *The Praetorian Prefect from Commodus to Diocletian*.

Humbert, M. (1988) 100.1 *MEFR*, 431-503, 'Le tribunal de la plèbe et le tribunal du peuple: remarques sur l'histoire de la *provocatio ad populum*'.

Hume, D. (1829[3], Edinburgh) *Commentary on the Law of Scotland respecting Crimes*.

Impallomeni, G. (1982) *St. Biscardi* III, 177-203, 'Riflessioni sul tentativo di teoria generale penalistica in Claudio Saturnino'.

Jackson, B.S. (1970) *GeorgiaJIntCompLaw*, 45-103, 'Some comparative legal history: robbery and brigandage'.

Jaeger, H. (1960) 38 *RHD*, 214-62, 'Justinien et l'*episcopalis audientia*'.

Jameson, S. (1975) 24 *Historia*, 287-314, 'Augustus and Agrippa Postumus'.

Johnson, A.C., P.R. Coleman-Norton. & F.C. Bourne (edd.) (1961, University of Texas, Austin) *Ancient Roman Statutes*.

Johnson, G.J. (1988) 47 *Latomus*, 417-22, '*De conspiratione delatorum*: Pliny and the Christians re-visited'.

Jolowicz, H.F. (1940, Cambridge) *D 47.2: de furtis*.

Jones A.H.M. (1960, Blackwell, Oxford) *Studies in Roman Government and Law.*
—— (1964, Blackwell, Oxford) *The Later Roman Empire*, 284-602.
—— (1972, Blackwell, Oxford) *The Criminal Courts of the Republic and Principate.*
Jones, B.W. (1990) 45 *PP*, 348-57, 'Domitian and the exile of Dio of Prusa'.
Jones, C.P. (1987) 77 *JRS*, 139-55, 'Stigma: tattooing and branding in antiquity'.
Jones, H. (1992) 51 *Latomus*, 753-61, 'L'ordre pénale de la Rome antique'.
Kaden, E.H. (1953) *F. Lewald*, 55-68, 'Die Edikte gegen die Manichäer von Diokletian bis Justinian'.
Kaser, M. (1949) 2 *RIDA = Mél. de Visscher* I, 511-50, 'Die Rechtsgrundlage der *actio rei uxoriae*'.
—— (1956) 73 *SZ*, 220-78, '*Infamia* und *ignominia* in der römischen Rechtsquellen'.
—— (1971 & 1975, Munich) *Das Römische Privatrecht.*
Keenan, J.G. (1989) 35 *ArchPapF*, 15-23, 'Roman criminal law in a Berlin papyrus codex (BGU IV 1024-1027)'.
Kelly, J. (1957, Weimar) *Princeps iudex.*
—— (1966, Oxford) *Roman Litigation.*
Kennell, S.A.H. (1991) 73 *Klio*, 526-36, 'Women's hair and the law: two cases from late Antiquity'.
Keresztes, P. (1967) 26 *Latomus*, 54-66, 'Hadrian's rescript to Minucius Fundanus'.
—— (1969) 28 *Latomus*, 601-18, 'The Emperor Maximinus' decree of AD 235'.
—— (1979) *ANRW* II.23.1, 247-315, 'The imperial Roman government and the Christian church: I, from Nero to the Severi'.
—— (1984) 43 *Latomus*, 404-13, 'Nero, the Christians and the Jews'.
Kinsey, T. (1980) 49 *AntCl*, 173-90, 'Cicero's case against Magnus [et al.] in the *pro S. Roscio Amerino*'.
—— (1985) 54 *AntCl*, 188-96, 'The case against Sextius Roscius of Ameria'.
—— (1988) 57 *AntCl*, 296-7, 'The sale of the property of Roscius of Ameria: how illegal was it?'.
Klingenberg, G. (1979) 96 *SZ*, 229-57, 'Das Beweisproblem beim Urkundendiebstahl'.
Kocher, E. (1965, Munich) *Überlieferter und ursprünglicher Anwendungsbereich der lex Cornelia de falsis.*
Köstermann, E. (1955) 4 *Historia*, 72-106, 'Die Maiestätsprozesse unter Tiberius'.
Kunkel, W. (1962, Munich) *Untersuchungen zur Entwicklung des römischen Kriminalverfahrens in vorsullanischen Zeit.*
—— (1963) 24 *RE*, '*Quaestio*' (= *Kleine Schriften* 1974, Weimar, 33-110).
—— (1966) 83 *SZ*, 'Das Konsilium im Hausgericht' (= *Kleine Schriften* 1974, Weimar, 117-49).
—— (1967a) 84 *SZ*, 'Ein direketes Zeugnis für den privaten Mordprozess' (= *Kleine Schriften* 1974, Weimar, 111-16).
—— (1967b & 1968a) 84 & 85 *SZ*, 'Die Funktion des Konsilium in der magistratischen Strafjustiz und im Kaisergericht' (= *Kleine Schriften* 1974, Weimar, 151-254).
—— (1968b) *Symbolae David* I, 'Prinzipien des romischen Strafverfahrens' (= *Kleine Schriften* 1974, Weimar, 11-31).

—— (1969) 'Über die Entstehung des Senatsgerichts' (= *Kleine Schriften* 1974, Weimar, 267-323).

Kupiszewski, H. (1971) *St. Volterra* IV, 601-14, 'Quelques remarques sur le *parricidium*'.

Kurylowicz, M. (1985) 102 *SZ*, 185-219, 'Das Glückspiel im römischen Recht'.

Labruna, L. (1971, Naples) *Vim fieri veto*.

Lacey, W.K. (1980) 14 *Antichthon*, 127-42, '2 BC and Julia's adultery'.

Laet, S.J. de (1945) 14 *AntCl*, 145-63, 'Où en est la problème de la juridiction impériale?'.

—— (1949, Bruges) *Portorium*.

Lamberti, F. (1990) 36 *Labeo*, 218-66, 'Riflessioni in tema di *litem suam facere*'.

Lambertini, R. (1980, Milan) *Plagium*.

La Rosa, F. (1957) 3 *Labeo*, 231-45, 'Note sui *tresviri capitales*'.

—— (1964) *Synteleia Arangio-Ruiz* I, 310-14, 'Note sulla *custodia* nel diritto criminale romano'.

Last, H. (1937) 27 *JRS*, 80-92, 'The study of the persecutions'.

—— (1949) 39 *JRS*, 1-5, 'Rome and the druids'.

—— (1951, Cambridge) *CAH* IX^1, ch. 1-4 & 6-7.

Lauria, M. (1932) 8 *AnnMacerata*, 'Appunti sul plagio' (= *Studii e Ricordi*, 1983, 185-92).

—— (1934a) 56 *AAN*, 'Accusatio-inquisitio' (= *Studii e Ricordi*, 1983).

—— (1934b) *St. Ratti*, 95-135, 'Calumnia' (= *Studii e Ricordi*, 1983).

—— (1938) 4 *SDHI*, 163-92, 'Contractus, delictum, obligatio' (= *Studii e Ricordi*, 1983).

—— (1968) 'Nomen cristianum' (= *Studii e Ricordi*, 1983, 477-).

—— (1970) 21 *IURA*, 182-6, 'Infames ed altri exclusi degli ordini sacri secondo un elenco probabilmente precostantiniano'.

Lawson, F.H. (1950, Oxford) *Negligence in the Civil Law*; 2nd ed. with B.S. Markesinis, *Tortious Liability for Unintentional Harm* (Cambridge 1982).

Lear, F.S. (1965, University of Texas) *Treason and Related Offences in Roman and Germanic Law*.

Lebigre, A. (1967, Paris) *Quelques aspects de la responsabilité pénale en droit romain classique*.

Lee, R.W. (1956, London) *The Elements of Roman Law*.

Lemosse, M. (1953a) 31 *RHD*, 430-9, 'Accusation calomnieuse et action d'injures'.

—— (1953b) 21 *TR*, 30-54, 'Recherches sur l'histoire du serment de *calumnia*'.

Levick, B. (1976) 35 *Latomus*, 301-9, 'The fall of Julia the younger'.

—— (1979) 28 *Historia*, 358-79, 'Poena legis maiestatis'.

—— (1983) 73 *JRS*, 97-115, 'The *senatusconsultum* from Larinum'.

Levy, E. (1931, Heidelberg) *Die römische Kapitalstrafe*.

—— (1933) 53 *SZ*, 151-233, 'Von den Anklägervergehen'.

—— (1936) *St. Riccobono* II, 77-100, 'Zur Infamie im römischen Strafrecht'.

—— (1938) 45 *BIDR*, 57-166, 'Gesetz und Richter'; 396-410, 'Statute and judge' [a resumé in English].

Lewis, A.D.E. (1989, Sevilla) *Estudios sobre Urso* ed. J. González, 41-56, 'Ne quis in oppido aedificium detegito'.

Liebs, D. (1969) 86 *SZ*, 167-91, 'Die Klagenkonsumption'.

Lilja, S. (1983, Helsinki) *Homosexuality in Republican and Augustan Rome*.

Linderski, J. (1990) 133 *RhM*, 86-93, 'The death of Pontia'.

Lindsay, R.J.M. (1949) 44 *CPh*, 240-3, 'Defamation and the law under Sulla'.

Lintott, A.W. (1968, Oxford) *Violence in Republican Rome*.

—— (1972) *ANRW* I.2, 226-67, '*Provocatio*: from the Struggle of the Orders to the Principate'.

—— (1978) 106 *Hermes*, 125-38, 'The *quaestiones de sicariis et veneficis* and the Latin *lex Bantina*'.

—— (1981) 98 *SZ*, 162-212, 'The *leges de repetundis* and associated measures under the Republic'.

—— (1990a) 80 *JRS*, 1-16, 'Electoral bribery in the Roman Republic'.

—— (1990b) 68 *RHD*, 1-11, 'Le procès devant les *recuperatores* d'après les données épigraphiques jusqu'au règne d'Auguste'.

Lippold, A. (1963) *RE* 24.1, 1162-6, '*Quinquevirale iudicium*'.

Lo Cascio, E. (1979) 57 *Athenaeum*, 215-38, 'Carbone, Druso e Gratidiano: la gestione della *res nummaria* a Roma tra la *lex Papiria* e la *lex Cornelia*'.

Lombardi, G. (1984) 50 *SDHI*, 1-98, 'L'Editto di Milano del 313 e la laicità dello Stato'.

—— (1986) 52 *SDHI*, 1-60, 'Dall'Editto di Milano del 313 alla *Dignitas Humanae* del Vaticano II'.

Longo, G. (1958) 61 *BIDR*, 103-207, 'La complicità nel diritto penale romano'.

—— (1970a) *St. Scaduto* III, 452-532, 'La repressione della violenza nel diritto penale romano'.

—— (1970b) *Sein und Werden: F. von Lübtow*, 321-38, 'Sulla legittima difesa e sullo stato di necessità'.

—— (1974) 13 *AnnFacGiurUnivGenova*, 381-482, '*Crimen plagii*'.

Lopuszanski, G. (1951) 20 *AntCl*, 5-46, 'La police romaine et les chrétiens'.

Lorenzi, C. (1991) 57 *SDHI*, 158-80, 'Coll. 4.8.1: la figla adultera e il *ius occidendi iure patris*'.

Lotmar, P. (1912) *Mél. Girard* II, 119-43, '*Lex Iulia de adulteriis* und *incestum*'.

Lovato, A. (1989) 55 *SDHI*, 423-37, 'Legittimazione del reo all'accusa e funzione emendatrice della pena'.

Lowe, J.C.B. (1991) 112 *AJPh*, 29-44, 'Prisoners, guards and chains in Plautus, *Captivi*'.

Lucrezi, F. (1986) 97 *AAN*, 171-98, 'Costantino e gli aruspici'.

Lugand, R. (1930) 32 *RevArch*, 36-57, 'Le viol rituel chez les romains'.

Luzzatto, G. (1956) 73 *SZ*, 29-67, 'Von der Selbsthilfe zum römischen Prozess'.

MacCormack, G. (1972) 3 *Index*, 382-96, 'Criminal liability for fire' .

—— (1978) 25 *RIDA*, 293-305, '*Usucapio pro herede, res hereditariae* and *furtum*'.

—— (1979) 26 *RIDA*, 239-60, '*Terminus motus*'.

—— (1982a) *ANRW* II.14, 3-28, 'The liability of the judge in the Republic and Principate'.

—— (1982b) 28 *Labeo*, 43-50, 'A note on a recent interpretation of *paricidas esto*'.

—— (1983) 51 *TR*, 271-93, '*Ope consilio furtum factum*'.

MacCoull, L.S.B. (1990) 20 *JJP*, 103-7, 'The Aphrodite murder mystery'.

McDermott, W.C. (1977) 120 *RhM*, 64-75, 'The Verrine jury'.

McDonald, W. (1929) 23 *CQ*, 196-208, 'The tribunate of Cornelius'.

McGinn, T.A.J. (1989) 16 *Helios*, 79-110, 'The taxation of Roman prostitutes'.

—— (1990) 107 *SZ*, 315-53, '*Ne serva prostituatur*: restrictive covenants in the sale of slaves'.

—— (1991) 120 *TAPhA*, 335-75, 'Concubinage and the *lex Iulia* on adultery'.

Mackenzie, G. (1678, Edinburgh) *The Laws and Customs of Scotland in Matters Criminal*.

MacMullen, R. (1963) 10 *RIDA*, 221-5, 'The Roman concept robber-pretender'.

—— (1966, Cambridge, Mass) *Enemies of the Roman Order*.

—— (1971) 2 *AncSoc*, 105-16, 'Social history in astrology'.
—— (1984, Yale) *Christianizing the Roman Empire*.
—— (1986) 16 *Chiron*, 147-66, 'Judicial savagery in the Roman Empire'.
—— (1988, Yale) *Corruption and the Decline of Rome*.
—— (1990, Princeton) *Changes in the Roman Empire*.
Magdelain, A. (1973) 22 *Historia*, 405-22, 'Remarques sur la *perduellio*'.
Manfredini A.D. (1976) *SDHI*, 99-148, 'L'editto "de coercendis rhetoribus latinis" del 92 a.C.'.
—— (1979, Milan) *La diffamazione verbale nel diritto romano*.
—— (1982) *St. Biscardi* III, 223-44, 'La testimonianza del liberto contro il patrono nel processo criminale die età classica'.
—— (1984) *Scr. Guarino – Sodalitas* V, 2209-25, 'Una questione in materia di naufragio'.
—— (1985) 32 *RIDA*, 257-71, '*Commutare cum feminis vestem*'.
—— (1986) ARC, 39-, ' "Ad ecclesiam confugere", "ad statuas confugere" nell'età di Teodosio I'.
—— (1987) 1 *AUFG*, 11-28, 'La donna incestuosa'.
—— (1991) 5 *AUFG*, 103-26, '*Ius gladii*'.
Mannino, V. (1984, Milan) *Ricerche sul defensor civitatis*.
Mantovani, D. (1988) *Idee* ed. Burdese, 171-223, 'Sulla competenza penale del *praefectus urbi* attraverso il *liber singularis* di Ulpiano'.
—— (1989, Padua) *Il problema d'origine dell' accusa popolare*.
—— (1990) 68 *Athenaeum*, 19-49, 'Il pretore giudice criminale in età repubblicana'.
—— (1991) 69 *Athenaeum*, 611-23, 'Il pretore giudice criminale in età repubblicana: una riposta'.
Marini Avonzo, F. de, see Avonzo.
Marino, F. (1988a) 105 *SZ*, 634-63, 'Il falso testamentario nel diritto romano'.
—— (1988b) 105 *SZ*, 771-5, 'Appunti sulla falsificazione del marchio nel diritto romano'.
—— (1988c) *Idee* ed. Burdese, 137-57, 'Cic. *Verr.* II 1.42.108 e la repressione del falso'.
Marotta, V. (1983-84) 12 *Index*, 405-46, 'Politica imperiale e culture periferiche nel mondo romano: il problema della circoncisione'.
—— (1988, Milan) *Multa de iure sanxit*.
Marshall, A.J. (1967) 17 *CQ*, 408-13, 'Verres and judicial corruption'.
—— (1990a) 9 *ClViews*, 333-66, 'Women on trial before the Roman Senate'.
—— (1990b) 44 *Phoenix*, 46-59, 'Roman ladies on trial: the case of Maesia of Sentinum'.
Marshall, Bruce A. (1975) 118 *RhM*, 136-52, 'Q. Cicero, Hortensius, and the *lex Aurelia*'.
—— (1985, U of Missouri Press) *A Historical Commentary on Asconius*.
Martin, T.O. (1948) 6 *Seminar*, 20-41, 'A curious parallel: D 48.19.5pr and *Matt.* 13.29'.
Martina, M. (1980) 26 *Labeo*, 155-75, '*Grassatores* e *carmentarii*'.
Martini, R. (1965) 16 *Jus*, 363-85, 'Alcune osservazioni sul Senatoconsulto Silaniano'.
—— (1976) *Accad. Romanist. Costant. Atti* II, 103-17, 'Sulla costituzione di Costantino in tema di parricidio (CTh 9.15.1)'.
Martino, F. de (1937) 3 *SDHI*, 387-418, 'L'*ignorantia iuris* nel diritto penale romano'.

—— (1938) *Scr. Massari = Diritto e Società*, 460-76, 'Note esegetiche sul SCo Liboniano'.

—— (1975) 21 *Labeo*, 211-14, 'I *supplicia* dell'iscrizione di Pozzuoli'.

Mattingly, H. (1969) 59 *JRS*, 129-43, 'The two Republican laws of the *tabula Bembina*'.

—— (1970) 60 *JRS*, 154-68, 'The extortion law of the *tabula Bembina*'.

—— (1975a) 25 *CQ*, 255-63, 'The extortion law of Servilius Glauca'.

—— (1975b) 34 *Latomus*, 726-8, 'The jury panel of the *lex repetundarum*'.

—— (1979) 107 *Hermes*, 478-88, 'The character of the *lex Acilia Glabrionis*'.

—— (1983) 111 *Hermes*, 300-10, '*Acerbissima lex Servilia*'.

Mayer-Maly, T. (1957) 23 *SDHI* 323-34, '*Servum sub poena vinculorum domino reddere*'.

—— (1961) *RE* 9A.1, 311-47, '*Vis*'.

Memmer, M. (1991) 108 *SZ*, 21-93, '*Ad servitutem aut ad lupanar*'.

Mentxaka, R. (1988) 30 *BIDR*, 277-335, '*Stellionatus*'.

—— (1990) 37 *RIDA*, 247-334, 'Algunas consideraciones sobre el *crimen de residuis* a la luz de la legislacion municipal'.

Messana, M.A. (1991) 41 *ASGP*, 63-208, 'Reflessioni storico-comparative in tema di carcerazione preventiva'.

Messer, W.S. (1920) 15 *CPh*, 158-75, 'Mutiny in the Roman army'.

Metaxaki-Mitrou, F. (1985) 54 *AntCl*, 180-7, 'Violence in the *contio* during the Ciceronian age'.

Meyer, H.D. (1978) 95 *SZ*, 138-57, 'Die Strafklagekonsumption beim Repetundendelikt und die Rechtsregel "bis de eadem re ne sit actio" '.

Millar, F. (1965) *Historia*, 362-67, 'The development of jurisdiction by imperial procurators: further evidence'.

—— (1977, London) *The Emperor in the Roman World*.

—— (1984) 52 *PBSR*, 124-47, 'Condemnation to hard labour in the Roman Empire from the Julio-Claudians to Constantine'.

Mitchell, T.N. (1971) 20 *Historia*, 47-61, 'Cicero and the *SC ultimum*'.

Molè, M. (1966) 170 *AG*, 116-66, 'Ricerche in tema di plagio'.

—— (1971) *St. Volterra* III, 69-104, 'Una "vexata quaestio" in tema di furto'.

Momigliano, A. (ed.) (1963, Oxford) *The Conflict between Paganism and Christianity in the Fourth Century*.

Mommsen, T. (1887, 3rd ed., Leipzig) *Römisches Staatsrecht*.

—— (1899, Berlin) *Römisches Strafrecht*.

Monaco, L. (1984) *Scr. Guarino – Sodalitas* IV, 2013-24, '*Veneficia matronarum*'.

Moreau, P. (1987) 65 *Athenaeum*, 465-92, 'La *lex Clodia* sur le banissement de Cicéron'.

Morgese, S. (1983) 49 *SDHI*, 147-78, 'Taglio di alberi e *latrocinium*: D 47.7.2'.

Mulroy, D. (1988) 118 *TAPhA*, 155-78, 'The early career of P. Clodius Pulcher. A re-examination of the charges of mutiny and sacrilege'.

Murga, J.L. (1979) 26 *RIDA*, 307-36, 'Délito e infracción urbanistica en las constituciones bajo-imperiales'.

—— (1987) 34 *RIDA*, 229-64, 'La *perclusio locatoris* como *vis privata* legitima'.

Musurillo, H. (ed.) (1972, Oxford) *The Acts of the Christian Martyrs*.

Nardi, E. (1968) *St. Grosso* I, 313-19, 'Credo stoico e portata delle leggi Cornelia e Pompeia sull'omicidio'.

—— (1980a) *ANRW* II.13, 366-85, 'Aborto e omicidio nella civiltà classica'.

—— (1980b, Milan) *L'otre dei parricidi e le bestie incluse*.

Nicholas, B. (1962, Oxford) *An Introduction to Roman Law*.

Nicolet, C. (1972) *ANRW* I.2, 197-214, 'Les lois judiciaires et les tribunaux de concussion'.

Niederländer, H. (1950) 67 *SZ*, 185-260, 'Die Entwicklung des *furtum*'.

Niedermeyer, H. (1930) *St. Bonfante* II, 381-417, '*Crimen plagii* und *crimen violentiae*'.

Nippel, W. (1984) 74 *JRS*, 20-9, 'Policing Rome'.

—— (1988, Stuttgart) *Aufruhr und 'Polizei' in der römischen Republik*.

Noethlichs, K.L. (1981, Wiesbaden) *Beamtentum und Dienstvergehen*.

Nörr, D. (1981) *IJ*, 350-64, 'The matrimonial legislation of Augustus'.

—— (1986a, Munich) *Causa mortis*.

—— (1986b) *The Legal Mind: St. Honoré*, 203-17, '*Causam mortis praebere*'.

North, J.A. (1979) 25 *PCPhS*, 85-103, 'Religious toleration in Republican Rome'.

O'Neal, W.J. (1978a) 55 *ClassBull*, 24-8, 'Delation in the early Empire'.

—— (1978b) 26 *RSC*, 359-62, 'Composition of the juries *de repetundis* from the *lex Calpurnia* to Sulla'.

Oost, S.I. (1956) 77 *AJPh*, 19-28, 'The date of the *lex Iulia de repetundis*'.

Pailler, J.M. (1986) 54 *PBSR*, 29-39, 'Caton et les Bacchanals'.

—— (1988, Rome) *Bacchanalia: la repression de 186 av. J.C. à Rome et en Italie*.

Palmer, R.E.A. (1980) *The Seaborne Commerce of Ancient Rome*, ed. J.H. D'Arms & E.C. Kopff, 217-33, 'Customs on market goods imported into the City of Rome'.

Pascale, M.R. de (1985) 31 *Labeo*, 57-61, 'Sul suicido del *miles*'.

Pavis d'Escurac, H. (1976, Rome) *La préfecture de l'annone*.

Pékary, T. (1987) 18 *AncSoc*, 133-50, '*Seditio*. Unruhen und Revolten im römischen Reich von Augustus bis Commodus'.

Peppe, L. (1984, Milan) *Posizione giuridica e ruolo sociale della donna romana in età repubblicana*.

Perrin, B. (1951) 29 *RHD*, 383-405, 'Le caractère subjectif de la répression pénale dans les XII Tables'.

—— (1966) *Mel. Piganiol* III, 1455-65, 'La responsabilité pénale du mineur'.

Pharr, C. (1932) 63 *TAPhA*, 269-95, 'The interdiction of magic in Roman law'.

Phillips, E.J. (1974) 56 *Klio*, 87-101, 'The prosecution of C. Rabirius in 63 BC'.

Piazza, M.P. (1991, Padua) *La disciplina del falso*.

Plescia, J. (1971) 30 *Latomus*, 120-32, 'On the persecution of Christians in the Roman Empire'.

Polara, G. (1974) 77 *BIDR*, 89-138, 'Marciano e l'elemento soggetivo del reato'.

Polay, E. (1986, Budapest) *Iniuria types in Roman law*.

Pommeray, L. (1937, Paris) *Études sur l'infamie en droit romain*.

Pontenay de Fontette, see Fontette.

Portmann, W. (1990) 39 *Historia*, 212-48, 'Zu den Motiven der Diokletianischen Christenverfolgung'.

Prete, P. del (1937, Bari) *La responsibilità dello schiavo nel diritto penale romano*.

Provera, G. (1965) *St. Biondi* II, 541-69, 'Riflessi privatistici dei *pacta de crimine*'.

Pugliese, G. (1948) *St. Solazzi*, 391-417, 'Figure processuali ai confini tra *iudicia privata* e *iudicia publica*'.

—— (1970) 21 *IURA*, 155-81, 'Aspetti giuridici della *pro Cluentio* di Cicerone'.

—— (1982) *ANRW* II.14, 722-89, 'Linee generali dell' evoluzione del diritto penale pubblico durante il Principato'.

Pulciano, C.E. (1913) *Il diritto privato romano nell' epistolario di Plinio il giovane*.

Pürkel, J.B. Ungern-Sternberg von (1970, Munich) *Untersuchungen zum spät-republikanischen Notstandrecht*.

Purpura, G. (1973) 34 *ASGP*, 165-275, 'I *curiosi* e la *schola agentium in rebus*'.

—— (1974) 35 *ASGP*, 225-67, 'Ricerche sulla *supplicatio* avverso la sentenza del prefetto del pretorio'.

—— (1976) 36 *ASGP*, 219-51, 'Il papirio BGU 611 e la genesi del SC Turpilliano'.

Radin, M. (1920) 10 *JRS*, 119-30, '*Lex Pompeia* and the *poena cullei*'.

Raditsa, L.F. (1980) *ANRW* II.13, 278-339, 'Augustus' legislation concerning marriage, procreation, love affairs and adultery'.

Rainer, J.M. (1987) 55 *TR*, 31-8, 'Zum SC Hosidianum'.

Ramsay, J.T. (1980) 29 *Historia*, 402-21, 'A reconstruction of Q. Gallius' trial for *ambitus*'.

Reggi, R. (1958, Milan) *Liber homo bona fide serviens*.

Reidinger, W. (1958) *RE* 8A2, 1732-53, *Vestales* [within Vesta].

Reimundo, B. (1984) *St. Biscardi* V, 239-66, 'Prohibición de *hereditatem capere* en el régimen del SC Liboniano'.

Reynolds, P.R.B. (1926, Oxford) *The Vigiles of Imperial Rome*.

Richardson, J.S. (1987) 77 *JRS*, 1-12, 'The purpose of the *lex Calpurnia de repetundis*'.

Richlin, A. (1981) 8 *Women's Studies*, 225-, 'Approaches to the sources on adultery at Rome'.

Rilinger, R. (1988, Munich) *Humiliores – Honestiores*.

Rizzelli, G. (1986) 28 *BIDR*, 411-41, 'Alcuni aspetti dell'accusa privilegiata im materia di adulterio'.

—— (1987) 29 *BIDR*, 355-88, '*Stuprum* e *adulterium* nella cultura e la *lex Iulia de adulteriis*'.

—— (1988) 30 *BIDR*, 733-43, 'In margine a PS 2.26.11'.

—— (1990) 210 *AG*, 459-64, 'Il *crimen lenocinii*'.

Robertis, F.M. de (1939) 59 *SZ*, 219-60, '*Arbitrium iudicantis* e statuizioni imperiali'.

—— (1942a, Bari = 4 *Ann. Bari* 1941) *Sulla efficacia normativa delle costituzioni imperiali*.

—— (1942b) 8 *SDHI*, 255-307, 'Dal potere personale alla competenza dell'ufficio'.

—— (1943, Bari) *Studi di diritto penale romano*.

—— (1948) *St. Solazzi*, 169-96, 'La funzione della pena nel diritto romano'.

—— (1954, Bari) *La variazione della pena nel diritto romano*.

—— (1971, Bari) *Storia delle corporazioni e del regime associativo nel mondo romano*.

—— (1974) 40 *SDHI*, 67-98, 'Interdizione dell'*usus equorum* e lotta al banditismo'.

Robinson, O.F. (1968) 15 *RIDA*, 389-98, 'Private prisons'.

—— (1973) 8 *IJ*, 356-71, 'Blasphemy and sacrilege'.

—— (1975) 10 *IJ*, 175-86, 'The Roman law on burials and burial grounds'.

—— (1981) 98 *SZ*, 213-54, 'Slaves and the criminal law'.

—— (1985) *St. Moschella* – 8 *Ann. Perugia*, 527-60, 'Women and the criminal law'.

—— (1990-2) 25-7 *IJ*, 269-92, 'The repression of Christians in the pre-Decian period: a legal problem still'.

—— (1991-2) 33-4 *BIDR*, 89-104, 'Some thoughts on Justinian's summary of Roman criminal law'.

—— (1992a, London) *Ancient Rome*.

—— (1992b) 60 *TR*, 29-38, 'An aspect of *falsum*'.
—— *JLH* (1996) forthcoming, 'The Senate and Roman criminal law'.
Rodriguez-Alvarez, L. (1979) 49 *AHDE*, 5-37, 'La tentativa di homicidio en la jurisprudencia romana'.
—— (1991) 37 *Labeo*, 305-38, 'Nueva aproximacíon al tema del *veneficum*'.
Rogers, R.S. (1933) 64 *TAPhA*, 18-27, 'Ignorance of the law in Tacitus and Dio'.
—— (1934) 65 *TAPhA*, lii-liii, '*Delatores* under Tiberius'.
—— (1935, Philadelphia) *Criminal Trials and Criminal Legislation under Tiberius*.
—— (1952) 83 *TAPhA*, 279-311, 'A Tacitean pattern in narrating treason trials'.
—— (1959a) 49 *JRS*, 90-4, 'Treason in the early Empire'.
—— (1959b) 90 *TAPhA*, 224-37, 'The emperor's displeasure: *amicitiam renuntiare*'.
—— (1960) 55 *CPh*, 19-23, 'A group of Domitianic treason trials'.
—— (1965) 96 *TAPhA*, 351-9, 'The case of Cremutius Cordus'.
—— (1966) 97 *TAPhA*, 373-8, 'The emperor's displeasure and Ovid'.
Röhle, R. (1988) 56 *TR*, 305-9, 'Zur Datierung des Reskriptes der *divi fratres* in D 48.12.3pr'.
Rosen, K. (1990) 21 *AncSoc*, 273-92 '*Iudex* und *Officium*: Kollektivstrafe, Kontrolle und Effizienz in der spätantiken Provinzialverwaltung'.
Rouvier, J. (1963) 41 *RHD*, 443-56, 'Remarques sur l'*actio vi bonorum raptorum*'.
Russi, A. (1986) 98 *MEFRA*, 855-72, 'I pastori e l'esposizione degli infanti nella tarda legislazione imperiale'.
Rutgers, L.V. (1994) 13 *ClAnt*(= *CalSt*), 56-74, 'Roman policy towards the Jews: expulsions from the city of Rome during the first century C.E.'.
Ryan, F.X. (1994) 89 *ClPh*, 159-62, 'The *lex Scantinia* and the prosecution of censors and aediles'.
Sainte-Croix, G. de (1963) 26 *P & P*, 6-38, 'Why were the early Christians persecuted?'.
—— (1964) 27 *P & P*, 28-33, 'Why were the early Christians persecuted? A rejoinder'.
Salerno, F. (1990, Naples) *Dalla consecratio alla publicatio bonorum*.
Salzman, M.R. (1993) 42 *Historia*, 362-78, 'The evidence for the conversion of the Roman Empire to Christianity in CTh XVI'.
Sander, E. (1960) 103 *RhM*, 289-319, 'Das römische Militärstrafrecht'.
Santalucia, B. (1979) 30 *IURA*, 1-33, 'La legislazione sillana in materia di falso nummario'.
—— (1988) *Idee* ed. Burdese, 5-21, 'Note sulla repressione dei reati communi in età repubblicana'.
—— (1989, Milan) *Diritto e processo penale nell' antica Roma*.
Saumagne, C. (1955) 33 *REL*, 241-57, 'La "passion" de Thrasea'.
—— (1962) 227 *RH*, 337-60, 'Les incendiaires de Rome et les lois pénales des romains: Tac. *Ann.* 15.44'.
—— and M. Meslin, (1979) *ANRW* II.23.1, 316-39, 'De la legalité du procès de Lyon de l'année 177'.
Scaffardi, G.P. (1981) 29 *St. Parmensi*, 237-49, 'CTh 9.16.1 e CTh 16.2.31. Note sui rapporti tra ideologia religiosa e legislazione penale'.
Schiller, A.A. (1936) *St. Riccobono* IV, 79-112, 'Trade secrets and the Roman law'.
—— (1953) 57-8 *BIDR*, 60-97, 'The jurists and the Prefects of Rome'.
Schumacher, L. (1982, Wiesbaden) *Servus index*.

Schwartz, J. (1966) *Mel. Piganiol* III, 1481-8, *'In Oasin relegare'*.
Seager, R. (1967) 16 *Historia*, 37-43, 'The *Lex Varia de maiestate'*.
—— (1994) *CAH* IX², 165-207, 'Sulla'.
Serangeli, S. (1968) 71/10 *BIDR*, 199-226, 'CJ 7.16.31 e le azioni contro il litigante temerario'.
Serrao, F. (1954, Milan) *La iurisdictio del pretore peregrino*.
—— (1956a, Milan) *Il frammento Leidense di Paolo: problemi di diritto criminale romano*.
—— (1956b) 151 *AG*, 16-66, 'Sul danno da reato in diritto romano'.
—— (1956c) *St. de Francisci* II, 471-511, 'Appunti sui patroni e sulla leggitimazione attiva all'accusa nei processi *repetundarum'*.
—— (1970) 73/12 *BIDR*, 125-96, 'Responsibilità per fatto altrui e nossalità'.
Sherwin-White, A.N. (1949) 17 *PBSR*, 5-25, *'Poena legis repetundarum'*.
—— (1952a) 42 *JRS*, 43-55, 'The extortion procedure again'.
—— (1952b) 3 *JTS*, 199-213, 'The early persecutions and Roman Law again'.
—— (1964) 27 *P & P*, 23-7, 'Why were the early Christians persecuted? An amendment'.
—— (1966, Oxford) *The Letters of Pliny: a historical and social commentary*.
—— (1972) 62 *JRS*, 83-99, 'The date of the *lex repetundarum* and its consequences'.
Shotter, D.C.A. (1966) 15 *Historia*, 312-17, 'Tiberius' part in the trial of Aemilia Lepida'.
—— (1980) 108 *Hermes*, 230-3, 'A group of *maiestas* cases in AD 21'.
Siber, H. (1936, Leipzig) *Analogie, Amstrecht und Ruckwirkung im Strafrecht des römisches Freistaates*.
Sinclair, P. (1992) 51 *Latomus*, 397-403, *'Deorum iniurias dis curae* (Tac. *Ann.* 1.73.4)'.
Sinnigen, W.S. (1957, Rome) *The officium of the Urban Prefecture during the Later Roman Empire*.
—— (1959) 80 *AJPh*, 238-54, 'Two branches of the late Roman secret service'.
—— (1961-2) 57 *CJ*, 65-72, 'The Roman secret service'.
—— (1962) 83 *AJPh*, 369-82, 'Three administrative changes ascribed to Constantius II'.
—— (1964) 57 *ByzZS*, 78-105, 'Chiefs of staff and chiefs of the secret service'.
Sirks, B. (1991, Amsterdam) *Food for Rome*.
Slater, W.J. (1994) 13 *ClAnt* (= *CalSt*), 120-44, 'Pantomime riots'.
Slob, E. (1986, Zutphen) *Luxuria*.
Smallwood, E.M. (1959 & 1961) 18 & 20 *Latomus*, 334-47 & 93-6, 'The legislation of Hadrian and Antoninus Pius against circumcision' & 'Addendum'.
—— (1976, Leiden) *The Jews under Roman Rule*.
Solazzi, S. (1930) 104 *AG* = *Scritti* III 1960, 357-77, *'Infirmitas aetatis* e *infirmitas sexus'*.
—— (1936) 69 *RIL* = *Scritti* III 1960, 547-55, 'Sul *crimen expilatae hereditatis'*.
—— (1937) *Scr. Massari* = *Scritti* III 1960, 563-6, 'D 48.4.7.3 e l'analogia nel diritto penale romano'.
—— (1943) 9 *SDHI*, 175-201, 'Glosse alle costituzioni imperiali'.
—— (1956) 22 *SDHI*, 345-8, 'La condanna ai *vincula perpetua'*.
Solimena, C. (1905, Rome) *Plinio il giovine e il diritto pubblico di Roma*.
Sordi, M. (1983, London) *The Christians and the Roman Empire*.
Spagnuolo Vigorita, T. (1978, Palermo) *Secta temporum meorum: rinnovamento politico e delazione fiscale agli inizi del principato di Gordiano III*.
—— (1984, Naples) *Exsecranda pernicies. Delatori e fisco nell'età di Costantino*.

Squires, S. (tr.) (1990, Bristol Cl. Press) *Asconius: Commentaries on Five Speeches of Cicero.*

Stangl, T. (ed.) (1964 reprinted, Olms, Hildesheim) *Ciceronis orationum Scholiastae.*

Staveley, E.S. (1953) 96 *RhM*, 201-13, 'Iudex selectus'.

Stockton, D. (1979, Oxford) *The Gracchi.*

Strachan-Davidson, J.L. (1912, Oxford) *Problems of the Roman Criminal Law.*

Talbert, R. (1984, Princeton) *The Senate of Imperial Rome.*

— (1985, London) *Atlas of Classical History.*

Tatum, W.J. (1990) 40 *CQ*, 187-94, 'Cicero's opposition to the *lex Clodia de collegiis'.*

Taubenschlag, R. (1916, Leipzig/Berlin) *Das Strafrecht im Rechte der Papyri.*

— (1953) *St. Arangio-Ruiz* I, 501-7, 'Il delatore e la sua responsibilità nel diritto dei papyri'.

— (1957) 8 *Éts. Pap.* 737-41, 'Die körperliche Züchtigung'.

Tellegen, J.W. (1979) 26 *RIDA*, 387-97, 'Captatio and crimen'.

Tellegen-Couperus, O. (1985) 53 *TR*, 309-20, 'Did the Senate function as a court of appeal in the Later Roman Empire?'.

Theisen, F. (1990) 37 *RIDA*, 419-46, 'Strafrechtliche Bestimmungen in römischen Stadtrechten'.

Thomas, J.A.C. (1961) 12 *IURA*, 65-80, 'Accusatio adulterii'.

— (1962a) *JR*, 127-48, 'Sutor ultra crepidam'.

— (1962b) 9 *RIDA*, 417-30, 'Prescription of crimes in Roman law'.

— (1963) 79 *LQR*, 224-37, 'The development of Roman criminal law'.

— (1968) 19 *IURA*, 1-32, 'Animus furandi'.

— (1970) *Éts. Macqueron*, 637-44, 'Lex Iulia de adulteriis coercendis'.

— (1976, North Holland) *Textbook of Roman Law.*

— (1977) 38 *Rec. Bodin – L'Enfant*, 9-31, 'Delictal and criminal liability of the young in Roman law'.

Thomas, Y.P. (1981) 93 *MEFRA*, 643-715, 'Parricidium'.

— (1984) *EFR Du Châtiment*, 499-548, 'Vitae necisque potestas'.

Thome, G. (1992) 35 *AC (SA)*, 73-98, 'Crime and punishment, guilt and expiation: Roman thought and vocabulary'.

Thompson, L.A. (1971) *St. Volterra* II, 479-85, 'A passage of Cicero relating to prosecutions *repetundarum'.*

Thurman, W.S. (1969) 100 *TAPhA*, 593-606, 'A law of Justinian on the right of asylum'.

Thurmond, D.L. (1994) 82 *Athenaeum*, 459-93, 'Some Roman slave collars in *CIL'.*

Tilli, G. (1977) 23 *Labeo*, 16-41, 'Dominus sciens e servus agens'.

Torrent, A. (1980) 50 *AHDE*, 111-30, 'El senadoconsulto Messaliano y el *crimen falsi'.*

— (1982) 52 *AHDE*, 223-42, 'Suppositio partus – crimen falsi'.

Treggiari, S. (1969, Oxford) *Roman Freedmen during the Late Republic.*

— (1991, Oxford) *Roman Marriage.*

Tyrrel, W.B. (1973) 32 *Latomus*, 285-300, 'The trial of C. Rabirius in 63 B.C.'.

— (1974) 91 *SZ*, 106-25, 'The *duumviri* in the trials of Horatius, Manlius and Rabirius'.

Vacca, L. (1965-68) 45 *St. Cagl.* 519-66, 'Ricerche sulla rapina nel diritto romano: l'editto di Lucullo e la *lex Plautia'.*

— (1972, Milan) *Ricerche in tema di actio vi bonorum raptorum.*

— (1982) *ANRW* II.14, 682-721, 'Delitti privati e azioni penali nel principato'.

Vandenbossche, A. (1952) 12 *AIPhO* = *Mél. Grégoire* IV, 471-516, 'Recherches sur le suicide en droit romain'.

Vanucchi Forzieri, O. (1982) 48 *SDHI*, 289-317, 'La legislazione imperiale del IV-V secolo in tema di divorzio'.

Vanzetti, M. (1974) 20 *Labeo*, 77-82, '*Iuvenes* turbolenti'.

Venturini, C. (1969) 11 *BIDR*, 19-87, 'La repressione degli abusi dei magistrati romani ai danni delle popolazione soggette fino alla *lex Calpurnia* del 149 a.C.'.

—— (1979, Milan) *Studi sul crimen repetundarum nell'età repubblicana.*

—— (1984) *St. Sanfilippo* V, 787-804, 'La orazione pro Cn. Plancio e la *lex Licinia de sodaliciis*'.

—— (1987a) *St. Biscardi* VI, 133-57, 'Concussione e corruzione'.

—— (1987b) 53 *SDHI*, 74-109, '*Quaestio extra ordinem*'.

—— (1988) 54 *SDHI*, 66-109, '*Accusatio adulterii* e politica costantiniana'.

—— (1991) 37 *Labeo*, 351-8, 'Edili e repressione criminale'.

Veyne, P. (1981a) 30 *L'Histoire*, 77-, 'L'omosexualité à Rome'.

—— (1981b) 36 *Annales* (*ESC*), 339-60, 'Clientèle et corruption au service de l'État'.

Villers, R. (1956) *St. de Francisci* I, 373-91, 'Appel devant le prince et appel devant le sénat'.

Vincenti, U. (1982) 85 *BIDR*, 101-26, 'Aspetti procedurali della *cognitio senatus*'.

—— (1984) 86-7 *BIDR*, 65-93, 'Per uno studio sugli appelli *ante sententiam*'.

—— (1985a) 88 *BIDR*, 347-58, '*Internecivi exerere actionem* e crimen suspectae mortis intendere (CTh 9.1.14)'.

—— (1985b) 205 *AG*, 113-44, '*Cognitio senatus* e *appellatio*'.

—— (1986) 32 *Labeo*, 55-67, 'Note sull'attività giudiziaria del senato dopo i Severi'.

—— (1988) *Idee* ed. Burdese, 23-43, '*Falsum testimonium dicere* (XII T. 8.23)'.

—— (1989, Padua) '*Duo genera sunt testium.*' Contributo all studio della prova testimoniale nel processo romano.

Visky, K. (1949) 3 *RIDA* = *Mel. de Visscher* II, 437-84, 'La responsabilité en droit romain'.

Visscher, F. de (1940, Louvain/Paris) *Les édits d'Auguste découvertes à Cyrène.*

—— (1963, Milan) *Le droit des tombeaux romains.*

—— (1964) 11 *RIDA*, 321-33, 'La justice romaine en Cyrènaique'.

Vitali, E.G. (1972) *St. Scherillo* I, 275-98, 'Sull'*impedimentum criminis* (adulterio e divieti matrimoniali)'.

Vitucci, G. (1956, Rome) *Ricerche sulla praefectura urbi in età imperiale* (sec. I-III).

Vitzthum, W. (1966, Munich) *Untersuchungen zum materiellen Inhalt der lex Plautia und lex Iulia de vi.*

Voisin, J.L. (1979) 38 *Latomus*, 422-50, 'Pendus, crucifiés, *oscilla* dans la Rome païenne'.

Volterra, E. (1929) 37 *BIDR*, 57-76, 'Intorno alla prescrizione dei reati in diritto romano'.

—— (1930a) 38 *BIDR*, 75-149, 'Osservazioni sull'*ignorantia iuris* nel diritto penale romano'.

—— (1930b) *St. Bonfante* II, 109-26, 'In tema di *accusatio adulterii*'.

—— (1934) *St. Ratti*, 387-447, 'Per la storia del reato di bigamia in diritto romano'.

—— (1949) 3 *RIDA* = *Mel. de Visscher* II, 485-500, 'Processi penali contro i defunti'.

Wacke, A. (1978) 13 *IJ*, 372-89, 'The *potentiores*'.

—— (1979) 26 *RIDA*, 505-66, 'Fahrlässige Vergehen im römischen Strafrecht'.

—— (1980a) *ANRW* II.13, 562-607, 'Die *potentiores* in den Rechtsquellen'.

—— (1980b) 97 *SZ*, 26-77, 'Der Selbstmord'.

—— (1983) *St. Sanfilippo* III, 679-712, 'Il suicidio nel diritto romano e nella storia del diritto'.

Waldstein, W. (1964, Innsbruck) *Untersuchungen zum römischen Begnadigungsrecht.*

—— (1972) 3 *Index*, 343-61, 'Zum Fall der *dos Licinniae*'.

Watson A. (1967, Oxford) *The Law of Persons in the Later Roman Republic.*

—— (1970a) *Sein und Werden, F. von Lubtow*, 381-7, 'Drunkenness in Roman law'.

—— (1970b, Southern Methodist Press, Dallas) *The Law of the Ancient Romans.*

—— (1991, University of Georgia) *Roman Law and Comparative Law.*

—— (1994) 62 *TR*, 113-25, '*Prolegomena* to establishing pre-Justinianic texts'.

Wieling, H. (1991) 38 *RIDA*, 385-420, '*Iniusta lex Maiorani*'.

Williams, G. (1962) 52 *JRS*, 28-46, 'Poetry in the moral climate of Augustan Rome'.

Williams, M.H. (1989) 48 *Latomus*, 765-84, 'The expulsion of the Jews from Rome in A.D. 19'.

—— (1990) 39 *Historia*, 196-211, 'Domitian, the Jews and the "Judaizers" – a simple matter of *cupiditas* and *maiestas*?'.

Winkel, L. (1982) 29 *RIDA*, 281-94, 'Quelques remarques sur l'accusation publique'.

Wittmann, R. (1974) 91 *SZ*, 285-359, 'Die Entwicklungslinien der klassichen Injurienklage'.

Wolf, J.G. (1988a, Heidelberg) *Das SC Silanianum und die Senatsrede des C. Cassius Longinus.*

—— (1988b) 105 *SZ*, 776-83, '*Martyres vindicati*'.

Wolodkiewicz, W. (1985) 63 *RHD*, 1-18, 'La préscription de l'action pénale à Rome'.

Wouw, J.A.C.J. van de (1973) 41 *TR*, 311-24, 'Papinians *libri duo de adulteriis*'.

Yaron, R. (1962) 30 *TR*, 243-51, '*Vitae necisque potestas*'.

—— (1964) 32 *TR*, 533-57, '*De divortio varia*'.

—— (1989) 57 *TR*, 313-16, 'Papinian D 48.5.12(11).7 from a different angle'.

Yuge, T. (1989) 17 *Index*, 283-, 'Soziale Gründe der Christenverfolgungen im Zweiterjahrhundert'.

Zilletti, U. (1961) 161 *AG*, 72-107, 'Annotazioni sul *crimen stellionatus*'.

—— (1963) 29 *SDHI*, 124-50, 'Sul valore probatorio della testimonianza nella *cognitio extra ordinem*'.

—— (1968a) *St. Grosso* II, 35-93, 'Note sulla *restitutio in integrum damnatorum*'.

—— (1968b) 34 *SDHI*, 32-109, 'In tema di *servitus poenae*'.

Zmigryder-Konopka, Z. (1939) 18 *RHD*, 307-47, 'La nature juridique de la rélegation du citoyen'.

Zucotti, F. (1991) 37 *Labeo*, 174-226, 'Il *furor* del patricida e il testamento di Malleoli'.

Zumpt, A.W. (1865-69, Berlin) *Das Kriminalrecht der römischen Republik.*

Index of Sources

References (in **bold** type) are to chapter and footnote numbers.

D 49.2.1.2 **I 108, 140**
D 49.2.1.4 **I 138**
D 49.3.1.pr & 1 **I 137, 138**
D 49.14.1 **VII 18**
D 49.14.1.3 **II 107**
D 49.14.15pr **VII 155**
D 49.14.22pr **VI 49**
D 49.14.46.2 **VI 98**
D 49.15.7.2 **I 146**
D 49.15.12.16 **III 153**
D 49.16.3.4 **VI 23**
D 49.16.3.10-11 **II 51 VI 24**
D 49.16.5.1 **VI 24**
D 49.16.6.1 **VI 25**
D 49.16.6.4 **VI 23**
D 49.16.6.7 **II 97**
D 49.16.13.4 **VI 25**
D 50.5.3 **VI 98**
D 50.6.6.12 **VI 72**
D 50.10.3.2 **VI 33**
D 50.10.4 **VI 33**
D 50.13.1.3 **III 118**
D 50.16.53.2 **II 35, 56, 60**
D 50.16.70pr **VII 64**
D 50.16.101 **V 71, 92, 247**
D 50.16.225 **VII 84**
D 50.16.226 **II 24**
D 50.16.236pr **II 22**
D 50.17.4 **II 90**
D 50.17.47 & 50 **II 63**
D 50.17.109 **II 63**
D 50.17.152 **II 70 III 78**
D 50.17.155.2 **I 201**
D 50.17.157pr **II 92**
D 50.17.167.1 **II 75**
FIRA i 7 (*tabula Bembina*) **I 13, 49 VI 84**
　vv. 1 & 78 **VI 85**
　v. 13 **I 47**
　vv. 16-17 **I 47 VII 28**
　vv. 23-6 **I 50**
　vv. 36-38 **I 59**
　vv. 51-54 **I 68**
　i 13 (*tabula Heracleensis*) **III 147**
　vv. 104 & 112-13 **VII 28**
　vv. 122-23 **V 230**
　i 21 (*lex Ursonensis*) c. 102 **I 65**
　i 30 (*SC de Bacchanalibus*) **VII 77**
　i 45 (*SCC de aedificiis non diruendis*) **VII 204**
　i 68 (Cyrene Edict V) **I 72**

　i 94 (*edict of Constantine*) vv. 12-14 **I 197**
Fragmenta Vaticana 6 **VII 61**
FV 197-8 **I 48**
Gaius
G 1.27 **VII 60**
G 1.53 **IV 27 VII 3**
G 1.58 **V 24**
G 1.61 **V 26**
G 1.62 **V 16, 24**
G 1.63 **V 24**
G 1.64 **V 42**
G 1.91 & 160 **VII 63**
G 2.52-7 **III 103**
G 3.189-92 **III 18**
G 3.198 **II 43**
G 3.199 **III 133**
G 3.209 **III 85**
G 3.213 **IV 25**
G 3.220 **IV 114**
G 3.220-5 **IV 107**
G 4.23 **VII 12**
G 4.44 **VII 66**
G 4.112 **II 11**
G 4.174-81 **VII 181**
G 4.178 **VII 134**
ILS 45 =*CIL* VI 1283 **I 40, 41 IV 10**
　47 =*CIL* VI 1311 **I 40**
　642 =*CIL* III 2, 824ff. **VII 10**
　1423 =*CIL* VI 1634 **I 116**
　1455 =*CIL* X 6662 **I 116**
　8506 =*CIL* III 2544 **III 126**
Institutions of Justinian
Inst. 1.3.4 **VII 62**
Inst. 1.10.1 **V 24**
Inst. 1.10.2 **V 26**
Inst. 1.10.3 **V 24, 26**
Inst. 1.10.4 **V 15**
Inst. 1.10.5 **V 24**
Inst. 1.10.6-7 **V 22**
Inst. 1.10.8 **V 26**
Inst. 1.10.9 **V 25**
Inst. 1.10.10 **V 4**
Inst. 1.10.12 **V 42**
Inst. 1.16.1 **VII 62, 64**
Inst. 2.6.2 **III 75**
Inst. 2.17.8(7) **I 115**
Inst. 4.1.8 **II 44 III 161**
Inst. 4.1.9 **III 133**
Inst. 4.2 **III 85**
Inst. 4.2.1 **III 92**
Inst. 4.2.2 **III 89**

General Index

This index includes some notes under the page from which they are referred.

pollution, 50
Pompey, 3; 83,85
popular actions, 32,39
postulatio (in an accusation), 8
potentes, 80
praefectus annonae, see Prefect of
  the Grain Supply
  praefectus praetorio, see
    Praetorian Prefect
  praefectus urbi, see Urban Prefect

  praefectus vigilum, see Night
    Watch, Prefect of the
Praetorian Prefect(s), 10-11,12; 32
praetors, and see Urban Praetor, 3-4
praevaricatio, and see procedural
  offences, 5; 65; 99,100
Prefect and prefecture, see Grain
  Supply. Night Watch,
  Praetorian, Urban
prescription/prescriptive periods,
  15,21-2; 47,48; 55,62,66,72; 84
prison, 6,13; 103
  prisons, private, 13; 49; 103
private criminal actions, 1; 41-2
procedural offences, see also
    calumny, *praevaricatio*,
    tergiversatio, 37; 99-103
procurators, imperial, 9; 32
prosecution, see accusation
prostitution, 14; 64,67,69-70
provinces, and provincials, 11-12; 81
provincial governors, see governors,
  provincial
provocatio, see appeal
public order, see *vis*
public records, misuse of, and see
  also *falsum*, 77,83
pupil, see children (and Glossary)

quaesitor (president of a jury court),
  4; 42
quaestio extraordinaria (special
  court), 1,2
quaestio/nes perpetua/e (standing
  jury courts), and see also under
  the various offences,
  1,2-6,7,8,10,12; 21; 89; 90

Rabirius, C., 2; 75
rape, 14; 48; 71-3

rapina (robbery with some violence),
  23,25,28-30; 44,48; 79
receiving stolen goods, see reset
receptio inter reos, 8
relegation, 6; 26,28,32,34,35; 51; 66
religion, offences against, in
    Christian Rome, 13; 84; 98
  in pagan Rome, 95-7
removal from rank (municipal,
    professional, senatorial) as a
    penalty, 26,27,32; 51; 82,86
reparation, 6,8; 16; 82,84; 99
[*res*] *repetundae* (extortion by
    officials), 2,3,6,8; 16; 30; 74,81-2
  quaestio de repetundis, 7
reset and resetters, 26,28,35
residuis, de (misappropriation of
    monies remaining), 3; 83-4
resolutions of the Senate, see
  SC/SCC
rhetoricians, 92
robbery, see *rapina*
Roscius Amerinus, 46
rustics, 17
rustling (*abigeatus*), 24,25-6

saccularii, 27
sack (*culleus*), 46,47; 67
sacral law, 95
sacrilege, 3; 25; 31; 84,88
Saturninus, 75
SC (= *senatusconsultum*; SCC =
    senatusconsulta; i.e. resolutions
    of the Senate), 9; 36,37;
    43,50,51; 79,80,81,82,85,87;
    91,93
  Calvisianum (4 BC), 7
  Claudianum, 45
  Claudianum on cohabitation (AD
    52), 57; 94
  Geminianum (AD 29), 37
  Hosidianum (AD 44), 104
  Libonianum (AD 16), 9; 20; 36-7
  Messalianum (AD 20), 37
  Neronianum, 45
  Pisonianum, 45
  Silanianum (AD ?10), 19,21;
    43,45; 61
  Turpillianum (AD 61), 32; 65;
    99,100,101,102
  Volusianum (AD 56), 104
Scantinius, a plebeian tribune, 70